RICHMOND
PEARSON
HOBSON
Naval Hero of
Magnolia Grove

RICHMOND PEARSON HOBSON
Naval Hero of Magnolia Grove

by

Harvey Rosenfeld

Yucca Tree Press

First Printing   February 2001

Rosenfeld, Harvey
    RICHMOND PEARSON HOBSON: Naval Hero of Magnolia Grove
        1. Hobson, Richmond Pearson.   2. U.S. - History - Spanish-
      American War, 1898 - Naval Operations.   3. U.S.S. Merrimac.
      4. U.S. - History - Women's Suffrage.   5. U.S. - History -
      Prohibition.   6. Narcotics trade, abolition of
      I. Harvey Rosenfelt.   II. Title.

Library of Congress Catalog Number:00-104714
ISBN: 1-881325-48-2

Cover photographs courtesy: Magnolia Grove Museum
Cover design Stephen M. Matson

I would like to express my gratitude to the good folks of Greensboro, Alabama, especially Gloria Cole, the curator at Magnolia Grove, for inspiring this biography; to Rick Wilson for his hospitality, and to the librarians at Hale County Library for their ready assistance. I would also like to thank the Pace University Library and staff for their valuable cooperation in the project; to Janie and Steve Matson at Yucca Tree Press; to Anatole of Any for his technical assistance; and Peri Hoffman of P. Hoffman & Associates/Periodicals, for their editorial expertise and professional advice. Most of all, I thank my wife, Pearl, and son, Robbie, for their continued support and assistance.

Table of Contents

Illustrations

Foreword

Dr. Harvey Rosenfeld's Richmond Pearson Hobson biography returns to Alabamans an important piece of forgotten history. Dr. Rosenfeld quoted a newspaper article bemoaning the diminished value placed on Hobson's accomplishments. Just as the South has been omitted from the annals of the progressive movement, Hobson has been overlooked in Alabama as one of its native sons who played a significant role in world issues. Dr. Rosenfeld thoroughly documented Hobson's heroic sinking of the *Merimac*, campaigns for a stronger navy, support of prohibition, prophesies about the dangers of Japanese, German, and Russian aggression, international battles against the narcotics trade, and the inclusion of women in our democratic governance.

Although woman's suffrage was a small part of Dr. Rosenfeld's biography of Richmond Pearson Hobson, including Hobson's role in the woman's suffrage movement is an appreciated gift to Alabama women and supportive men who have worked tirelessly for women's issues. In our story telling of our struggles for equality, we too often have only negative legends to share. Stories about Alabama legislators hiding in Tennessee to avoid a quorum in the Alabama legislature so the Nineteenth Amendment would fail to be ratified in Alabama, or tales about the Alabama governor forgetting to sign the Marital Rape Bill are all too common.

Dr. Rosenfeld has given us some positive stories for our history of struggle. His descriptions of Hobson's participation in the 1913 suffragette march in Washington are reminiscent of recent marches in support of women's issues. Dr. Rosenfeld's vivid narrative of the derision and criticism leveled against Hobson and other woman's suffrage marchers could well have been descriptions of similar actions against ERA marchers in Washington more than seventy years later. Hobson's efforts helped women ultimately achieve the right to vote. In addition, Rosenfeld's gift of forgotton history helps Alabama women and men know the struggle is not merely a recent occurrence, nor one that has only taken place in other places by other people. We can now realize the continuity and longevity of the women's movement, and we can feel connected with the entire struggle and not feel isolated and alone in our efforts.

In addition to giving us a gift of lost history, Dr. Rosenfeld's example has challenged us to remember other heroes and heroines. I have worked in Alabama for nearly three decades for such women's issues as ratification of the Equal Rights Amendment, marital rape laws, women's health programs, domestic violence legislation and programs, and hate crime bills. These endeavors were recognized during the George Bush presidency when I was honored by being named one of the Points of Light. As I reminisce about those years of struggle, I remember so much derision and criticism. I also remember so many heroes and heroines who struggled in smaller arenas than did Richmond Pearson Hobson, and like Hobson, they have been forgotten. Also like Hobson, they suffered the consequences of their efforts. He lost his last election to continue as a United States legislator because of his support of woman's suffrage.

In summary, Dr. Harvey Rosenfeld described Richmond Pearson Hobson's progressive efforts and global concerns in a way that gives all Americans, particularly Alabamans, the opportunity to learn both historical and personal lessons. As is always the case in looking back over time, some criticisms about the subject of a biography may be warranted. History has judged Prohibition to be a failed experiment. The question of race always seems to awkwardly position historical figures between one movement and another. Some actions are too radical for the era from which one is emerging, yet too conservative for the period into which one is evolving. We must understand the process of history and employ historical perspective in judging a hero. Almost everything Hobson predicted has become reality. The seeds he planted decades ago have grown today into a strong navy, international laws against narcotics, and inclusion of American women in our democratic government. Dr. Harvey Rosenfeld has given us far more than a mere history lesson by writing a meaningful biography of Richmond Pearson Hobson. He has taught us the value of remembering and bringing to others' attention the contributions of forgotten heroes and heroines who planted the seeds in the soil that produced the benefits we all now enjoy.

M. Carolyn Thomas, Ph.D.
Professor of Counselor Education
Director, AUM Counseling Center
Auburn University Montgomery
Montgomery, Alabama

Richmond Pearson Hobson, circa 1903.
Courtesy: Magnolia Grove

Prologue

Santiago de Cuba ... June 3, 1898

"Valiente! Valiente!"

It was early in the morning, just past daybreak, near the entrance of Santiago harbor. Just minutes before, the eight men floating on the small catamaran—all that remained of the dilapidated old collier *Merrimac* they had just succeeded in intentionally sinking—were readying themselves to die. They had seen the squad of riflemen on the Spanish launch they were hailing form into a semicircle. They had heard them shout the dreaded instructions: 'Load ... ! Ready ... ! Aim ... !'"

"The miserable cowards," Lieutenant Richmond Pearson Hobson, senior officer of the crew, had thought bitterly. "A brave nation will hear of this and call for an account."

But no account was to be reckoned, for the command to "fire!" was never voiced. A most distinguished looking and elegantly dressed Spanish Admiral and two of his junior officers leaned out of their cabin and called the firing squad off. Lieutenant Hobson responded by quickly removing his revolver-belt, glasses, canteen, and life preserver and surrendering himself and his crew. Their nearly suicidal mission to block the Spanish fleet had not succeeded as hoped, the rescue plan did not materialize as planned, and now they had no choice but to turn themselves over to the enemy.

The Spaniards looked on in amazement as Contraalmirante Pascual Cervera y Topete pulled the strikingly handsome American naval officer and his seven crew members out of the water. Who were these Americans, dressed only in long woolen underwear with revolvers and lifebelts strapped under their stomachs, that had dared to execute—and nearly successfully complete—such a suicidal mission? Their astonishment turned quickly to civility, kindness, and outright praise as they chanted in unison, applauding the *Merrimac* crew's act of courage, "Valiente! Valiente!"

Lavish praise notwithstanding, Richmond Pearson Hobson and the *Merrimac* men were now prisoners of the Spanish military, on their way to incarceration at Morro Castle ... .

1

SOMETHING TO SAY FOR HEREDITY

"Under Providence ... some have the privilege of dying, others the privilege of living for country and humanity. Those who die have a simpler part. Those of us who live must make good our part ..." writes Hobson in his *In Line of Duty*.

So lived the Hobson family, priding itself in its roots. While one Hobson ancestor placed the first British flag on New Zealand soil, another fought for American independence from the British in the Revolutionary War. Each made good his part.

James Marcellus Hobson was born in 1840, the son of a planter. When he was twenty-one years old, having graduated from the University of North Carolina, he enlisted as a private in the Confederate Army. Despite being wounded during the Battle of Malvern Hill, and again at the Battle of Chancellorsville, he continued fighting, rising to first lieutenant before he was wounded, again, at the Battle of Spotsylvania. This time he was captured, and for the fourteen remaining months of the war, Lieutenant James Hobson was a prisoner.

Returning home following his release, Hobson began reading law under North Carolina State Chief Justice Richmond Mumford Pearson. When Justice Pearson retired from the bench and settled in the North Carolina hills, young James was one of a select group of prodigies for whom Pearson built a series of cabins. To the good fortune of our country, it was more than a legal education James acquired by studying with Pearson. His admission to the bar in 1867 was followed closely by marriage to his mentor's daughter. The union of Sarah Croom Pearson and James Hobson, which brought together two of Carolina's most illustrious families, would lead to the birth of an American hero.

Magnolia Grove . . . 1863 - 1882

Less than fifty miles by carriage from the Mississippi border, one comes upon Greensboro, Alabama, with its post-Civil War population of fewer than two thousand souls, most of them black. Greensboro lies in the heart of the area known as west central Alabama's Black Belt, so called because of its dark, fertile topsoil and not at all for the color of the majority of its inhabitants' skin. The closest 'major' city to Greensboro is Montgomery, boasting a post-war population of only slightly more than ten thousand souls.

In *Buck Jones at Annapolis*, Hobson describes Greensboro as "... a typical old Southern town. Little has changed since pre-Civil War days in this quaint college town "of unusual culture." The dwellers spend their days as planters nearby, and they help form one big family. Many left to go to other cities with a wider business horizon, particularly the young men, but no one would ever think of starting a cotton mill or other industry in Greensboro itself. The old families that had produced great statesmen, jurists, generals, are rearing a new breed amid less wealth but under the same old traditions."

On the western end of what is destined to become Greensboro's historic district is Magnolia Grove, its magnificent Greek revival mansion sitting on a modest fifteen-acre estate, fronted with six stunning stuccoed Doric columns. Magnolia Grove, on a site earlier known as McAlpine's Grove, was built sometime in the late 1830s or early 1840s by a wealthy North Carolina attorney and planter named Colonel Isaac Croom who would use it as his town house, fifteen miles from his plantation.

Colonel Croom's wife, Sarah Pearson Croom, is known to have diligently inspected each and every brick—all of them made on the property—as they went into the structure. The planning and design for the estate has been credited to one Dr. Drisch, a physician and builder from Tuscaloosa.

Standing in the gateway, one snatches a simultaneous glimpse of the mansion's spreading portals, its stretching white columns and its white facade. The handsome exterior delights in its temple style pediment, a fine wooden balustrade and small porch over the entrance. Notable inside are the unsupported curving staircase, expansively large rooms, and exhilaratingly high ceilings.

One takes the gentle slope for a leisurely walk beneath the mansion's immediate park. The sweetgums and white water oaks stretch their limbs gracefully, along with those of the pecans, mock oranges and cedars. Most majestic, of course, are the magnolias, whose seed pods remind one of sword hilts, beautifully adorned with pearls of brown.

Magnolia Grove dominates and overwhelms its ante-bellum surroundings, a tribute to Colonel Croom. Croom had settled in Greensboro to be near relatives, but flourished well beyond his expectations, becoming Alabama's largest landowner, president of the State Agricultural Society and the State Historical Society, and a state representative for the county.

Isaac Croom died in 1863, and his beautiful, young niece, Sarah Croom Pearson, came to live with the aunt for whom she was named. When the War Between the States finally ended a year or so later, Magnolia Grove was—thankfully—one of the relatively few Southern homes that had survived its devastation.

It was here, to Greensboro, Alabama, and Magnolia Grove, that Sarah chose to return with her husband, James Hobson, after they were wed in 1867. And it was in Greensboro, Alabama, that James Hobson, following the footsteps of both his ancestors and Sarah's, launched his career as a lawyer, later to become probate judge and state representative. James's uncle on his mother's side was North Carolina's former Governor John Motley Morehead, and two of his mother's cousins, also named Morehead, were former governors of Kentucky. In addition to being the daughter of a Chief Justice, Sarah could trace her ancestry back to Elder William Brewster of the *Mayflower*. A maternal great-grandfather was Colonel James Motley, who served with George Washington during the French and Indian Wars and a paternal great-great-grandfather was

Colonel John Williams, a U.S. Senator from Tennessee and heroic commander under Andrew Jackson during the War of 1812. His wife, Melinda White Williams (Sarah's great-great-grandmother), was the daughter of General James White, founder of Knoxville, and the sister of Hugh Lawton White, Chief Justice of Tennessee.

It was in the grandeur of Magnolia Grove and the glory of their illustrious heritage that Sarah began raising her family. James Marcellus, Jr. ('Mr. Gus'), was the first child born to Sarah and James Hobson (in all, there would be seven—four boys and three girls), but it was their second child, and second son, Richmond Pearson, who would bring them the most glory.

Shortly after Sarah gave birth to Richmond on August 17, 1870, a member of the household took the baby to introduce him to 'Mr. Gus' and was heard telling him, that his little brother would be somebody important some day. Speculation is that the household 'prophet' was either Tom Tap or Aunt (Mammy) Tap. Tom and Mammy, former Hobson slaves who came to Magnolia Grove with James, were not exactly family members, but they were considered as much fixture and family as anyone else in the household.

Ole Aunt Tap, as Mammy was affectionately known, had nursed the Hobson family for two generations. She was a little woman, with her head encased in a colorful bandanna and a spotless white kerchief around her neck, who responded graciously and efficiently to all the calls she heard from a special bell on the back porch.

Tom Tap had saved James Hobson's life in the Battle of Chancellorsville. One of James' and Sarah's daughters, Margaret, wrote a poem about Tom's heroism and devotion.

> *"How He Saved Marse Jim's Life"*
> Dem waz stirrin' times, I tell yer
> De wust yer ever saw;
> I followed my young Marster
> All thr'u dat bloody war
>
> De day we went ter jine de troops
> Ole Mistis sez, sez she:
> 'Stay wid him, Tom, thr'u ev'ything
> An' bring 'im back to me ... .'

I prayed ter God in heaben
Do I couldn't see His face
Ter he'p me ter pertect him;
Ter giv' me stren'th an' grace.

An de Marster up in heaben
Must'a hyeard dis niggar's prayer:
I knowed dat he wuz watchin'—
I could feel His lovin' care ... .

One day it seem de battle
Wuz ragin' wust uv all,
When I seed er bullet hit him—
An' I seed Marse Jimmy fall.

I ain' never stopped er minnit—
I jes dashed right into hell—
Brought him back upon my shoulder
Thr'u all dat shot an'shell

I nussed him mighty keerful,
An' dat night I heard him say:
'Tom, I don't know how yer did it—
But yer saved my life terday.'

I could feel ole Marster up in heaben
Lookin' at me wid er smile—
An' He sent er blessin' ter me
For savin' uv His chile ... .

It wasn't long before everyone agreed that young Richmond showed signs of later distinction. In *The Lower South in American History*, William Garrett Brown, who claims to have known the youngster when Richmond worked in the cotton fields with black sharecroppers, described him as "formal, grave faced, precocious, with a smoldering fierceness in his eyes ... ."

> His manner was stiff and formal; his conversations, almost comically stilted. One might have thought him heavy natured if it had not been for his eyes. In them there was a smoldering fierceness which I did not understand, for his bearing was modest to gentleness,

and his voice had all the drawling sweetness of the leisurely civilization out of which he came. Sometimes,
however, in baseball and other sports, it had a tone
of authority which provoked less resistance than an
attitude of superiority is apt to provoke among people
in whom association with a subject race has bred an
imperious temper.

For the rest, he stood out from his fellows chiefly
by reason of the steadfastness with which he kept in
mind the possibility of an honorable career and the fear-
lessness with which he addressed himself to the more
serious concerns of boyhood. That attitude toward life
was somewhat remarkable, for the shadow of defeat,
the reality of suffering made doggedness commoner
than ambition.

A close look at Brown's words does not convincingly demonstrate that historians fully understand the young Hobson: Not surprising! From his youth, Richmond Pearson Hobson was a complex character, a blend of contradictions and paradoxes. He felt
the need to excel and outshine everyone else to reflect his illustrious heritage. His education and religious training advanced his moral
and religious commitment. Moreover, he worshipped his mother
and transferred this worship to his wife whom he deeply loved.
These feelings had a profound influence on his public life. But, he
had to harmonize his values with the Southern mores and the flex-
ibility required in political life: A most difficult feat!

Sarah Hobson remembers that her son took an interest in things
that interested her. She was quoted in the *Saturday Evening Post*: "As
I was always very proud of Magnolia Grove, he, too, began to be
proud of it and to care for it. Some of the old trees had fallen
down, and he and I together planted several others which he watched
over and nursed. Now they're grown up and tall and beautiful and
we call them 'Rich's trees.'"

Richmond's sister, Florence Hobson Morrison, told of his
affection and concern for his mother when he was four. "When
Dad worked in his office, he would come in to Mother and assure
her, 'Mother, I will stay here to watch over you until Father comes.'
The little soldier fell asleep on Mother's arms."

One Christmas, she related, "Samuel Augustus and Richard went to see what Santa had brought them. Well, it was two white goats hitched to two wagons. Samuel Augustus got immediately on the goat, driving it as if he were a king on a chariot. However, Richmond left for town to bring bundles up for Mother for the fireplace."

H. G. Benners wrote in the *Greensboro Watchman*, that young Richmond took part in

> ... the usual small boy activities: gathering the chest-nuts at Magnolia Grove, dodging Aunt Croom, and slip-ping off after muscadines in the woods near Station Hill; plum hunting in the Cherry Field, hunting for jay birds and yellow hammers; the anti-profanity league, with a penalty of three slaps on the shoulder for each infrac-tion; finding Indian arrows near the depot, damming the ditch in the pasture to make a 'wash hole'; slaying robins with sling shots, and larks, with our little muzzle loaders ... having weekend visits to Mrs. Pros Nelson at Sun-shine [the uncle's plantation home near Greensboro] and Mrs. Charles Stickney's class at St. Paul's Sunday School, where we memorized 'The Collect for the Day' and a hymn for each Sunday, and Dr. Richard H. Cobbs ques-tioned us in the church catechism ... fishing at Cocke's Pond, Flinn's Mill, Millwood, usually reached afoot by us.

Like other Greensboro lads, young Hobson went barefoot all summer. As boyhood friend, Benners, further recalls in *Demorest's Family Magazine*, "All the boys went barefooted all summer, and sometimes in winter, not from poverty, but because our parents thought it made us hardier."

During young Hobson's days, Greensboro was the terminus of the Selma and Greensboro Railroad. "One of young Hobson's great delights," reminisced Benners, "was to slip down to the de-pot in the evening and help the train crew, the help consisting of riding up and down on the switch-engines until the time came to turn it, and then how he used to push away at that old turn table lever until she swung clear around and headed for Selma once more. We boys were more hindrance than help, but we thought we were 'the whole thing.'"

The young Richmond Pearson Hobson is also recalled by Hobson himself in his *Buck Jones at Annapolis*. While the work is not a bona fide autobiography, Richmond's son, George, argues for the similarities between Buck and young Richmond. Speaking from his home in Falls Church, Virginia, George Hobson said, "My dad never claimed that *Buck Jones* was a retelling of his youth and later years. However, many of the incidents in the book did happen, and the personality presented was that of Dad."

Richmond's childhood recollections are captured in Chapter II, "Buck's Boyhood Trials." "'Buck' (the young Richmond), and brother 'Hugh' were renowned, not only in their native 'Sumter' but also throughout the country: for academic achievement in Sunday school and in athletics, especially fishing, hunting, and swimming."

According to a report in the *Birmingham Age-Herald*, teachers, schoolmates, and friends called Rich the fastest runner, the best swimmer, and the most accurate rifleman. But he never boasted about his qualities. He was humble, considerate, and a good friend, "... ever the quiet, resolute, purposeful, intrepid youth. He had great endurance." The report continued, "On Saturdays, his day off from school, he went into the woods, or fished, or walked some 20 miles and would not be fatigued in the least."

While Rich did not seek fights, if challenged he demonstrated exceptional boxing skills. His sister, Florence, related a story told her by a neighbor: Two boys would regularly return home from school and when they reached a certain spot, the older boy would start a quarrel and then begin to torment and fight the younger lad. Young Rich heard about the Greensboro bully. One day, when the appointed time and place for the fight arose, Rich was waiting. "He stepped out," related the sister, "and gave the larger boy such a thrashing he would never forget. After that he never again tormented the smaller boy."

Rich's mom not only accepted her son's occasional fighting, but she was proud—under the proper conditions. As she told the *New York World* in 1898, "He could always take care of himself in a fight at school, and he did, too. It's no disgrace to a boy if he does have a little fight now and then at school, providing he doesn't get licked and he is in the right."

Rich developed quickly and rapidly caught up with his older brother, James, Jr. For three years, Rich had effectively used the Indian hug to contend in wrestling and was even able to throw his brother, who was considered the best town wrestler in his age group. However, 'Buck' could never overcome his brother on a regular basis.

A traumatic episode in young Richmond's life concerned his beloved dog, Hugo. The tale is relayed in *Buck Jones*.

> One day while they were out hunting, 'Buck' noticed a rabbit that had just jumped into a pile of brush. Because it was bad for bird-dogs to see, 'Buck' would usually not fire at rabbits in front of Hugo. For some reason, this time he violated his own rule, thinking, 'As this fellow comes out of the brush I will get him before Hugo comes up.'
>
> 'Buck' miscalculated and wound up shooting his most valuable friend. 'O Hugo!' the boy cried, and his heart stopped beating. A terrible fear seized him. He stood riveted, paralyzed. The dog dragged himself up slowly, with a gaping wound in its shoulder, but never uttered a cry. His liquid brown eyes looked up at 'Buck', standing motionless, without any reproach, only with affection as much as to say: 'Don't be sad; I know you did not mean to do it.'
>
> He soon realized that he had killed Hugo, who he had loved more than any other pet. 'Buck' brought his friend home and buried him in his garden, with Christian burial, under the large apple tree at the head of his watermelon patch.

Hobson's upbringing had been firmly rooted n his belief in God, but he, as young 'Buck,' faced a great crisis after the death of Hugo:

> 'It is not so much about poor Hugo,' ['Buck'] told his Mom, sobbing, 'but I have come to doubt God. One of the seniors has been telling me lately that there is no God, that religion is only superstition, that it is all nature and natural law. When I called out to God, there was no answer.' 'Buck' was now buffeted by the mystery of creation, the mystery of life, the mystery of death.

His mother kissed and reassured a doubting youngster. 'Yes, darling. There is a God I *know*,' she reassured
her son, 'and He is good and merciful, and if we do our
part well, He will take care of us all and all will be well
in the end.'

The mother gently stroked his hair, wet with tears.

Years later, Mrs. Grizelda Hobson, Richmond's wife, in praising her mother-in-law cited the words of Dr. Richard H. Cobbs,
son of the Greensboro Bishop, who said, "To come into her presence is like one kneeling for a benediction." Adding her own words,
Grizelda Hobson continued, "Perhaps she realized that in this hour,
her boy was going through his last childish struggle, that it was the
last time she would help him master a situation. Perhaps, unconsciously, she was giving him that benediction."

The end of the chapter in *Buck Jones* informs us, "A still doubting 'Buck' promised his Mom, 'I can't tell, Mamma, about God,
but I *am* going to do *my* part.'"

That episode ended Rich's childhood. This was the last struggle
in which anyone was to help the youngster. And it was, perhaps,
this early end of his childhood that helped propel Richmond
Pearson Hobson to his destiny.

left: Richmond Pearson
Hobson, age 2.
below: Hobson's Mother and
Father. Source: *The Southern
Review.*

2

EDUCATION FOR LIFE

Like the other Hobson children, Richmond was tutored at home. In particular, his very devout mother, along with the Episcopal Church, gave him his religious training.

Mrs. Hobson was asked by the *New York World*, "Did you set before your son a great man as a hero to be imitated?"

She responded, "Never! I read with him Abbot's *History of England*, histories of Napoleon, and other great men and generals. I always kept before him men who had accomplished some great deeds. But I've not done any better than many other mothers."

What she stressed was the teaching of religion and proper values. "Teach boys first to fear God and serve Him," she'd say. "Teach them to be upright and to do their duty always and to be frank and amiable. A mother should be a companion to her sons. There's a great deal in that. By companionship with him, a mother keeps her boy's confidence. Give him the best books to read—books that will give him high ideals, high purposes; books that will stimulate him and teach him never to fall short of his most lofty purposes."

Pope's "Essay on Man" so stimulated the youngster that he knew it as well as the Catechism. In particular, he recited the part beginning: "Lo, the poor Indian, whose untutored mind/Sees God in clouds and hears Him in the wind."

Beyond his tutoring at home, young Hobson completed primary studies in the private school of Miss Kate Boardman and Miss Mary Avery and from the start led all classes in his studies.

Southern University . . . 1882 - 1885

At age twelve, in 1882, Richmond enrolled in Southern University, then in Greensboro. His academic record was outstanding. Most valuable were the oratorical skills he developed on campus, which would be a hallmark of his public career. He won a declamation medal, the sophomore prize, for "The Curse of Regulus," a Roman general, who fought and was captured by Carthage in 255 B.C. Hobson was "full of the fire and zeal of Regulus himself," wrote H.G. Benners in *Demorest's*, "flashing on the audience the hatred and loathing due the people of Carthage." Then at age fifteen, in 1885, he gave one of the most remarkable displays of true eloquence. One professor told the *New York Tribune* that rarely was such eloquence "heard from schoolboy lips."

Socially, he was active in Kappa Alpha fraternity. In 1884, Richmond—accompanied by his father—was one of a party of students who visited the New Orleans Exposition. They strolled to the Canal Street wharf and were looking at the ships anchored in the Mississippi when he heard a man shouting, "Visit the man-of-war for 25 cents." Excitedly, he jumped at the chance. To Hobson, the old flag-ship *Tennessee* was the most magnificent ship ever afloat. A fascinated teenager studied the warship. A blue-jacket took the visitors on the ship and answered the teen's endless questions, as he took out pen and paper and detailed its construction, operation, and maintenance. Richmond spoke enthusiastically about entering the Navy.

After graduating in 1885, Richmond set out to follow his plans of attending a military academy. The youngster was fascinated by all matters related to the miliary, his father told the *New York Tribune* in 1898. "Richmond was always interested in Army and Navy matters and in soldier business," said the senior Hobson. Would it be the Point or the Naval Academy? Actually, as revealed in *Buck Jones*, the youngster Rich had made the choice before his eleventh birthday. Since Rich's brother Hugh had opted for West Point, Rich felt it was his "duty to go to Annapolis."

Sadness turned to joy when Dad, portrayed in *Buck Jones* as 'Major Jones,' told his son of the importance of the ocean in the life history of America. "The United States is essentially the ocean's country," asserted the Major. "You will find, my boy, that naval operations have played a far more important part in the life and history of America than people realize. America's whole naval history is like a romance." 'Major Jones' had "electrified" his son. And then the youngster recalled his mother's words. "I did my part, my duty, in accepting Annapolis ... Mother is right ... . If we do our part, it will all turn out for the best in the end."

Annapolis . . . 1885

Entry to Annapolis was decided by competitive examinations in the applicant's Congressional district. For Richmond Pearson Hobson, it was the Sixth Congressional District, which included Greensboro. Richmond was the youngest competitor. While the other boys had studied for months, having begun as soon as they heard of the exam date, Rich did not start studying until six weeks before the test. He had first learned of the exam while reading the newspaper.

Hobson, age fourteen, entered Annapolis under appointment by Congressman A.C. Davidson. The day before leaving his Greensboro home, he gathered his possessions: a little carpet bag which he had used for fishing and hunting, along with a package of food, and a Bible given him by his mother the previous year. Relates Mrs. Grizelda Hobson in her *Memoirs*: "All the little town turned out at the depot to see him off. They brought Confederate flags to wave to him—the only ones they had in the little town. Rich was deeply stirred when one by one his family told him goodbye. He was especially moved by his father, who looked lovingly at him, as he clasped his hand, and his mother, who held him one last moment in her arms tightly. Then the train whistle blew; all waved flags as Rich stepped aboard, holding his head up, but swallowing hard!"

Upon arrival, he had an appointment, as did all applicants, at the Navy Department with the Secretary of the Navy. He passed a familiar type of house—a little like that at home—white, with large columns. "Who lives there?" he wondered. Who could he ask?

Richmond Pearson Hobson during
his first year at the Naval Academy.
Courtesy: Magnolia Grove

He noticed a black man across the street, raising feelings of home, with Tom and Aunt Tap. "Uncle," he addressed the man, "will you tell me who lives there?"

Snapped the man, "I ain't no uncle of yours; when I want to claim kin I'll let you know."

The young Hobson was angered. "Do you know to whom you are talking?" he exclaimed.

"Scuse me boss," said the man civilly. 'I didn't mean nothing. I thought you was trying to guy me. The President lives there, suh, and that's the White House."

His adolescent routine all but stopped. No more athletics. Aside from meals and a few hours of sleep, Richmond only allowed himself the 'luxury' of a two-mile jog around twilight.

Hard work paid off. He reported to the Naval Academy in May, 1885, three months before his 15th birthday. Courses in sail-making and knot tying had been replaced by the traditional, familiar courses in engineering principles and methods. This was evident in the texts used during the late 1800s: *Principles of Machine Construction, Manual of Spherical Trigonometry, Treatise of Hydromechanics, Treatise on Analytic Mechanics, Ganot's Physics, Elastic Strength of Guns, Navigation and Nautical Astronomy*.

Richmond's scholastic intensity prepared him well for the academic rigors. He was the youngest member of his class, but that did not have a direct relationship to the difficulties awaiting him. According to Richard Sheldon, who studied Hobson's progressive policies in Congress, life at Annapolis became difficult because of the young midshipman's "pride, personal habits, high ideals, and romantic outlook on life."

In fact, he endured brutal hazing from his own classmates and from upperclassmen. As he related in the 1910 *Congressional Record*, he had "run the gamut of hazing at Annapolis in perhaps its severest form." In particular, his abstinence from drink, his daily prayers, and reading from the Bible were derided by his classmates.

On one occasion Richmond was approached by a fellow midshipman: "Mister, did I see you drinking milk?"

"Yes, sir."

"What do you mean by it? Knock it off."

One evening as time for taps approached, Richmond scanned the deck to see if his mates were preparing to say their prayers. All was fun and laughter on board, and they began to climb into their hammocks. The narrative is developed in *Buck Jones*: "'Shall I say my prayers in my hammock? That is what the rest are probably going to do ... .' Still, no one commenced their prayers. He had always knelt down to say his prayers. It went against his grain not to do so now, yet he hesitated. Then with sharp self-scorn he suddenly knelt down, with his elbows on his camp stool on the open deck, and said his prayers."

Richmond was spotted by the non-worshippers and targeted for jeering. Said one idler, "'Did you know we had a parson on board?'" he roared, sneeringly. The young midshipman quickly became known as "Parson." However, he did gain a measure of respect when he saved a classmate from drowning. He was now 'Parson Tough.'

Richmond never hazed others. He considered this a crude and inhumane form of discipline. As a Congressman in 1910 he supported a bill to impose tough penalties for hazing.

All of this did not deter 'Buck' from devotion to church and country. He described the call for service, initiated by the quartermaster's raising the church flag to the yardarm: "'It is very beautiful,' he thought, as he watched the quartermaster bend on the ensign. The Nation's flag began to go up slowly, very slowly. 'Buck' held his breath, as it stopped reverently just beneath the church pennant, the glorious flag, flying there proudly, but looking up in humility to the flag of the blue cross above ... . It seemed to 'Buck' that the Infinite was all about them and God seemed present and very close."

On another occasion, Richmond finished his supper and hurried on deck for the Chaplain's service. "The sunset was weird and unnatural," marveled Richmond. "All hands uncovered and the Chaplain offered up thanks. The lad had never felt so close to nature and to nature's God ... . All heads were bowed in silence. The only sound made by man was the Chaplain's voice, as he besought guidance from the Almighty during the perils of the night."

That night "the mystery and wonder of the universe" filled 'Buck.' He realized that the universe "was organized with a Divine plan ... [and 'Buck' himself] was a part of that plan." This realization remained with the midshipman throughout life.

One of his friends had not been to church for twenty years, but he carefully scrutinized Richmond throughout the service and was impressed. Said the skeptic, now 'converted': "'I like the lad's religion ... . Whatever it may be, it's not cowardly. He holds his head up and looks straight out. Even when bowed in prayer his eyes are still open.'"

No episode in *Buck Jones* so stirred the midshipman as the experience on a cruise a week before graduation: "The water rose, the breaking sea swept by. He struck out, half swimming, half wading across the wreckage, climbed the tottering chart house, broke in, found an ensign, dashed back, climbed the forerigging, then out on the foreyard, and lashed the Stars and Stripes, to the fore life. Higher still, above the din, the voices rose: 'Oh, say, does that Star Spangled Banner yet wave o'er the land of the free and the home of the brave?'

"Under the light of a vivid flash, all eyes turned to the national flag fluttering above them in the gale."

Nothing, however, at Annapolis was of as much moment as Hobson's being "put in Coventry," or being ostracized. He refused to compromise his absolute sense of duty and honor. During his second year, he was named Officer of the Day, an assignment he did not relish. As a plebe, 'Buck' saw the effects of banishment. One student had cheated in a secret poker game. Rather than report the matter to authorities, participants turned the affair over to the class, which put the cheater in Coventry. No one spoke to the scoundrel again: "'Buck' remembered the look of scorn as everyone turned away. This appeared to him as the most terrible punishment possible on this earth."

The news of his assignment depressed him. "'It was an overcast afternoon,' recalled 'Buck,' with black, tragic clouds out toward the horizon. The face of the earth and of the heavens seemed weird and dark and threatening ... . During supper he made an effort to appear light-hearted, but his heart was as heavy as lead."

Two ringleaders decided to test the young officer's resolve. They were joined by some two dozen supporters. In violation of the rules, they were smoking in the washroom. 'Buck' told the twenty-one culprits they would be reported for smoking. One ringleader mocked the officer and told his buddies, "['Buck'] would go to any length to get a chance to report a classmate and curry favor with the Superintendent and Commandant."

'Buck' was not done. Four were reported for being late to breakfast formation. Another was reported for wearing a nonregulation uniform. The list of rule breakers became immense. Two large pages listed more rule-breakers for that one day than for the previous two weeks. The two ringleaders spread their venom in the Annapolis halls. Rather than performing his duty, the incensed cadets insisted, 'Buck' was following self-serving goals: "He wants to show off his authority. He's working for promotion."

"He hates the class, and is taking it out this way.'"

"He thinks he is the whole thing—greater than the customs, greater than the class."

The ringleader, also class president, had stirred up the men. How dare 'Buck' report infractions? It was simply not done. The decision was Coventry. As 'Buck' was completing his report, the other ringleader gave him the news: "Mr. Jones ... I have been sent as a committee to notify you that the class has put you in Coventry."

Immersed in fulfilling his duty, 'Buck' had no immediate reaction. But when he came to the end of his report, the idea sunk in. "'In Coventry. In Coventry,' he repeated."

As he prepared for his night's rest, 'Buck' realized that he had more space than in past days. The men had moved their hammocks away. The next morning, a classmate disregarded his "Good morning." Those he met stared at him coldly and then turned away. When he washed his hands, the basins on both sides emptied. No one sat at his table. His work partner in the blacksmith shop asked for reassignment. When he jumped into the pool, all left the water.

For the first three days of Coventry, he spoke to his classmates seven words the first day; three, the second; none, the third. "He went about in silence, treated with scorn and contempt."

"'O God!' he lamented. 'I've tried to do my part.'"

'Buck' observed that no cadet had ever been able to sustain Coventry for any long period at Annapolis. "It is a punishment beyond anything conceived of elsewhere."

The twenty-one expected Hobson would be angry, glum, and hopelessly depressed, and finally give in to resignation from Annapolis. However, they did not know 'Buck.' The cadets "were surprised to see him go his way, holding his head and eyes erect, as he carried out a routine—an hour's work, a half hour in the gym, a 20-minute swim, and twice weekly horseback rides: 'And during the other spare hours ... he studied and read some interesting books, notably the classics and the standard novels he never had time to read before. He began to delve into the theory of the steam engine, and take up theoretical naval architecture and nautical astronomy.'"

The ringleaders were more incensed now than when they had condemned 'Buck.' If 'Buck' did not crack, of what value would Coventry be? And they became even more infuriated when one of the twenty-one began reporting all violators when he became Officer of the Day. Of course, he was put in Coventry.

The ostracized 'Buck' now had a companion and soul brother, who was known in *Buck Jones* as Catell. Mrs. Grizelda Hobson in her *Memoirs* identified him as Cadet Sumner Kitelle, later Admiral Kitelle, who remained faithful to Hobson through the banishment. Said Catell, "'I've come over to join you, 'Jones.' I didn't have the courage the first time; but since they put you in Coventry I have been impatient for my turn for duty to come again.'"

The next week 'Buck' had two companions, both in Coventry. The Coventry roster kept growing. By summer's end, nineteen had joined 'Buck.' Reflected 'Buck,' "'They were a concrete illustration of the great fact that the highest and truest happiness even for youth can only come in the path of rectitude and duty.'"

The banishment had little effect on 'Buck,' both socially and academically. He had now matured physically, resembling his father. Aside from the friendship of Catell, 'Buck' enjoyed the social life in the Academy YMCA and became its president. In his final year he commanded the cadet battalion.

"Sometimes little things would happen at the Academy that would make friends for him," Richmond's mother told the *Saturday*

Evening Post. "He always wrote of them to me. Once, the boys asked him to play ball, not thinking that he was very well fitted for it, on account of his close application to his studies, but they were much surprised when he took his place as catcher, refusing the ordinary protection of gloves and mask, and showed himself quite efficient. For that they always said he had tremendous nerve, but of course they did not know that he had shown that same nerve in things he did when at home."

Years later, one of his classmates, Admiral Vesey Pratt, wrote to Grizelda Hobson about the young midshipman:

> We were classmates of the graduating year of 1889. It seems only yesterday when we all gathered together as plebes to begin what was to be our life work ... . I remember well his proficiency in all his studies, especially in mathematics, and I often wondered how a man so young could do so much better than those four years his senior. Often when I was struggling over a problem which Professor Hendrickson had given us to solve, I, with mine not half completed, would look around and see Hobson with his completed, standing ready to recite.
>
> These were the days when every man near the top was on his honor never to lie or cheat, but to help others less fortunate, which your husband did often to my knowledge. He was always a crusader, always honest, always fearless, and because he was in a way different, he was not appreciated at that time by all of his classmates, to whom mediocrity and personal property meant more than honor.

After Hobson's war exploits, the *New York Times* reported, without confirmation, that his classmates had voted to remove his banishment. Hobson said, "No." They had rejected him and he did well without their comradeship. "Gentlemen," he said, "you have gotten along without me for a year; I shall manage to worry on without you for the remaining year." He would continue to thrive without them.

Mrs. George E. Sledge of Greensboro, who knew many members of the Hobson family, compiled a brief history of "The

Hobson Family of Greensboro." According to Mrs. Sledge, when the cadets found out that the youngest member of the class was also the highest in rank and honors: "They met, and by a series of resolutions confessed the wrong they had done him and asked his friendship and forgiveness. He met the overture with dignity and courtesy, but with manly spirit of self-reliance and independence."

Indeed, 'Buck's' classmates received him warmly. He was cheered loudly by his fellow graduates as the youngest graduate in the class and first in his class of '89. No hard feelings, Hobson records in *Buck Jones*. In fact, the lesson was valuable: "We unconsciously come to love a place in proportion to our character growth while there ... the *dear* old Naval Academy."

While not proven, some Greensboro citizens have conjectured that the Coventry experience influenced Hobson to choose the more intellectual, introspective Construction Corps career rather than line duty in the Navy, the career choice for most of his fellow cadets.

Richmond Pearson Hobson as an
Ensign in the United States Navy.
Courtesy: Magnolia Grove

3

CAREER CHOICE: NAVAL CONSTRUCTOR

For more than twenty years, the U.S. Naval Academy had sent its top-ranking graduates to Europe for additional study in construction and ship design. Annapolis did not have the resources to offer such a course on the European level. This was also testimony to the sophistication that advanced technology had brought to the field of naval warfare. All this suited Richmond Pearson Hobson well, for the Naval Academy graduate who studied under this program became a naval constructor. According to an article in the 1904 *New York Times* by Edwin Bjorkman, no Annapolis man had ever turned down the opportunity of studying in Europe under the European program. The only unhappy men were the regular naval officers, who lamented the loss of the best personnel for the fighting force.

Aboard the U.S.S. Chicago ... *1889-1890*

After graduation, Hobson went on the customary midshipman's tour of duty aboard the *U.S.S. Chicago*, the Flagship of the Squadron of Evolution in the Atlantic Ocean, from July 1889 to October 1890, under the command of Rear Admiral John C. Walker.

Hobson and seven of his Annapolis classmates were given many duties: gun duty in the engine room, service in the powder division, and electrical or torpedo duty. Whether at port or at sea, the men had little leisure time aboard the *Chicago*. Naval life was best described by Admiral French Ensor Chadwick, commander of the *New York* and chief of staff to Admiral William T. Sampson. It was a regimen that "brooks only the qualities that make for a man, for most certainly the sea is not for weaklings. the daily life demands courage, resolution, and resourcefulness that comes with a strong character."

Young Hobson took on many responsibilities as assistant navigator. The *Chicago* visited numerous South American and Mediterranean ports and was present at the ceremony in Brazil of the Recognition of the Flag of the Republic.

While in Corfu he experienced an incident that deepened an already overwhelming patriotic spirit. The citizens ashore were celebrating a feast day. A hoist of flags flew over the governor's palace, with the American flag about halfway up. Four flags flew above the Stars and Stripes. An incensed Admiral Walker summoned his lieutenant and ordered the governor be awakened and told as follows: "If he wishes to hoist the flag at all, he must put it at the top. That spirit of the Navy today is, and has been, the spirit of the Navy from the very beginning. Before we had a flag, John Paul Jones, then a lieutenant, hoisted the rattlesnake flag on the flagship *Alfred* of the first Colonial fleet, with the motto, 'Don't tread on me.' Our flag stands for great principles of human liberty and self government, upon which hangs the welfare of humanity. This is the secret of the superhuman devotion shown by our people whenever the flag is in peril. Our Navy stands between the Nation and the powerful enemies of our institutions ... . No flag under Heaven and made by the hand of man shall fly above the Stars and Stripes."

Europe . . . 1890-1893

In November, 1890, Hobson arrived in Paris. He spent one year at the Ecole Nationale Supériere des Mines and two years at the Ecole d'Application du Génie Maritime. He took twenty-three courses, including one in hypnotism. His friends claimed that he was the only American to ever be in Paris and not visit the Moulin Rouge.

An article in the 1899 *Saturday Evening Post* offered a vignette from a Hobson acquaintance who met him while in Paris. Knowing of the lieutenant's interest in machinery, the tourist met Hobson at a watering resort: "Do you know," he announced to Hobson, "that there is a piece of American machinery in this town."

"Is that so?" responded the Alabaman enthusiastically "I haven't seen it, and I should like to very much."

"Then, come with me," said the friend. He took him to a barber shop which featured a pair of shears stamped with a house of Providence, Rhode Island.

"That's American machinery, indeed," said the amused Hobson, "and I am thrilled to see it."

He graduated from Génie with distinction, the first American to ever earn honors. Instead of vacationing after graduation in 1893 Hobson spent the summer months in the French shipyards to gain first-hand knowledge of ship building. His studies having been completed in September, 1893, Hobson accepted a brief assignment at the American Embassy in London. Once more, he seized the opportunity for first-hand viewing of English shipbuilding.

However, Hobson did not completely bury himself in his books or withdraw to the shipyards of France and England. He returned to his boyhood love of soccer and joined the Parisian White Rovers Soccer Club. His fierce play, however, was not appreciated by opponents. *London To-Day* presented the following observations by an English adversary: "He always played as though he did not know on which side he was on. He kicked all over the place, and among the most celebrated of these kicks was one that put a prominent member of our club to bed for six weeks."

Back Home—A Taste of Bureaucracy . . . 1893-1897

After more than four years abroad, Hobson returned to America in December 1893, for a near-five-year prelude to his heroics in the Spanish-American War. His first American assignment was in Washington with the Navy Department's Bureau of Construction and Repair. For eighteen months he supervised work on new vessels under construction at Navy yards across the country. He received his first taste of government bureaucracy when, in October 1894, he requested that Secretary of the Navy Hilary Herbert send him to Asia as an official U.S. observer during the Sino-Japanese War.

Four days later, Hobson was irritated that the Secretary did not respond to his letter, so the young naval constructor confronted his fellow Alabaman in person. Fine, said the Secretary, but only if China and Japan agreed in writing, The determined Hobson received permission from the belligerents. However, the Chief of the Bureau of Navigation involved himself in the affair. He did not take kindly to Hobson's by-passing chains of command in appealing to the Secretary of the Navy.

A brief note to Hobson from Bureau Chief Francis Ramsey was a clear no: the Department deemed it unnecessary to send a Naval Constructor to the Asiatic Station.

Hobson was not unsettled by the turndown. The next fall he asked Herbert once more, this time for assignment in Europe, where Hobson thought a yes was likely. Once more, a "No." However, Hobson would not accept this and turned to Congress and Uncle Richmond Pearson to intervene. The young man learned quickly that he was creating enemies within the service because of his pushy and maverick tactics. Herbert relayed this message to the Congressman: Your nephew might be a genius but has to learn protocol in military officialdom. "Young Hobson," said the Secretary, "had disregarded that entente cordiale or that sense of subordination with and to [his] superiors which the discipline and good of the service require."

The villain in the affair might have been Francis T. Bowles, also a naval constructor in the Construction Corps. More traditional than Hobson and ten years his senior at the Naval Academy, it was perhaps Bowles who rallied the Corps against the Alabaman. He and others had good cause to be jealous of Hobson.

In 1894 Hobson wrote a major article in *Proceedings of the U.S. Naval Institute* titled "A Summary of the Situation and Outlook in Europe." In short, concluded Hobson, war was imminent in Europe, with the threat coming from France and Russia. In particular, Russian expansion posed the most serious threat to Western civilization. Granted that the Sino-Japanese War had ended after submission of his article, Hobson was still convinced that Russia's absorption of Southeastern and large additional portions of Central Europe appeared inevitable. Whether Western Europe was to follow would depend on the capacity of the Western nations for union. The "coming war," predicted Hobson, "will be on a scale incomparably greater than any in the world's history."

Having been turned down twice already, Hobson became pragmatic and sent a new proposal through regular channels. Naval constructors, he said, should be assigned sea duty so that they could observe ship performance under actual conditions, and, of course, he proposed himself for the assignment. This was a keen proposal and was accepted. Hobson was detailed to the *New York*, an armored cruiser, flagship of the North Atlantic Squadron, commanded by Admiral Francis M. Bunce.

Hobson led a busy life in the capital as a member of the Metropolitan Club and of the Army and Navy Club. A much-sought after Navy man, Hobson stood 6 foot, 180 pounds, with tender, sympathetic brown eyes. Having learned dancing at Professor Bayol's Dancing School in Greensboro, Hobson led many cotillions. He also excelled as a horseman and fencer.

During 1895-96 he served at the Brooklyn Navy Yard and later was Officer in Charge of Construction at the Navy Yard in Newport News. He was asked by Naval Constructor Francis Bowles and Assistant Constructor Hobbs to act as their counsel in the case of a Court of Inquiry into the installation of the turret guns of the *Puritan*. The case arose from charges by Commodore Sperry against Bowles.

Evidence of Hobson's writing skills and naval insights was again shown in articles for *Proceedings of the U.S. Naval Institute*. One article dealt with "The Disappearing Gun Afloat;" a second article, also technical, was published in 1896 and examined "The Yacht Defender and the Use of Aluminum in Marine Construction."

While Hobson had accumulated enemies in the service because of his unorthodox approach to fulfilling his requests, the imbroglio in 1897 with Joseph J. Woodward was of an entirely different nature. Woodward accused Hobson of neglect of duty because defective castings of parts for two ships had been inspected by the junior constructor and approved. More than just castigating him,

Woodward put a series of technical questions before his subordinate so as to embarrass and humiliate Hobson in the eyes of his colleagues, especially younger colleagues and secretaries.

Hobson had few problems responding to the questions on machine tool practice. But Hobson would not let the arrogance of Woodward go unavenged, Within a few weeks Hobson composed a 47-page document that featured a detailed explanation why the defects were not his fault. Most important to Hobson was his vigorous assertion that Woodward's examination insulted both Hobson and, more importantly, the U.S. Navy. Hobson directed his remarks to the Secretary of the Navy.

That role was then being filled by Theodore Roosevelt, Acting Secretary. This initiated a career-long relationship with the Roosevelts, first Teddy and then FDR. The first contact was most gratifying to Hobson, for the Acting Secretary fully vindicated Hobson's complaints. Wrote Roosevelt, "After careful consideration of your letter ... as well as of the statement in regard thereto submitted by Naval Constructor Woodward, that officer has been informed that his conduct on the occasion in question merits and receives the Department's unqualified reprobation."

Back to "Annapolis" ... 1897-1898

Hobson gained an added measure of satisfaction that year with the acceptance of his proposed three-year postgraduate course in naval construction, at Annapolis. The Naval Academy could now rid itself of dependance on Europe's naval schools, where Hobson himself had been trained. Hobson organized the course and suggested that it be run by one professor and, not surprisingly, Richmond Pearson Hobson's name was put forward by Richmond Pearson Hobson.

The inaugural class was taught by Hobson in the fall of 1897. During the summer the class visited various Navy Yards, shipyards, drydocks and engine companies.

The sinking of the battleship *Maine* in Havana harbor brought conflict between America and Spain closer. Continuing hostility changed Hobson's focus. In the spring of 1897 he had requested that the commandant of the New York Navy Yard transfer him to the Line and that he be assigned duty afloat in the Squadron to be actively engaged in prosecuting the war.

War was not declared until April 1898, but Hobson was most eager to take his students to Key West, Florida, to join the North Atlantic Squadron, and continue the graduate course. "Although my father had been vindicated by the Secretary of War," said George Hobson, "and although Dad felt pride in that his course proposal was accepted, he still was stung by Woodward's behavior. He saw the approaching war as a means of totally wiping out that unfortunate incident."

Hobson began to study Spanish and instructed his class to determine the weaknesses of the Spanish navy. Readying himself for possible future action, he hoped this preparedness would make him and his students valuable. It turned out as planned.

Not only did Hobson continue his course, but he was also assigned the direction of a naval station at Key West. More important for Hobson's future was his attachment to the *U.S.S. New York*, the flagship of William T. Sampson. The naval constructor had succeeded in convincing the Secretary of the Navy of the value of assigning a naval architect to observe ships under war conditions.

There were great advantages of having a naval constructor at sea. Before war was declared, Hobson had sent several confidential reports to Sampson on the weaknesses of the Spanish fleet, especially their lack of protection above the protective deck. Hobson recommended battle tactics to direct rapid fire and machine guns to the upper works just above the protective deck. Hobson's reports proved invaluable and were so described in 1901 by Sampson when he was Commandant at the Boston Navy Yard. Had Spain more aggressively challenged the American Navy, Sampson told the media, the Admiral would have followed the battle tactics recommended by the naval constructor.

In the Right Place . . . 1898

Where was Richmond Pearson Hobson when the U.S. declared war on Spain, April 21, 1898? Historically, and personally, he was in the right place. He was aboard the *U.S.S. New York*. The next day,

Sampson's squadron left to blockade Havana and other ports east and west of the Cuban capital.

What did Hobson do after the declaration of war? He offers some answers in *Line of Duty*, an autobiographical follow-up to *Buck Jones at Annapolis*. 'Buck' was assigned to the *U.S.S. Oregon* and left for the Caribbean from the West Coast. He was later a participant (historically incorrect) at the Battle of Santiago.

'Buck' received a packet of letters from his Mother: "It is a holy war, my son," she wrote him a day after war was declared. "Go forth and do your duty. God will take care of you."

Mrs. Hobson told the *Saturday Evening Post* in 1899, "Richmond was always longing for an opportunity to be of service to his country. It was a righteous war, a war for humanity, and I was as glad as he that he would help free the oppressed. I wrote to him after the war opened that I hoped he would do his duty and that he would refrain from unnecessary rashness. I cannot say that I was afraid— it was a holy war, and he was in God's care."

Sampson's squadron shelled Matanzas on April 27. He moved his squadron to Puerto Rico upon hearing that Cervera was headed for the Caribbean with a swift fleet. Learning of Sampson's movements, Cervera headed for Santiago de Cuba, which was not yet under American blockade, and arrived May 19. Sampson's squadron had arrived at San Juan on May 12, but not encountering Cervera's fleet, was ordered to return to Key West, where it arrived May 18. Also at Key West was the Flying Squadron led by Commodore Winfield Scott Schley. Sampson ordered Schley to head for Cienfuegos in hopes of locating Cervera.

Before learning of Cervera's whereabouts, Sampson sailed for Cay Frances to guard Havana's eastern approaches. When he learned that Cervera was actually at Santiago, he ordered Schley to head for the Harbor. The Flying Squadron arrived in Santiago, May 24 but, inexplicably, neither the Flying Squadron nor the auxiliary cruisers at Santiago made any attempt to search for Cervera's fleet. While en route back to Key West, Sampson had cabled Schley to blockade Santiago. Navy Secretary John D. Long also cabled Schley to remain at Santiago, intending to sink a collier in the entrance to the Harbor. But Schley had left Santiago on May 26 and did not receive the cable.

4

SINKING OF THE MERRIMAC

On May 29, Sampson was back at Key West. With Schley having missed Long's cable, the command of the sinking operation at Santiago fell to William Sampson and Richmond Pearson Hobson. The story of Hobson's heroics unfold in the naval constructor's narrative, *The Sinking of the Merrimac*. It is clear in the narrative that the plan for sinking the *Merrimac* was Sampson's, not Hobson's; however, "The Hobsons of Greensboro" insists, without proof, that the naval constructor "was the instigator as well as the executor of the plan," and during a 1941 ceremony honoring his former Annapolis teacher, Joseph W. Powell agreed that Hobson had "instigated" the plan.

In actuality, Sampson consulted with Hobson and asked him for a report, which was approved by the Admiral. At the time Hobson was planning his own report "the reduction of Havana." "[W]hile I was preparing this report ... the admiral first proposed to me his scheme of sinking the *Merrimac* at Santiago," reported Hobson.

The Alabaman presented an intricate plan for destroying Havana : "I ... set to work on the problem of clearing a channel of torpedoes and mines. The result was the outline design of a craft especially constructed to be unsinkable, having the general form of an iron canal-boat, operating by its own motive power, rendered unsinkable by being stowed with air-tight cans a foot long, and made indestructible be [sic] special arrangements in construction by the use of wire cables. I had elaborated a plan for the use of five such unsinkable craft, to precede the fleet in entering the harbor of Havana."

Sampson listened politely, but his interest was in a sinkable ship, not an unsinkable vessel, and the site was Santiago, not Havana. Cervera had evaded America's blockade, and while his fleet was no match for the American Navy in numbers and strength, Sampson did not want him to escape and prolong the war. Sampson sought to strangle Cervera and his fleet.

"Wouldn't it be more advisable to destroy the fleet rather than tying up the Spaniards?" asked an astonished Hobson.

"You are absolutely right," responded the Admiral, "but we do not expect Admiral Cervera to leave his protection and fight us. It would be suicide for Spain."

Sampson then picked Hobson's brain. "As a clever naval constructor," asked Sampson, "let me hear your ideas on how to sink a ship."

"It is not so simple, sir," said Hobson. "It is easy to scuttle a ship, but not quickly. To block the channel completely, the ship must be placed in the proper position and all this must happen in a few minutes."

"Can it be done?" wondered Sampson. "Study the question carefully and report back to me."

The next day, May 30, Hobson presented Sampson with a complete plan, including "the choice of circumstances, and the navigation and manoeuvering of the vessel, as well as the method of sinking." Sampson gave full approval.

The old coal ship *Merrimac* seemed ideally suited for the mission. With a faulty engine and a bottom half filled with coal, the collier could be relied on to remain at the bottom—without drifting—at the designated site.

The constructor had proposed two methods for sinking the vessel: driving off the bottom plates and using a series of torpedoes. The torpedoes was the quicker method, so Sampson agreed to that plan. Hobson added, "I propose to place the ten torpedoes to be tied against the outside of the ship, about twelve feet below the water line ... . To discharge these torpedoes, wires from each will run to a small generator bridge. They would be fired simultaneously. If all the torpedoes went off, the *Merrimac* would sink in a minute and a quarter."

Aside from Hobson's *Sinking of the Merrimac*, the constructor's plans are fully sketched in a notebook, preserved by his wife Grizelda

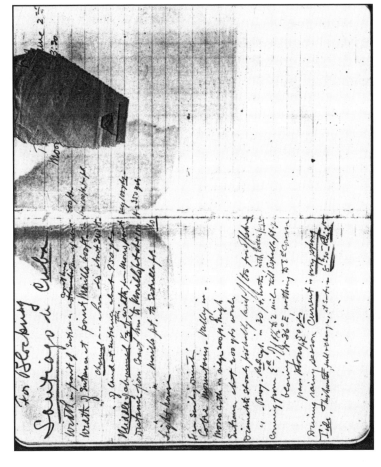

Excerpt from Hobson's logbook on the blocking of the Santiago de Cuba harbor.

Source: Magnolia Grove.

Hobson, and now at Magnolia Grove. An entry of June 2 is called "For Blocking Santiago de Cuba."

Sampson approved the plans, but said no to Hobson's request for adding two warheads from the torpedoes on the *New York.* When Hobson pleaded that this would provide a "positive means" of sinking the *Merrimac,* that if all else failed, "we could blow the bottom out of the *Merrimac* with those,"

Sampson replied, "No, I cannot let you have them. Two hundred pounds of guncotton on the inside would blow everything to the devil. This is a dangerous mission, but I will not allow an American crew to commit suicide."

Having so meticulously devised the plan, Hobson assumed he would command the mission, as did James M. Miller, who was commander of the *Merrimac.* "As commanding officer of the *Merrimac,* Commander Miller has a claim that can not be disregarded," Sampson reminded Hobson.

"I am well aware of this," answered Hobson, presenting his case. "I would be pleased to have the Commander as a passenger, because he is totally unfamiliar with the plans. To make this mission work, the ship needs an officer with engineer training and expertise in ship construction. I do not know Commander Miller personally, but it would very unlikely that the Commander as a line officer of that rank [would] possess these qualifications."

Commander Miller took his case to Sampson. "I agree that I and my officers are not familiar with the details of the mission," conceded Miller. "But why can't I and my officers go along on this mission? This is still our ship."

The request was refused. Hobson insisted—and Sampson agreed—that the crew should be young and athletic. Anyone the age of the commander and the officers would not be able to cope with the physical strain and exposure. It had to be every man for himself. Any time spent on possible rescue of the commander and the officer might bring the loss of the entire crew.

But who would Hobson choose? Seven was the requisite crew number. The mission was near suicidal, but there was no shortage of volunteers. "The call for volunteers had been made by signal," said Hobson, "and names were pouring in by the hundred. It may be said broadly that the bulk of the fleet was anxious to go."

The commanders of the blockading squadron proposed that each ship would send one sailor. Said Captain Robley Evans of the *Iowa*, "I was naturally anxious to send a man who would die reflecting credit on the ship." However, Evans did not know who to choose since all 600 of his crew members volunteered. After selecting one volunteer, another sailor offered $150 for his place on the ship. "No," said the selected seaman. "The [rejected] sailor wept," related Evans, because "he had lost a chance to get his head shot off."

Hobson himself selected the crew. The lucky seven were: George Charette, 31, of Lowell, Massachusetts, gunner's mate on the *New York*: Randolph Clausen, 28, coxswain of the *New York*; Osborn Warren Deignan, 24, coxswain of the *Merrimac*; Francis Kelly, 35, of Glasgow, Scotland, a water tender; Daniel Montague, 29, of Brooklyn, New York, chief master-at-arms of the *New York*; J.C. Murphy, coxswain of the *Iowa*; and George F. Phillips, 36, of Boston, Massachusetts, machinist on the *Merrimac*. Hobson tapped those he felt had the needed skills, were the most reliable, and those who were familiar with the operations of the *Merrimac*. Deignan was chosen on the recommendation of Captain Miller, who said that Deignan was an excellent quartermaster and coxswain on the *Merrimac*. Hobson disappointed many, among them his former students at the Naval Academy, Joseph W. Powell and Ernest F. Eggert, who now were assigned to the *U.S.S. New York*.

Hobson's target for departure was June 1, midnight. That was frustrated by an insufficient quantity of wire. It took Herculean effort to ready the *Merrimac*. Stripping parties and work gangs vied for space on board to complete their tasks: shifting of coal, removal of watertight doors, preparing charges and rigging anchors. Other unforeseen problems included the inability to shift the large anchor aft and the failure to find an electrical detonating machine. "We will use batteries," said Hobson. After much effort, enough batteries were located to detonate six of the ten charges. How reliable were these batteries?

The *Merrimac* neared the entrance of Santiago harbor around dawn on June 2, 1898. The historic moment had arrived, or so thought Hobson and his crew. "The admiral said good-bye with a simple word of kindness," related Hobson. "With us who knew him, such a word from Admiral Sampson would outweigh a

Members of the *Merrimac* sinking crew.
clockwise from the top: George Charette, J.C. Murphy
George F. Phillips, Francis Kelly, Osborn Warren Deignan,
Randolph Clausen, *(center)* Daniel Montague.
Source: Hobson, *The Sinking of the Merrimac.*

volume. The propeller fouled one of our lines, delaying matters one-half hour."

History, however, would have to wait one more day. The torpedo boat the *Porter* came tearing up, with an announcement by Lieutenant John C. Fremont, her commander, that Sampson had ordered the *Merrimac* to return. The commander was worried that the Spanish had too much visibility.

Hobson's first impulse was to disobey orders. Who knew if there would be another opportunity? "Please ask the Admiral if he will reconsider. I am sure we can get in the harbor." The Admiral would not budge. "We should have to wait another day," an unhappy Hobson told his crew. A cloud of gloom and disappointment beset the men, recalled Hobson. "No one spoke a word. Every man lingered near his post for some time, not wishing to make the effort necessary to get into a position of comfort. I knew how the men felt." Hobson told the crew to relax, lie in the shade, think of nothing, and sleep if they could. All to no avail. The men were too tense and anxious.

As for Hobson himself, *Merrimac*'s commander was at peace with himself because he felt inspired by the spirit of God and nature. "These were hours of interesting experience before the start. There was no diversion of the senses, and this fact and the feeling of loneliness seemed to deepen the impression of the closeness of God and nature. My business affairs had been disposed of at the beginning of the war and I had no disquieting thoughts as to the past or the future. The mind and the heart accepted the reality of things with deep, keen exquisite delight."

Physically, Hobson was well prepared. "Do not tire yourself out," advised a fellow officer. Hobson assured him of being "in excellent shape, with pulse normal, nerves steady—if anything a tinge phlegmatic—brain as clear as a bell—in fact, only in 'second wind,' as it were, while the limit of endurance was not in sight."

As the crew awaited orders, important developments unfolded on the *Merrimac*. The men attempted to tow a lifeboat on for possible escape, but that scheme failed when the lifeboat capsized and broke loose. A boat was put on the deck of the *Merrimac* instead and later they added a catamaran.

After midnight on June 3, the men enjoyed a cheerful, relaxing breakfast of sandwiches and coffee. Were Hobson and his men nervous? The press assembled on the *New York* to record the last words of the gallant eight, who obviously, reporters felt, were fated to disaster.

"I shall go right into the harbor until about four hundred yards past the Estrella battery, which is behind Morro Castle," Hobson told. "I do not think they can sink me before I reach somewhere near that point. The *Merrimac* has seven thousand tons bouyancy, and I shall keep her full speed ahead ... . [Then, when] the narrowest part of the channel is reached I shall put her helm hard aport, stop the engines, drop the anchors, open the sea connections, touch off the topedoes and leave the *Merrimac* a wreck, lying athwart the channel, which is not as broad as the *Merrimac* is long."

After Hobson detailed the mission, one young reporter asked, "Is it possible to survive?"

"Ah! That is another thing," chimed Hobson. "I may jump before I am blown up. But I don't see that it makes much difference what I do. I have a fair chance of life either way if our dinghy gets shot to pieces. We shall try to swim for the beach under Morro Castle ... . We shall fight until the last, and we shall only surrender to overwhelming numbers, and our emergency will only take place as an almost uncontemplated emergency."

An amazed journalist studied Hobson's demeanor. "No doubt about it. That young officer was as cool as a cucumber."

The *Merrimac* eight sailed into history about 1:30 a.m. on June 3, 1898. The men had precise responsibilities. All had assignments before each would explode his torpedo. Coxswain Murphy, of the *Iowa*, had the most dangerous job. After cutting loose the bow anchor with an axe, he would be exposed to enemy shelling as he made his way across the forecastle. He would have to dodge the rising chain and break hawsers. Finally, he would arrive at portside and detonate his torpedo, situated beneath himself, under the collision bulkhead. Coxswain Deignan and Hobson were to remain on the bridge. Those who survived the mission would be picked up by a launch from the *New York*, which was following the *Merrimac*.

Countless disappointed sailors were not on the *Merrimac*, but perhaps there was not a more frustrated civilian than Byron R. Newton, a reporter for the Associated Press. He told his unhappy story in a Letter to the Editor of the *New York Times*, in 1933: According to Newton, the U.S. Navy prevented him from joining the *Merrimac* mission. Hoping to beat all newspapers in the country, Newton then sought to get an advance story through an exclusive interview with Sampson. That failed too. "Instead of interviewing Sampson," said Newton, "he interviewed me, and discovering that I knew more about the affair than he thought I should know, I was detained on the flagship, practically a prisoner until after the *Merrimac* was sunk. When I protested against being a prisoner, the Admiral politely explained, 'My dear sir, you are not a prisoner, merely my guest by compulsion.'"

Newton did not think he was courageous for seeking to accompany the mission. "My offer to accompany Hobson on the *Merrimac*," said the journalist, "was not, however, any evidence or exhibition of great courage. Any newspaper man in the fleet would have jumped at the chance of an exclusive story ... . The thing had all the makings of a whale of a story, and that was what the country and our newspapers wanted."

The *Merrimac* sailed away from the squadron. Hobson expected the collier would be spotted by the enemy within 2,000 yards of the shore. Actually, the *Merrimac* was within 400 yards of the harbor entrance when a small picket boat opened fire. The target was the exposed rudder of the collier. The enemy intensified its fire from all directions.

Hobson's lament is recorded in *The Sinking of the Merrimac*: "If we only had a rapid fire gun, we could have disposed of the miserable object in 10 seconds; yet, there he lay unmolested, firing point blank ... . A flash of rage and exasperation flashed over me."

However, the *Merrimac* remained focused. The double bottom was already flooded, and when the seacocks were opened at the right moment, Hobson gave orders to detonate the first torpedoes. The time had come for sinking the ship. The engine stopped. Hobson ordered the final turn to starboard.

"Meet her! Meet her, Sir!" shouted Hobson. The sky opened up beyond Morro Castle. "Hard aport! Hard aport, sir!" continued Hobson. Silence. "Hard aport, I say."

"The helm is hard aport, sir, and lashed," responded Coxswain Deignan.

Unfortunately, the collier would not turn. The enemy had destroyed the steering gear in three places. "Oh, heaven" moaned Hobson. "Our steering gear is gone, shot away at the last moment, and we are charging forward straight down the channel."

The vessel moved down the channel at six knots, with both anchors torn loose. Torpedo No. 1 had gone off promptly and surely. Undaunted, Hobson gave the order to detonate the remaining explosives. It was useless. Enemy fire on Socapa slope opened up at full blast. Projectiles exploded and clanged. "It was Niagara magnified," said Hobson.

"Torpedoes 2 and 3 will not fire," reported Mate First Class George Charette. "Very well," said Hobson. "Lay down and underrun all the others, beginning at No. 4, and spring them as soon as possible."

Coxswain Osborn Warren Deignan had waited to hear Nos. 2 and 3; when he didn't he tried his own and it, too, failed. He then went down to Coxswain Randolph Clausen who got off No. 5. But six of the eight torpedoes failed. "With only two exploded torpedoes," thought a dejected Hobson, "we would be some time sinking, and the stern-anchor would be of first importance." He resolved to go down aft and stand over to direct it personally, letting go at the opportune moment.

More bad news for Hobson and crew. "The escape boat has been wrecked, sir," advised Clausen. The stern-anchor was gone. But hope was not lost for the mission. "Looking over the bulwarks," said Hobson, "I saw that we were just in front of Estrella [Point], apparently motionless, lying about two-thirds athwart the channel, the bow to the westward. Could it be that the ground-tackle had held?" He told the crew, "We will sink by the bow and the stern will probably stay out of the water. Then we should block the channel after all."

But the planned sinking seemed unlikely to materialize, Hobson quickly realized. "We were helpless," related Hobson. "The bow moved, the stern moved—oh, heaven! the chains were gone! The signal-cord from the bridge had been broken. A large projectile from ahead over the port bow, apparently from a ship, had exploded aft, wrecking everything in the vicinity and cutting the lashing that held the anchor!"

As success began to slip away, Hobson wondered sadly, "What if Admiral Sampson had granted us warheads. They would blow the bottom out and we would sink in less than half a minute!"

He told his men, "Yes, we will sink, in about eight or ten minutes. However, that will only happen after we float into the channel beyond Estrella. In any event, it will be almost impossible for us to block the channel."

The *Merrimac* hastened to a rendezvous with historical frustration. The men could clearly see Castle Morro. They would reach the channel in less than three minutes. The ship was now at the mercy of enemy fire. The Spaniards tattooed the *Merrimac* at point-blank range. "The deafening roar of artillery," said Hobson, "came just opposite our position. There were the rapid-fire guns of different calibers, the unmistakable Hotchkiss revolving cannon, the quick succession and pause of the Nordenfelt multi-barrel and the tireless automatic gun. "A deadly fire came from ahead, apparently from shipboard. These larger projectiles entered, exploded, and raked us. Those passing over the spar-deck apparently passed through the deck-house, far enough away to cause them to explode in front of us ... the Socapa batteries with plunging fire, the ships' batteries with horizontal fire, the striking projectiles, and flying fragments all produced a grinding sound with a fine ring in it of steel on steel."

The *Merrimac* was hit hundreds of times. Suddenly, a cataclysmic jolt shook the collier out of its foundation. It had hit a mine. All told, a minimum of ten remote-controlled mines ripped apart the collier.

The *Merrimac* was prepared for failure; the crew expected physical annihilation. "I waited to see one man's leg, another man's shoulder, the top of another man's head, taken off," feared Hobson. "I looked for my own body to be cut in two diagonally, from the left hip upward, and wondered for a moment what the sensation would be. Not having pockets, tourniquets had been carried loosely around my left arm, and a roll of antiseptic lint was held in my left hand. These were placed in readiness."

However, all hope was not lost. The collier moved. The ship headed right down the channel where its width increased. Would the channel be blocked?

Failure! "A great wave of disappointment set over me," recounted Hobson in his book. "It was anguish as intense as the exultation a few minutes before. On the tide set us, as straight as a pilot and tugboats could have guided ... we approached the bight leading to Churruca Point to the right, and the bight cutting off Smith Cay from Socapa on the left causing the enlargement of the channel. I saw with dismay that it was no longer possible to block completely. The *Merrimac* gave a premonitory lurch, then staggered to port in a death-throe. The bow almost fell, it sank so rapidly."

Having failed to block the harbor, the *Merrimac* was now beset with other problems. The heavily shelled vessel reeled to port. "She is going to turn over on us, sir," an unidentified crew member reported to Hobson. "No, she will right herself in sinking," a confident Hobson asserted, "and she will be the last spot to go under." He was right. The shelling ceased, and the *Merrimac* started downward, righting as it went.

Survival was the question. The life-boat had been carried away, so the crew gathered about the catamaran. "What shall we do now that the boat is gone, sir?" wondered the men. "Shall we swim for the shore?"

"We will never make it, against the tide," asserted Hobson." The shores are lined with troops, and their small boats will be looking for victims that might escape our vessel. We are only a mile from the mouth of the channel and day will be here in a few minutes. Remain where you are. As long as the stern remains out of the water, we can drop down the hatch and burrow in the coal.

"Even if the Spaniards board, they will not be likely to search our vessel, certainly not in the beginning. Right now, let's conceal ourselves till nightfall. Afterwards, we will reconsider our plans. It would seem that our only chance lays in remaining undetected until the coming of the reconnoitering boat. Hopefully, we will be able to surrender without being fired on and killed."

The men waited for dawn hanging onto the bottom of the catamaran in the icy waters.

A launch to rescue the *Merrimac* had been set up under the command of Lieutenant Joseph Wright Powell, a close friend of Hobson. The launch had followed the *Merrimac* to the mouth of the harbor and then left for a safe position to monitor the action. If the *Merrimac* crew had needed to abandon the vessel on a raft when the torpedoes exploded, then Powell would dash to the rescue.

Because the crew did not abandon the *Merrimac* before the raft was washed overboard, Powell concluded that all the heroes were dead. An admiring Powell reported to the fleet about what he considered his lost friend: "He was brave to the end."

Powell recalled these moments at an address during the 1941 christening of the *U.S.S. Hobson* at the Charleston Navy Yard: "At long last, those of us who had kept ship all night left the *Merrimac* in my launch and she swung in to her appointed end. As the ship neared the harbor entrance, she was lost in the shadow of the hills. The Spanish lookout discovered her while she was still some distance from the mouth of the harbor, and the stillness of the morning hours was broken by a shot—and then another—followed by a sheet of flame and a roar of guns, awe-inspiring in their extent and volume. From both sides of the narrow channel, scarcely a discus-throw away, the sharp crack of the Mauser rifle of the infantry added to the din that grew to a crescendo, and then—after what seemed like hours—gradually died away to nothing.

"I believed that I was seeing the inevitable end of my heroic friend. Our patrolling launch continued until daylight on the chance of finding the cutter, or picking up a lone swimmer, but it seemed a hopeless one, and when we were driven off after daylight, my launch crew and I believed that we had seen a great man and his devoted followers sacrifice their lives to the call of duty. When the chivalrous foe, under a flag of truce, late that day reported all the crew captured, none seriously hurt, and Richmond Hobson untouched by that inferno of fire, I felt as if I had news of the resurrection from the dead. That was the bravest deed it has been my privilege to witness in a long life."

Hobson and crew continued to rest on the catamaran. The serenity was broken by the sighting of a Spanish launch.

Blowing up the *Merrimac* at 4 a.m., June 5, 1898.
Source: *Images of the Spanish-American War,*
April-August 1898—A Pictorial History.
Courtesy: Stan Cohen

Merrimac crew in water.
Source: Hobson, *The Sinking of the Merrimac.*

"A steam-launch is heading toward us," announced a crew member. "No time for careless actions now," thought Hobson. "It is a launch of large size," reported the *Merrimac* commander, "with the curtains aft drawn down. It is approaching from the bight around Smith Cay and heading straight for us."

When it was about thirty yards off, Hobson hailed the launch. The launch came to a halt, as if frightened, and backed off furiously. "A squad of riflemen are on board," a worried Hobson told his men. "They are forming a semicircle on the forecastle. I hear their instructions: 'Load! Ready! Aim!'"

The men murmured, "They are going to shoot us." But the Spanish volley never happened.

"Is there an officer on the boat?" shouted Hobson to the enemy. "If there is, I am an American officer who wishes to speak to him with the purpose of surrendering himself and his seamen as prisoners of war."

Obviously, Hobson had no choice but to surrender. The phrase "Hobson's choice" has been generally traced to Cambridge, England, and Thomas Hobson, who owned livery stables and let horses in strict order according to their position near the door. Hence, the phrase means a choice of taking what is offered or taking nothing at all. However, "Many people have attached 'Hobson's choice' to the choice of Richmond Pearson Hobson," said Gloria Cole, the on-site manager of Magnolia Grove. "He had the unhappy choice of surrendering or challenging Rear Admiral Cervera."

It was at this point that Contraalmirante Cervera y Topete leaned out to call off his firing squad and, as Hobson and the *Merrimac* crew surrendered, and amazed Spanish crew chanted, "Valiente! Valiente!" to applaud their enemy's act of courage. Who were these Americans who had dared to execute—and nearly successfully completed this suicide mission? Their astonishment turned to civility, kindness, and outright praise.

Prisoner of War . . . June 3, 1898

In spite of the high regard with which they were held, the *Merrimac* men were now prisoners at Morro Castle. Still, the

Rescue of the *Merrimac* crew by
Contraalmirante Pascual Cervera y Topete.
Source: Hobson, *The Sinking of the Merrimac.*

manner of the captors was so courteous, related Hobson, "We might have been guests coming to breakfast."

Hobson was visited by a disbelieving Captain of the *Reina Mercedes*, Emilio Acosta y Eyenmann. "You had no guns and sunk your own ship?" the Spaniard asked in wonderment. Hobson was permitted to write to Admiral Sampson that the *Merrimac* was sunk in the channel. "No loss, only bruises."

Hobson had intended to write as follows: "... sunk in the channel—not where planned, but the best that could be done ... ." However, Spanish hospitality induced Hobson to forego those additions.

For a moment, Hobson had false hopes about the mission's success. "But he says positively that the channel is blocked," Hobson had overheard a conversation between officers. The attribution was from an army engineer assigned to examine the matter.

"My heart leaped," exulted Hobson. "Could it be, after all, that the channel was completely blocked?" But sober thought again reasoned: "No. They may think so for a while—may continue to be in doubt ... but each time the inevitable conclusion came back that the blocking was incomplete. Hard and bitter was the thought, beyond the comfort of philosophy."

Hobson wrote in his book: "As I reviewed the experience, a flood of bitterness swept over me. These remarkable adverse coincidences could never happen again. As I saw the tug with a flag of truce going out to the fleet, I thought if I could only be exchanged quickly, or escape, the Admiral would let me take in the other collier, with the same plans and arrangements, and the same crew. Another time, I would guarantee complete blocking."

Through the graciousness of Admiral Cervera, Hobson and his crew were given healthful and nutritional conditions while in captivity. The amenities were more than satisfying through added involvement of British Consul Frederick W. Ramsden. The men were allotted ample furniture; each man was given a hammock and blanket. The Consul found two boxing-gloves in town and the men were able to get in sparring exercises.

Hobson himself did not lack anything: "I was not allowed to exercise outside, but the room was large, and I took exercise with the regularity of meals—going through setting up exercises, fencing, broadsword, and boxing ... . Mr. Ramsden had been able to get me a bath-tub, and a cold douche twice a day ... . As a matter of fact, the conditions were better than those on board ship, and I had more muscle and had better form when I came out than when I went in."

The junior Spanish officers were anxious to please, offering the crew ample cigars and cigarettes. The Spaniards would literally beg their superiors to be allowed to meet, and shake the hands of, celebrity prisoner of war Hobson: "My visitors were of all grades," related Hobson, "and many came from a distance. Officers, nearly all my seniors in age and rank, would beg as they put in warm and dignified words, to be allowed to shake my hand. There can be no question that the Spanish character is deeply sensible to a genuine sentiment. The history of warfare probably contains no instance of chivalry on the part of captors greater than that of those who fired on the *Merrimac.*"

On June 7 Hobson and crew had been transferred from Morro Castle to Santiago. Aside from more comfortable quarters, Hobson, from his window, was able to catch glimpses of the July 1 battles at El Caney and San Juan.

While Hobson was a naval officer and had a taste of battle on the *Merrimac*, he had never before seen the cruel side of war. The Spaniards were in retreat, and the Americans acted nobly under horrific conditions.

> Then I saw in all its force that cruel side of war, the suffering inflicted on the non-combatants—women, children, old men, invalids, almost all afoot, struggling to take along some needed article. Not until later did I see that other, most remarkable of all sights, the feeding of this population by our army, when the conditions for its own food-supply were the most difficult. When, in all the history of the world, has a besieging army ever before relieved a beleaguered city of its hunger—one of the strongest factors in a siege—taking upon itself in a distant and invaded land the burden of relief? War is harsh, and must remain harsh; the righting of wrong will always entail harshness, but we have surely turned a new page in the methods of warfare.

Contraalmirante Pascual Cervera y Topete.
Source: Hobson, *The Shinking of the Merrimac.*

Facsimile of Hobson's first draft of his
dispatch to Admiral Sampson
Source: Hobson, *The Sinking of the Merrimac.*

Admiral Cervera was developing into America's most glorious 'enemy.' More than bestowing lavish praise over the American heroes, he was willing to exchange them so they could return to their homeland.

"In recognition of their bravery," Cervera himself wired Sampson and offered to exchange the Americans for American-held prisoners in Atlanta.

However, many anxious moments passed before the exchange was realized. Sampson sent the *Vixen* with a flag of truce to Santiago Harbor, seeking to exchange the crew for some prisoners taken from a prize of *Marblehead* off Cienfuegos. Cervera notified Sampson that he was powerless to decide. The decision rested with Captain-General Ramon Blanco y Erenas.

And was it Blanco or Cervera who was responsible? Sampson charged that Hobson and his fellow prisoners were human shields at Morro Castle. Press reports and statements on June 17 attributed to the American admiral indicated that whenever the Americans bombarded Santiago, they were avoiding hitting Morro.

One naval officer was happy with Sampson's concern but unhappy with the war strategy. "If that report is true," he said, "it is creditable to Admiral Sampson's humanity, but it is not war. If Admiral Cervera has put the American prisoners in a fort subject to bombardment, and keeps them there for the purpose of exposing them to the danger of being killed by American shells, the Admiral is inhuman and his conduct should subject him to the condemnation of all civilized people."

And if this was the mind set of Cervera, argued others, what would stop him from putting each prisoner in a separate fort to escape bombardment. "Of course," said the naval officer, "this inhuman treatment of prisoners ought not to be possible, but Admiral Sampson ought to notify Admiral Cervera to take the prisoners to a place of security when another attempt at shelling is about to be made."

None were more unhappy than the citizens of Hobson's hometown in Greensboro. The town paper *Alabama Beacon* ran a page one special, Latest Bulletin: "Sampson sent word to Cervera holding him personally responsible for Hobson's safety. It is suggested Spaniards might kill him before evacuating or surrendering Santiago."

Negotiations hit a low point on June 20. Commodore John Watson cabled the War Department: "Captain-General [Blanco]

Contraamirante Cervera visits prisoner Hobson
at Morro Castle.
Source: Hobson, *The Sinking of the Merrimac.*

states Spanish Government refuses to exchange prisoners." The British Consul at Santiago, F. W. Ramsden, advised Washington to offer a ransom for the release of the prisoners. The Navy and War Departments agreed that the Spaniards realized how appreciated Hobson's services were and, therefore, were looking for a better deal from the Americans.

The Madrid correspondent of the *London Times* speculated that Madrid was wary about information the prisoners had about Spain: "Spain's refusal to exchange Lieut. Hobson and his companions of the *Merrimac* is easily explained and justified. Without any intention of acting as spies, they must have seen many things in or around Santiago which American naval and military authorities would gladly have information about."

Doubts still lingered on July 4th, but a day later Americans had ample reason to extend their Independence Day celebration: First was a crushing naval victory over the Spanish fleet and then, finally, freedom for America's heroes of the *Merrimac*.

Freedom . . . July 5, 1898

Having spent the war on the *Merrimac* and in prison at Morro Castle, it wasn't until July 5 that Lieut. Richmond Pearson Hobson first had a chance to marvel at the quality of the American soldier, as he gained his freedom in an exchange for Spanish prisoners.

"We passed close at hand the squad that came as escort— magnificent looking group of fellows! I saw at once that we had recruited from the very best manhood of the country, and all along in my subsequent ride, marveled to see men with muskets whose faces spoke indubitably of the highest walks of life. But it was not until my subsequent mission to the front, when privation and hardship were at their worst, that I came to appreciate fully the depth of their patriotism."

The prisoners were exchanged under a ceiba tree near San Juan road, between the Spanish and American lines, two-thirds of a mile between the entrenchment occupied by Col. Leonard Woods' Rough Riders, near Gen. Joe Wheeler's headquarters, and the

Reception of Hobson and his crew by
American soldiers after their release by the Spanish.
Source: Hobson, *The Sinking of the Merrimac*.

center of the American line. The American prisoners left the Reina Mercedes Hospital, on the outskirts of Santiago, at 2:45 in the afternoon. They were accompanied by Spanish Major Luis Yrles and walked to the meeting place and were not blindfolded.

On the other hand, the Spanish prisoners were mounted and blindfolded and were led by Col. John Jacob Astor and Lieut. John D. Miley. The Americans had brought three Spanish prisoners to exchange for the *Merrimac* men, but the Spanish only took one prisoner. Actually, that soldier was the only one among the three Spanish POW's who cared to return to his homeland:

Reflected Hobson, "The men who were to be exchanged seemed much downcast. Apparently, there was no vision of happy return on their minds. Doubtless, what they had seen of strength and morale had convinced them that their fight was hopeless ... . It was impossible not to feel sympathy for these men in their dejection. The evidences of meager fare and hard service were plainly visible on their faces ... . Their feeling was in great contrast to that of our men, who were on the tiptop of exultation, with beaming faces."

Hobson and his companions first were received by Gen. Joseph Wheeler, Capt. French Chadwick, and finally Maj.-Gen. William R. Shafter. "No interviews now," said Hobson to the press corps. "First, I must send a report to Admiral Sampson."

However, Hobson did speak of his experiences as a POW and spoke of his high regard for Cervera: "During the first four days ... the Spaniards did not exactly ill-treat us, but it took them some time to recover from the shock caused by what most of them considered our Yankee impudence in trying to block the harbor ... .

"For Admiral Cervera, I have nothing but the highest admiration and personal regard. His act in informing Admiral Sampson of our safety I regard as that of a kindhearted, generous man and chivalrous officer. I expressed to him my sincere thanks of relieving the anxiety of our shipmates and our friends at home. He repeatedly spoke to me of his admiration of what he called one of the most daring acts in naval history."

Hobson maintained contact with Cervera long after his release from Morro. They only met once the following month, before the naval constructor returned to Santiago on a ship-salvaging mission. The Admiral was at Annapolis under house arrest. Before boarding the train, he told reporters, "The American public never knows just how they owe to him for the way they treated and protected the prisoners in Santiago." Added Hobson, "He is a grand old man, I tell you, and I will never forget him for his kindness to me. When I came to New York I sent him a telegram, telling him that when I had the chance I would thank him in person. I want to take that chance now."

Hobson's joy in meeting with Admiral Cervera was akin to a father and son reunion. Wrote a correspondent, "It was like that of father and son. The grey-bearded Admiral first laid his hands on the shoulders of the young hero and then embraced him with Spanish fervor, and the conversation began on the most friendly terms. Reminiscences were conned over between them, and memories that had made their careers touch each other were recalled. The meeting ended with an invitation by the Spaniard that Hobson visit him at his home in Spain."

A waltz written in honor of Lt. Hobson after his
release from Morro Castle prison.
Courtesy: Magnolia Grove

5

ADORATION OF A HERO

Once free, Hobson lost no time in visiting Admiral Sampson. After reporting fully on the sinking of the *Merrimac*, Hobson made no requests for himself but asked that the crew be relieved of duties so that their heroism would receive the proper recognition and reward.

"There is letter for you," said the Admiral, not wanting to overlook the *Merrimac* commander. This letter from Secretary of the U.S. Navy John T. Long, praised the naval constructor's "extraordinary heroism ... readiness for emergency, fertility of resources ... under a most galling fire from the shore batteries of the enemy, at the risk of almost certain death to yourself and your brave associates on this duty." The just-freed Alabaman still had not fully grasped the epic hero he had become. Certainly, he marveled at the number of correspondents who covered the exchange of prisoners and could not miss the enthusiasm of the American troops in greeting him and his crew on July 6.

Celebrated New York *Herald* war correspondent Richard Harding Davis reported:

> Hobson's coming was the one dramatic picture of the war. The sun was setting behind the trail and as he came up over the crest he was outlined against it .... For a moment he seemed to sit motionless and then the waiting band struck up 'The Star Spangled Banner.' The strange thing was that no one shouted or cheered or gave an order, but everyone rose to his feet slowly, took off his hat slowly and stood so, looking up at him in

absolute silence. It was one of the most impressive things I ever saw—no noise, no blare, no shouted acclaim. What meaning of the depths of feeling there was in that silence.

Then a red-headed, red-faced trooper leaped out into the road and shouted, 'Three cheers for Hobson.' The men roared and cheered. The Rough Riders gave a cowboy yell and officers with sons of their own in West Point leaped up and down and a foreign attaché threw up his helmet into the air. Hobson rode down between the lines, raising his cap and smiling ... . They were men ... who knew a brave man because they were brave ... .

It was the most wonderful ride a young man of 28 has ever taken. To ride through the enemy's country guarded by your own countrymen. On every side to hear cheers and approval. At every step to know that your work was done, and well done. To know the weary days in jail were over. To feel the situation and see the great mountain peaks and royal palms bending benediction under a soft blue sky. Best of all when he rode through the twilight and reached the coast and saw again in the offing the lights of the flagship, his floating home, and then, from there across the water, came the jubilant cheer of the blue-jackets who could not even see him, who did not know him, but who cheered because he was coming, because he was free. (Brown, 396-97.)

Author of *Red Badge of Courage* and noted journalist and short story writer, Stephen Crane, also covered the war for the New York *World* and depicted the enthusiasm of the troops in greeting Hobson. However, Crane is not all laudatory in his comparing Hobson to Boulanger (either Gustave or Louis), the showy French painter:

The army was majestically minding its own business in the long line of trenches when its eye caught sight of this little procession. 'What's that? What they goin' to do?' 'They're goin' to exchange Hobson.' Wherefore everyman who was foot-free staked out a claim where he could get a good view of the liberated heros ... . There was a very long wait through the sunshiny afternoon ... . But suddenly the moment came. Along the cut roadway, toward the crowded soldiers, rode three men, and it could be seen that the central one wore the undress uniform of an officer of the United States Navy. Most of the soldiers were sprawled out on the grass, bored, and wearied in the sunshine. However, they aroused at the old circus parade, torch-light procession cry, 'Here they come.' Then the men of the regular army did a remarkable thing. They arose en masse and came to 'Attention.' Then the men of the regular army did another thing. They slowly lifted every weather-beaten hat and dropped it until it touched the knee. Then there was a magnificent silence, broken only by the measured hoofbeats of the little company's horses as they rode through the gap. It was solemn, funereal, this splendid welcome of a brave man by men who stood on a hill which they had earned out of blood and death.

Then suddenly, the whole scene went to rubbish. Before he reached the bottom of the hill, Hobson was bowing to right and left like another Boulanger ... . (Brown, 397.)

Nicholas 'Lawyer' Cobbs, a member of one of Greensboro's oldest families, recently articulated a unique aspect of Richmond Pearson Hobson's place in American history: "Richmond was the first Southerner who became a national hero. America was wracked by the Civil War. After the *Merrimac* episode, Richmond became a hero across America: from North to South, from East to West. His heroism was so valuable as a step in the healing process of a nation."

The adulation of the American troops was but a brief introduction to the overwhelming adoration that Richmond Pearson Hobson would receive in the press, in the communities, and among individuals throughout America and worldwide.

Perhaps Hobson had no time to read and digest the reaction of citizens across America. While Hobson and his crew languished at Morro Castle, crates of poems and letters were delivered for Hobson to the attention of Admiral Cervera. To make sure that these missives were not lost, admirers sent copies to the attention of Admiral Sampson.

"Richmond Pearson, you are the bravest and most daring man in the world," began one letter. Another admirer opened: "What a pleasure it is to be writing to such a gallant man! Even more than the Kings of the Earth!" "I must admit," gushed another correspondent, "your eyes appeal to me in some strange way." These damsels certainly could not kiss him—at this point. What did they want? They would be thrilled if he could only send an autograph, photographs, or just a few words.

To celebrate America's newest hero, families named their sons Richmond Pearson or simply Hobson. Many popular Hobson ditties sprang up. For example, women sang: "You're a dandy; you're a peach. And the brightest blooming pebble that is shining on the beach." Richmond Pearson Hobson had been transformed from small-town Greensboro citizen to instant naval icon, shaped in large measure by an American press ravenous for sensationalism.

After his release from Morro Castle, cheering and applause came from many directions and took varied forms such as congratulatory messages and admiring letters, and composition of heroic verse, albeit second-rate efforts. Government officials insisted that words were not enough. They called for material rewards for the super naval constructor.

In the Limelight . . . 1898

The adoration of Hobson began as soon as reports came out about the near-suicide mission in Santiago Harbor. But why all the uproar?

America was hero-starved. No slight was intended for the Manila master Dewey, but the Philippines were too far away for immediate hero worship. America had triumphed in Cuba. The Puerto Rico campaign would run until early August. The Philippines were a battleground for several years. And here was Hobson, gorgeous in appearance, God-fearing through and through, and brainy as attested by his place at the top of the U.S. Naval Academy, Class of '89.

Ironically, the press had at first recorded the success of the *Merrimac* in blocking Santiago harbor. Associated Press correspondent George Edward Graham reported that Spain had called the blocking successful when they first dispatched that the *Merrimac* crew were all safe. It was only in mid-July that the truth was revealed, because the Spanish fleet was not trapped and indeed did leave the harbor.

Previously assigned to the Brooklyn Navy Yard, Richmond Pearson Hobson received his first congratulatory message from the Southern Society of Brooklyn, according to Walter Pittman, who has written on Hobson's naval record. The letters and wires came from all over the world; from former U.S. President Harrison, who termed Hobson's feat as having few, if any parallels in the history of the world; to governors of American and Mexican states and countless social and fraternal clubs.

Call it hyperbole if you like, but Richmond Pearson's father, Judge James Hobson, captured the mood of the country in idolizing his son. After warmly congratulating his son, Judge Hobson observed:

> The town and country are in a perfect ferment. Your name is on the lips of every person and the central word in the headlines of every newspaper in the United States. Telegrams and letters of congratulations are pouring in upon us from every quarter ... .
>
> Papers and magazines throughout the U.S. are telegraphing every few minutes for your photographs and unfortunately, we had but few to furnish, and they want sketches of your life and character. Some of your friends are very busy furnishing the latter.

The hero's brother, James Hobson, Jr., also wrote Richmond Pearson and proudly proclaimed, "The world *now knows* my brother. I have known him *all my life*. The world now sees in him that determination, that disregard for danger, and that self-sacrifice which I have always known him to possess. His courage founded upon his keen sense of duty, his knightly and chivalrous and generous spirit, his intellectual ability, his scientific investigations, his purity, his love of mankind, his family devotion, and his true nobility have always been known to me."

The swelling local pride in Greensboro was captured by Judge Edward de Graffenroid, whose letter was cosigned by four other prominent citizens. "Every paper in the United States," they wrote, "has had something good to say about you. Your name has been on the lips of Cleveland and Harrison, and President McKinley, Secretary Long ... and other persons of distinction have wired to your father and mother of your brilliant conduct and your safety. The continent of Europe took up the story, and you will live in History." Not surprisingly, 'best friends' and classmates turned up to tell the media about their one-time buddy. One cigar manufacturer created a new line of 'Hobson's Choice.'

But, shockingly, the family of America's newest hero almost found itself homeless, according to newspaper reports. A story with a Cincinnati dateline said that the homestead in Greensboro was heavily mortgaged, and a popular subscription was begun to release it. Hearing this report, the *Cincinnati Times Star* wired the editor of the Greensboro *Beacon* for the facts. "All was well," came the answer: "Your inquiry received. Judge Hobson has tendered to the mortgage company the amount due on the mortgage. There is a dispute as to the amount of the debt, but money is in hand to pay any amount due, and no aid is needed of any sort." The note was signed by *Beacon* editor H. G. Benners. Nicholas Cobbs is at a loss to understand those stories. Because of the realty arrangements, he said, there had never been any concern about the family losing Magnolia Grove.

The versifiers lost no time in composing tributes. Certainly, no poem was more filled with local pride than "The Greensboro Boy," dated July 4, 1898, by Gilby C. Kelly:

> Tell how, ere the dawn had fairly stole
> O'er the Caribbean waters blue,
> He was steaming for the storm-burst goal—
> Hobson with his sacred seven crew—
> And kindly add, This youth of renown
> Is Dixie born, of Greensboro town.
>
> How he entered Santiago Bay
> Under the fire of wakened, wrathful guns,
> Sunk the *Merrimac* at break of day.

Flung himself among the wondering Dons—
In passing say, This youth of renown
Learned how to dare in Greensboro town.

Thrilling, tell how his disciplined brain
Planned the scheme to shut Cervera in,
How he asked that he might bear the strain
That required the stake of his life to win—
And post-write, that this youth of renown
Learned of the Christ in Greensboro town

Aye, recite the story over how he,
Yet a stripling naval engineer,
Has become the hero of the sea,
Made his name a star by which to steer—
And mention of the youth renown,
His mother lives in Greensboro town.

Let his country speak his name with pride,
And her muse recount his deed in song;
Let the sea winds whisper far and wide
Of the young lieutenant wise and strong—
And further add, This youth of renown
First went to school in Greensboro town.

Let the President commend his worth,
And the Senate vote him his due reward;
Let his name resound through all the earth,
And his fame the nation's honor guard—
Add, Uncle Sam's pride—the youth of renown
Is of Confederate stock and Greensboro town.

Professional Recognition . . . 1898

As personally pleasing and flattering as all these messages and
poems were to the youthful hero, he could not have been more thrilled
than with the professional critiques of his mission. There is no paral-
lel to the achievement in the history of naval warfare, insisted
naval historian Park Benjamin. His comments were cited in the July
1898, issue of *Review of Reviews*, titled "Lieutenant Hobson."
Benjamin observed: "Somers showed a like magnificent daring
when he blew up the ketch in the harbor of Tripoli; and Cushing's

dash upon the *Albermarle* was superb. But these men had simply to go to a definite point and destroy quickly, trusting to good fortune to escape with their lives. Both of these crept to their destination in little vessels under cover of the night. Hobson steamed into that channel with a huge 4,000-ton ship in plain view of the batteries, moved to a particular spot, maneuvered his vessel in a particular way, and sank her in a particular position under a hail of shot and shell which rendered the chances of success apparently infinitely remote. To conceive that the thing could be done at all was an inspiration; to be willing to attempt it argued a degree of personal courage which is heroic; to do it coolly, deliberately, and with pro-fessional certainty under that fearful fire showed an intelligent in-trepidity which is marvelous."

Few tributes were as meaningful to Hobson as those that came from patriotic and war groups. A few days before the fighting ceased in Puerto Rico, the Women's Patriotic Relief Association spon-sored a lawn party in Central Park, between 65th and 70th Streets, to show appreciation for the invalid soldiers and sailors who had returned from the front. The wounded men limped on the lawn, most on crutches; others were sadly crippled. They were the center of attraction. Each one gave his autograph for those in attendance. They delighted themselves with ice cream, cake, and cigars.

Mrs. Howard Carroll, president of the Association, traveled 200 miles from Fultonville, N.Y., to be with these heroes. Who would be the most desired speaker—Constructor Hobson, of course. But he sent his regrets in a letter that was read on the occasion: "I beg to express my thanks and appreciation for the kind invitation to the fete next Tuesday ... and regret very much that duty interferes and will prevent my being present for your noble cause, which appeals to my deepest sympathies. Wishing success to all your devoted efforts."

Resounding cheers followed the reading, and as a treat, Mrs. Samuel Miller, in charge of the souvenir department, promised that each soldier and sailor would receive a facsimile lithographed copy of Hobson's letter as a souvenir.

A full minute of applause followed that announcement.

While the praise rolled on endlessly, Hobson admirers called for appropriate material awards. The *Merrimac* crew were awarded

Medals of Honor, as well as promotions with increased salaries. Officers could not receive that honor, according to 1898 practice, so Hobson would have to wait until 1933. As for promotion, the Navy was uncertain how to elevate him. He was at the top of the list of assistant naval constructors; only eight officers of higher rank were above him in this corps. Would he be jumped over officers ahead of him? Would he choose promotion in a line other than construction?

Secretary Long was in a quandary. He wanted to reward Hobson appropriately, but he did not want to do injustice to other meritorious, veteran officers. In the Navy, promotion involved being advanced in rank and by number, moving ahead of other officers. Hobson supporters asked for a promotion of 344 numbers on the list of the Naval Construction Corps and twenty years in time. This would mean that Hobson would become a senior officer in the Navy in about fifteen years. Because of his youth, Hobson would keep that place for at least twenty years—unprecedented in the American Navy. Even Admiral Dewey gained only ten numbers for his heroics in Manila, and that is precisely what Richmond Pearson Hobson gained.

Debate began in the Capitol on June 17, 1989; after much discussion, on March 1, 1899, President McKinley nominated Hobson for an advancement of ten numbers. This nomination placed Hobson, 29, above all the lieutenant-commanders and nearly at the top of the commander's list. According to the *National Cyclopedia of American Biography*, this "was said to constitute the greatest material promotion in the history of the Naval service." Some Naval historians have challenged that statement with the promotion of Stephen Decatur for his heroics during the Tripolitan War in 1804.

Aside from the personal and professional enmity that arose among the officers, the nomination limited his future as a naval constructor. Hobson, therefore, applied for a transfer to the line. He was turned down, later to be assigned as Inspector of Spanish Wrecks at which time his duties, simply described for now, would involve salvaging the Spanish ships sunk in the Battle of Santiago on July 3, 1898.

Stopover in New York ... Summer, 1898

On July 22 Hobson left Washington for New York after conferring with Navy officials about the salvaging project. Only the *Maria Teresa* and the *Cristobal Colon* could be saved, Hobson concluded. To continue his project, he was leaving for Santiago, with a stopover in New York.

How would the Northerners in the Empire State receive the Southerner, now an all-American hero? From the moment he was spotted, he was overwhelmed with a rousing welcome.

His arrival was unexpected and unannounced. His actual purpose for the stopover was to complete arrangements with Merritt & Chapman Wrecking Company to save the warships. He arrived on the auxiliary cruiser *St. Paul*, which dropped anchor off Tompkinsville, Staten Island. Hobson was met by Dr. Doty, Health Officer of the Port, and Rochester Congressman James W. Wadsworth.

"Say, Hobson," said the Congressman. "I ... ."

Before a conversation could continue, all at the Port knew Richmond Pearson Hobson was on New York soil. The *New York World* was on hand to report the ebullient mood:

> 'Hobson's on board.' The words went along the boat's dock like lightning, and everyone crowded to the two who were standing near the bow of the *Castleton*, the boat that would take Hobson to Manhattan. 'Three cheers for Hobson!' yelled somebody, and men, women, and children joined in. The officers of the boat caught the spirit of the moment and the whistles of the old ferryboat tooted jubilantly. The boat was hero-mad in a second. Everybody wanted to shake Hobson's hand.
>
> 'Hooray for Hobson!' shouted a deck hand, who pressing forward, was the first to grasp the hero's hand. That was the signal. Hobson had to hold a reception then and there. How they crowded up! Millionaires and poor people, cottagers and excursionists—it was all the same. Among those on board were a detachment of men from the *Newport*, the United States vessel lying off Tompkinsville, near the *St. Paul.*

'Hobson!' cried a grimy stroker from the *Newport*, forgetting the 'Mr.' and the disparity of rank. 'I want to shake your hand. You're a hero!'

And Hobson, forgetting in his turn the rigid etiquette of the Navy, seized the fist outstretched hand and wrung it heartily. Again, the cheers and again much confusion on the part of Hobson. He could not budge by this time, so thick had the crowd clustered around him. The boat was slowly putting into her slip. The people on shore could hear the cheering. The words, 'Hobson is coming' brought great crowds outside the ferry-house.

'Here he comes!' screamed a newsboy. 'Hooray!'

The crowd on shore, where Hobson would catch a train, waited breathlessly and impatiently for the arrival of hero Hobson. The boat emptied. The crowd groaned. Almost all New Yorkers were unfamiliar with the handsome face of Hobson. They expected a gold lace uniform, a weather-beaten face of the sailor, and the like. And the Congressman did not say the magic word, 'Hobson.' He was shabbily dressed, in borrowed clothes; his face was pale, perhaps from his days in prison.

However, an unidentified reporter from *The World* knew Hobson and cornered him. Only one person caught the conversation, and appropriate for the Big Apple, it was old Lucy, who had been selling apples at the ferry for 20 years. She nearly threw herself into the cab taking Hobson and his company to the train.

'It's a great man you are sire,' she cried. 'We'll make you President, by helping you, sir.' Hobson took her hand, smiled, and wrung it warmly, while the crowd cheered gain wildly, and tears came again to the hero's eyes.

No one recognized hero Hobson on the train. However, upon arrival, he was recognized—without explanation—by a black porter." *The World* told this poignant vignette simply with its subhead: 'Southerner and Negro shake.'

The newspaper reported the dialogue: "'Am dis Mr. Hobson what wrecked de *Merrimac*?' he asked.

"'Yes,' replied the young man quietly.

"'Den, sah,' said the porter with a grin. 'I'd like de great honah of shakin' yuh hand.'"

Hobson bowed assent, and there in the sight of a crowd of people the Southerner and the Negro shook hands.

An older gentleman viewing the interchange made these comments, cited by many a 100 years later, especially in the South, to emphasize the historical importance of Richmond Pearson Hobson: "Such scenes as that do more to cement the North and the South than a thousand years of clap-track political talk."

The Hobson appearance was a quickie, but his arrival on August 4 was unequaled in its day in New York City—and few have surpassed it in the outpouring of enthusiasm that it generated. Hobson, understandably, was besieged with requests for press interviews and appearances by organizations from all over America. They were quickly turned down. He was busy on the assignment of salvaging the Spanish ships.

However, his Metropolitan Opera appearance was something special because proceeds would benefit the New York Soldiers and Sailors Families Protective Association. These groups aided monetarily and emotionally the relatives of those who served their country.

All New York dailies—*The New York Times, The Sun, The World, The Evening Journal,* and even the Yiddish-language daily, *The Forward,* which began printing in 1898—were on hand. No doubt, it was a media event.

The New York Times had been very low keyed—to this point— about the heroics of Hobson, more so than the enthusiastic reporting of the *World* and *Evening Journal,* for example. But the *Times* left no doubt about the star of the evening on that torrid summer night: "The men, women, and youngsters who looked up from the Paraquete into Hobson's quiet, earnest face or craned their necks from the heated galleries to catch his words saw more than a brave man, more than a man of brains and force. They saw a man whose gallant act has typified the feeling of the whole country and taught that the Yankee's aptitude for business has not yet choked his devotion to the flag."

The *Sun* observed, "There was such a display of patriotic feeling ... as this city has not seen for years and years ... . It was a continuous outburst of the strongest, warmest kind of national feeling, and of generous tribute to the men who have shown their gallantry in the war ... . This spectacle of a great audience of enthusiastic Americans rising to their feet, waving their handkerchiefs, and shouting three big American cheers at the mere mention of the name of the man [Admiral Cervera] who made the strongest fight that has been made on the sea against the United States during this war was equally significant and remarkable."

In describing the sinking of the *Merrimac*, reported the *World*, "[Hobson] held his audience as if every individual was hypnotized. It was one of the most impressive recitals that has been heard in the city in many a day."

McKinley was cheered, Dewey was cheered, and Cervera was cheered.

It was Lieutenant Hobson's night, however, rightly stated the *Sun*. "This world-famed naval officer, who looks more like a diffident young minister than a war hero, faced several thousand persons in the Metropolitan Opera-House last night, and gazed calmly around while they shouted for him, cheered for him, waved flags and handkerchiefs at him and they behaved as Americans always do when they desire to honor a brave man."

All seats had been sold, although the owners of a handful of boxes in the first and second tiers did not show. People stood in the rear, behind the seats on the main floor and in the galleries, and the stage was bursting with people. For the first time the hero of Santiago told of his experiences on the *Merrimac*, not as his own singular heroism, but as a testimony to the gallantry of the American sailor. It was a wonderfully impressive recital, and it was heard with breathless interest.

Hobson entered the hall in a dress suit with white tie of lawn, somewhat of a disappointment to those who wanted him in naval uniform. But no matter. "Three cheers for the hero of the *Merrimac!*" bellowed a man in a front row, joined by cheers that lasted for nearly five minutes.

"The man who had faced death so calmly seemed somewhat uncomfortable," observed the *Sun*. He was shown to a chair by Major John Byrne, "... and he seated himself as one glad to be hidden for a moment from that sea of faces."

The Alabaman was introduced by Major Byrne. Every mention of Hobson's name or his naval feat was the signal for rounds of thunderous applause. The introduction came to a close with deafening applause and the playing of "Way Down in Dixie."

Three times he tried to speak, but Hobson was drowned out in applause. Finally, he had his moment. Never lacking a sense of humor, he hollered to the band, "Don't you know that we want a Yankee Doodle." The band obliged.

While he retraced the heroics of the *Merrimac* incident, he moved the throng with an incident from his training days. "I was at the Naval Academy," he said, "when as a naval cadet I saw an incident of the American sailors' pluck. Our ship was about 500 yards from shore when a man unable to swim fell overboard. The boat was hoisted to the ship's side, as a sailor immediately sprang after him. Another man followed overboard, and one after another they went until the officer of the deck gave a stern command, 'No more men overboard.'

"This was my introduction to the question of what we call Jackies—the sailors. Another year passed and these conclusions were confirmed. I have had occasion to see Jacky, under conditions in which Jack was brave, as I have referred to him."

In his review of the *Merrimac* heroics, he spoke of the gallant, manly chief of the Spanish forces, Admiral Cervera, but when he referred to the "Spaniard," hissing ensued. Quickly, Hobson stopped and looked angrily at the audience. The hearers took note and great applause came from the assembled.

As for his compatriots, he said, "Now these men are samples of the knights of our Navy. If you will properly look upon the little incident of the person willing to die under any condition that may come, you will have an accurate idea, more or less of the American sailor."

At the end of the evening, a resolution was passed thanking Admiral Cervera for his courtesy to Lieutenant Richmond Pearson Hobson.

The festivities formally closed with the singing of "America" by the New York Bank Clerks Glee Club. When the Seventy-First Regiment Band attempted to play "When Johnny Comes Marching Home," the crowd frustrated the players by swarming over the footlights to the stage and grasping hero Hobson by the hand. They swarmed around him so that he could scarcely breathe. Women tossed flowers at him, and men patted him on the back, some chanting, "You're a peach, old man."

The police came to Hobson's rescue, as they got on the stage and forced people into a single line. Persistent women pleaded to at least have a few words with the hero. One proved a precursor of things to come: "May I kiss you?" begged the pretty lass. A jealous rival pushed her aside saying, "You fool, don't you know he's married?" A verbal battle ensued between those of the women idolizers willing to wager he was married and the hopefuls who insisted he was an eligible bachelor.

While the argument continued, a group of enterprising well-wishers found an open door on 40th Street and surged into the building to shake Hobson's hand. Hobson might have been hopelessly trapped if the police had not rushed in and bellowed, "All out!"

With every seat filled inside the Metropolitan Opera House, Capt. Price of the West 30th Street Station and a detail of twenty policemen had no problem with crowd control—no one was left waiting outside. The police assignment was to maintain some order among the fakirs, peddlers, and ticket speculators outside. There was much hawking of fans; souvenirs of the meeting in the form of flags—ten cents each; buttons; handkerchiefs; and, obviously, the most grabbed up items were photographs that somewhat resembled Hobson.

Why weren't there more people outside, wondered Capt. Price. "Well, I guess," answering his own question, "Coney Island and cheap beer are greater attractions than the sidewalk."

By any yardstick the evening was an unqualified success: the enthusiastic audience at the "standing room only" Opera House; the enthusiastic patriotism; the thrill-of-a-lifetime glimpse of superhero Hobson; and the $3,500 raised for the New York Soldiers and Sailors Families Protective Association.

Hobson's mother, who had traveled with him to New York for the occasion, was greatly pleased at the reception given her son. His sister, Annie, who was visiting in New York with a cousin, Miss Patton of Morristown, N.J., joined them as well.

Perhaps the most important occurence of the evening, especially where the personal life of Richmond Pearson Hobson concerned, was when he met Miss Grizelda Hull, who would later become his wife. Miss Hull was among the crowd of women who stormed the stage hoping to glimpse, or better yet talk with, the gallant Alabaman. Hobson stood with quiet amazement—the center of a wildly patriotic, shouting, cheering, pushing crowd. Having not expected this adoration, he simply looked about him, shaking hands automatically as the police pushed the crowd along.

Suddenly, a young girl stopped in front of him. "I'm proud to be a Southern girl," she said quietly. They shook hands. As Grizelda Hull Hobson relates in her *Memoirs*, "The hero rather lingered over it—and as I turned away, his eyes followed me. Several policemen were heard to whisper— 'Who is she?'— What did she say to him?— See how he is following her with his eyes.— He hardly knows he is shaking hands as they come at him.—See him.'"

Grizelda Hull was hurried away from the stage by her father, who had stood aside while his daughter went to meet hero Hobson. "What did you say that made him look so after you, dear," he asked. Grizelda repeated her words. Her *Memoirs* continue: "That evening the young lieutenant thought more than once of her. He always declared that his imagination had been instantly stirred, that his impulse was to follow her, that he kept recalling for days her brown hair that moved about her face ... her dress ... her smile. 'I must find her again,' he kept thinking. And she, in turn, that evening, put away the little white glove that had touched his hand."

After the program, Mrs. Hobson returned to the Waldorf-Astoria while Richmond, his sister Annie, and Miss Patton visited the residence of Mrs. Frederick T. Van Beuren, the mansion at 21 West 14th Street, where they entertained several friends of their hostess.

Before leaving the hotel the next day, Hobson told the press from his third-floor room, "That meeting was the largest and most enthusiastic one I ever attended. I haven't much experience, you know, in attending big meetings. I was delighted with my reception and shall always remember the experience as one of the most pleasant of my life.

"No, I did not experience stage fright. I felt pretty much at home before such an appreciative audience."

Having triumphed in New York, Hobson and his entourage left for Long Island, where he was instantly recognized and cheered, as was becoming usual. "Take good care of Hobson," said one man to the train conductor. "We will, my boy," came the response. "Don't you worry."

After Richmond Pearson Hobson left the New York Metropolitan area, the literature of heroism continued to grow. According to reports, while he was in New York, he visited New Jersey, without explanation. A story came to light a few days later because of witnesses of an incident in Newark.

After descending from the Pennsylvania Railroad Station at Market Street, Hobson tried to catch an Orange car. Realizing he needed the car at another point, he changed direction. Walking near Hobson was Patrick Halloran, a cripple on crutches.

As Halloran turned to catch the car, he found himself directly in front of a quickly approaching trolley car. Alerted by the outcries of the crowd, Hobson whizzed around, jumped on the track, lifted Halloran and together sprang back from danger, as the trolley whirled through. Hobson shook hands with Halloran, bid him farewell, and hopped on the next Orange car.

How was the obscure Greensboro native handling his new-found fame? He had displayed singular daring and heroism on the *Merrimac*, he was a hero, and he had perfect right to enjoy his praise from all directions. However, the press had so deified the naval constructor that a falloff was inevitable, a sort of "national indigestion," as Richard Sheldon called it. Hobson's public career certainly benefitted from this magnification, but it had its peril, and Hobson victimized himself.

As Sheldon writes,

> He refused to play the simple hero's role while it was demanded of him, and to sink back to obscurity when the public tired of him. He knew there was greatness in himself, and he knew it was not because he had done a single heroic act. That he had volunteered for a dangerous mission and had carried it off was simply a natural continuation of the established course of his life.
>
> That he survived it was a freak of nature, an unexpected twist of fate, which propelled him suddenly onto a larger stage, directly before the public. He was to find that the attention of the public, while offering great potential opportunities to an ambitious man like himself, was unfortunately a two-edged sword.

6

AMERICA'S MOST KISSED MAN—EVER

After he left the stage of the New York Metropolitan area, Richmond Pearson Hobson had a clear picture of the national icon he had become. But he was not prepared for the kissing craze that was to ensue. When Hero Hobson died in 1937, the Alabaman was celebrated by the *Herald* of Union Springs, Alabama, as being "kissed by more women than any other man who ever lived."

It was quite a tribute to the unassuming naval hero of the *Merrimac.* While the "kissing craze" excited America and Europe during 1898-99 and thrilled the lasses who smooched the handsome Southerner, it was a source of discomfort and embarrassment to Richmond Pearson Hobson and his family. This was so even after the craze disappeared. Decades after the episode, Hobson's sister, Margaret Hobson, turned down a request to have Magnolia Grove listed in the National Register of Homes because the interviewer prefaced her appearance with a reference to the "home where that kissing hero was raised." Even today, grandson Houston Stokes observes that "family members are still uneasy about those days."

Long Beach, New York . . . August 5, 1898

August 4 and 5 were two momentous days in the story of Richmond Pearson Hobson. On August 4 he met his future wife, Grizelda Hull of Tuxedo, New York. The next day came the "Kiss That Echoed Round the World," which many call the inception of the kissing craze.

Ironically, the hero had had a foreboding of the impending craze and in seeking to escape, he fell right into the kissing net. After his speech at the Metropolitan Opera House, the crowd, led by worship-seeking women, had rolled over the floodlights to greet him. One audacious gal had even asked for a kiss, but was turned down. Finally, he had arrived at his hotel room—only to be confronted by piles and piles of letters pledging never-ending love to America's most eligible bachelor.

"I have got to rest somewhere," thought Hobson, and the sea resort of Long Beach, New York beckoned.

He was the guest of an old friend, Edward James Gavegan, a New York attorney. From the train, they went into the waters of the Atlantic and the excellent swimmers headed toward the Rockaway Inlet. However, someone must have tipped off the summer vacationers, and attendance records were set at the beach that day.

Later, Gavegan took his visitor for a reception at the Long Beach Hotel. The 800 guests decided to take a collection and presented Hobson with a $300 sword. "I cannot adequately express my appreciation and my thanks," responded the honoree. "I have only to say, as long as my career shall continue, this emblem shall be dearly cherished and I shall ever recall this occasion and this spot on the Atlantic."

Hero Hobson must have sensed an exceptional interest in his person. Admitted S. S. McClure, editor of *McClure's Magazine*, to the lieutenant: "My daughters like all the rest of the people in Long Beach ... were half-crazy with pleasure at seeing you."

It was a most inspiring day at the Long Beach Hotel. Patriotic songs—especially "Yankee Doodle Dandy," "Dixie," and "Star-Spangled Banner"—never ceased from the band. Our hero was very accommodating. The men got handshakes; the children got kisses and autographs.

Enter Emma Arnold of St. Louis and summer resident of Long Beach. The lass was charmingly attired in a dark blue and green gingham dress with a white yolk and sleeves. Her jet black hair was brushed back in a pompadour, all collected under a dark straw hat. As she watched the kisses, she became jealous. When she was introduced to Richmond Pearson, she said impulsively, with a little sigh, 'I almost wish I were a child again.'

Lieutenant Hobson bestows a 'patriotic kiss' upon
Emma Arnold at a Long Beach, New York, resort,
thus beginning the kissing craze.
Source: *New York Evening Journal*

The gallant Hobson responded, innocently, "Then let me treat you like one," and kissed her.

The kissing craze was now let loose. The press had their "story." The war in Cuba was long over. Mopping operations were nearly done in Puerto Rico. New York—where Hobson kissed—and St. Louis—where the kissed resided—gave their readers all the news and features worthy of being read.

Carrying an August 6 dateline, the *Post-Dispatch* ran a special for the home folk. It forecast many kissing days ahead:

> Now that the fair Miss Arnold of St. Louis has started the kissing of Lieut. Hobson there is no telling where it will stop … .
>
> 'What do you think of Miss Arnold and the kiss she gave you last night?' he was asked by a reporter of the *Post-Dispatch*. The lieutenant's face reddened and he became much embarrassed. 'I guess you will have to ask her about that,' he said smiling. Then he added: 'I do wish people would remember that I am only a sailor, that I am here on duty, and that I have many things to attend to. I do not wish to be appear ungrateful for all the kindness that has been showered on me, but I do not see what earthly interest the people have in me.'

How unknowing our hero was! By August 7, J. Getcher Gunn, described as the "highly imaginative poet" of the Sunday *Post-Dispatch*, had already put the episode in verse. It was titled "How it Happened," as she "pictured" that kiss:

> Oh the glamor
> And the clamor
> Of the Hobson-Arnold kiss
> Lovely Emma
> Sweet dilemma,
> Which the hero couldn't miss!
>
> At the seaside
> On the leeside
> Of a summer hostelry.
> Came the issue.
> 'May I kiss you?'
> Chirped the maid to Richmond P.

Eyes appealing
Set him reeling—
Luckiest he of living men!
Cuss the Dago!
Santiago
Had no charms for Richmond then.

For it true is
That the St. Louis
Girls are neater, sweeter far
Than all others
(Like their mothers)
Makes no difference who they are

So the maiden
Beauty-laden
Glued a kiss upon the lips
That were cheerful
'Neath the fearful
Rain of lead from Spanish ships.

Hobson, go! You
Have all we owe you
What are shells that madly whirl
To the blisses of the kisses
Of a sweet Missouri girl?

The St. Louis lass was well researched by the *Dispatch*. She was the daughter of the late Lee L. Arnold and Amelia Arnold. Her brother, Fred, worked at the Olive Street furniture house. Several years earlier she had been the queen of a major ball at the Columbian Club. Miss Arnold, wrote the paper, "is as noted for the originality and beauty of her gowns as for the loveliness of her face and form. She travels 'in the most exclusive Jewish circle.'"

The front page of the *Dispatch* featured a drawing of the patriotic spirit of St. Louis, with a very detailed description of her now-famous costume. Proclaimed the headlines: "She Thought of Hobson the Hero, not the Man" and " ... Patriotism Was Her Only Reason."

Appropriately, a story of a famous kiss began with a quote on kissing by Ninon de l'Enchos (a courtesan in the court of Louis XIV, no one could doubt her expertise): "A kiss is an alms which enriches him who receives without impoverishing her who gives."

Certainly, any maiden like Miss Arnold would enrich the kissed: "... a look at her is calculated to fill the masculine bosom with a huge desire to be a Hobson himself. She has dark eyes, large and luminous; poets might liken them to the enticing green of a glade, to the depths of dark water, to the still glory of night. At any rate, they are the kind of eyes that a man may not forget in an hour or so."

In short, Hero Hobson "kissed the prettiest pair of lips at Long Beach." According to the *New York World*, "Who could resist? ... Challenged to a kiss by a pretty girl, Lieut. Hobson proved his gallantry again."

The *Dispatch* elaborated on Miss Arnold's patriotism. The reporter asked her directly, "Did a motive go along with a kiss?" She conceded it was "on the spur of the moment."

Continued Miss Arnold: She kissed the deed, not the man, "Pure patriotism was the motive ... . I am a patriot. It just made my blood tingle when I read about Hobson taking the *Merrimac* and sinking her so coolly under that fearful storm of fire ... . To me that seemed the greatest feat of bravery of the whole war ... . It made me proud to think I was an American ... . So, you see it was Hobson's deed I kissed and not Hobson."

Could she describe the kiss? asked inquiring reporters. Was it a special kiss? "No, just a plain ordinary one."

Continued the press: "Did he kiss you, or did you kiss him?"

"Why, he kissed me, and I kissed him."

The *New York Journal* offered no more details, but titillated with its headline: "How Hero Hobson Kisses."

How did the hometowners react to the Arnold smooch? The *Dispatch* asked the views of three "society folk." She had two supporters and one detractor. Said "the man," Lester Crawford, "Miss Arnold acted on a patriotic impulse, which was admirable, and, Hobson, as usual, showed good sense in accepting the kiss from such a pretty girl. About two years ago [Ignace, a Polish pianist] Paderewski was kissed blue by New York society women after a performance and nothing came of that."

Matron Mrs. Arthur Gale was accepting because "it was the act of an impulsive girl possibly in good taste, according to the judgment of any majority of women to whom you might submit the question ... . [S]omething must be allowed youth, impulse, and enthusiasm."

However, 'Maid' Corinne Francis gave a resounding nay to the maiden."A kiss is much too sacred to be used in such a manner," opined Miss Francis. "I do not think it was at all a proper tribute for Miss Arnold to kiss Lieut. Hobson."

No one was more unhappy than brother Fred Arnold. When first hearing the reports, he dismissed them. "I know my sister, well," he assured the family. But the truth came out to the stunned Fred. He got to the telegraph office and wired her his sentiments. He would not reveal the contents, but he issued this statement: "I know her intentions were good, but it is very unfortunate. She is an impulsive girl who doesn't always stop to consider the consequences of her acts. She is intensely patriotic, and I suppose when she met Lieut. Hobson, she was completely carried away by her admiration for his gallantry."

What a cad, editorialized the *New York Evening Journal* in "The Great Hobson Kiss." What nerve to give his sister a "severe reprimand." Fred Arnold owes "his generous and patriotic sister a humble apology. Obviously, the fellow does not understand the patriotic fervor in America:

"Further, this young man is of small and narrow a mind that he cannot grasp what everyone else has grasped—that the kiss his sister gave Hobson was symbolic and vicarious and in no sense personal, just as was the acknowledgement of the gift by the hero of the *Merrimac*.

"The Long Beach Hotel kiss is immortal. It has resounded throughout the country. It has echoed in every American heart. It expressed the sentiment of a nation.

"The young man who is judging it by the cannons of convention and by the precepts of ordinary propriety, is making himself ridiculous."

Miss Arnold became an instant Long Island celebrity. The summer folk within a dozen or so miles of Long Beach either drove or rode by her house to catch a glimpse of her. Said the *Dispatch*: "They walked around her two or three times, and some of the most particular sat down near by and inspected her. She endured the microscopic scrutiny with a polite indifference." Daughter and Mother Arnold remained in Long Beach until August's end, when they headed for Saratoga, never to be heard from again in the literature of the kiss.

As for the object of her attention, Lieut. Hobson, mother, and friends all left Long Beach on August 7 for New York City. Hero Hobson left for Washington to continue his salvaging assignment. Those who date the beginnings of the kissing craze to those August days admit there were few headlines after the Long Beach episode. However, these kissing historians emphasize Hobson's increased popularity. Wherever he traveled there were huge crowds and backpounders and handshakers, albeit few kissers. Still, Emma Arnold and Long Beach provided the proper prelude for the fast-paced kissing days to come in December 1898.

Chicago, Kansas City, Topeka and the Kansas Prairies ... December 1898

Less than six months had passed since Richmond Pearson Hobson was released from Spanish captivity. He had had his fill of adulation, so he was very appreciative of the orders to head for the far off Philippines to engage in the raising of Spanish ships sunk by Admiral Dewey.

All went well at a stop in Atlanta, where Hobson was invited to the Peace Jubilee Parade on December 15, and joined with President McKinley and Southern war hero General Joseph Wheeler. He was told that the Georgian women had created the Hobson Waltz in his honor. It was a tasteful celebration, sans "incidents." His destination was San Francisco and then the Philippines by ships.

But first was a stop in Chicago, and that's where the kissing saga reached its most fascinating turns. The date was December 18, 1898; the place was the Union League Club; and the theme, the necessity of a larger U.S. Navy. The program had been arranged by the Naval Reserve Association of Illinois.

The concluding ceremonies are described by General John McNulta, president of the reserve group, in the Hobson Papers in the Library of Congress. A long line of well-wishers readied themselves to shake the speaker's hand after the talk. As he surveyed the line, Richmond Pearson recognized two elegant, refined young ladies—Mary Fowle and Mrs. Thomas McDermott—as the daughters of a distant relative, former North Carolina Governor Daniel G. Fowle.

"Hey, ladies," McNulta encouraged the kinswomen, "why don't you kiss America's great hero?" The kissing cousins obliged. This seemingly innocent affair seemed to put a wrap on a very serious program. However, noted McNulta, the other fair women waiting in line for a handshake were moved to considerable merriment, and were not agreeable to settle for a mere handshake.

Noting the mood, McNulta shouted, "Listen, why don't you try for a kiss, too?" The good-natured general saw no problem. He was certain there would not be any more criticism of these acts than would be given to any ordinary country frolic. The audience concurred and each kiss brought loud applause from the audience.

However, the media was on hand, and the *Chicago Post* and *Times Herald* failed to see the good taste of the kissing. All told, they estimated that one hundred fair lasses were kissed by Hobson that evening. However, one meticulous police sergeant swore that he counted 163 kisses.

The stories whetted the kissing appetites of the fair sex and the stories moved beyond the confines of Chicago. In fact, the Chicago meeting included delegates from Kansas City, Hobson's next stop westward, and they spread the word to those who were planning to hear Hobson's talk. But the Kansas City belles would not wait for a talk. Who could blame them? They crowded and pushed for position at the railroad station. One account put the total at 417 women kissed, while another reporter insisted the number was 419. The totals were falsified, claimed McNulta. It was competition: Who had better kissers, those in Chicago or those in Kansas City? Said the general, "To give zest to it, the facts were exaggerated, in the nature of a pleasantry or competition between Kansas City and Chicago."

After Kansas City, it was Topeka. The numbers: either 200 or 350; in Kansas, the sum of smooched Kansans was 1,000. As one newspaper report beamed: The Prairies are not so dry.

Indeed, the media did engage in exaggeration or mock-satire, if you will. The *New York Tribune* reported on December 23 that Hobson himself rushed over to the women and kissed them, and if, for some mysterious reason, they refused him, General McNulta assisted him in pinioning the prisoners.

One group of Hobson supporters maintained that these women had kissed Hobson; he did not kiss them. Whatever the preciseness of the happenings, Hobson was often portrayed as unscrupulous and lecherous. The *Birmingham Age-Herald* castigated the hero for spreading devastating diseases.

Previously dubbed "the Modest Hero," the media now adapted the names "the kissing-bug" and "the hero of the merry smack." One story tried to capture the flavor: "Then the kissing fever seized the women, and Hobson made no resistance. In fact, he seemed to like it, and as each woman came up he grasped her hand and drew her toward him and smacked her soundly upon the lips." Another reporter studied a flustered hero: "They waited not, but rushed in, striking him on the nose, between the eyes and in the mouth with the protruding front of their elaborate millinery creations."

Roared one headline about the itinerant kissing hero: "Hobson Is Kissing His Way to Manila; Lieutenant Hobson Again Afflicted." One of the celebrants, reported the media, was famed opera singer Pauline Hall, who not only kissed Richmond Pearson, but, sad to say, fell upon his neck. The press printed a supposed interview with the *Merrimac* hero, who told of enjoying all that kissing but with a confession about the ennui of the pastime: "When the kissing is fast and furious it sometimes gets just a little tiresome, and it sometimes happens that [when] some rather ancient lips are presented I would fain pass them by unkissed, but when it starts in I have to take them in as it comes. There is no selecting: everything goes: the number of luscious lips always outnumber any others."

Was he tiring of all this? wondered one eager correspondent. Supposedly Hobson responded, "No, haven't yet; have thoroughly enjoyed it so far. I suppose if I kissed one woman as often as I have kissed different women, I would be thoroughly exhausted. But the constant change is delightfully exhilarating."

*　　*　　*

Eventually, Richmond Pearson Hobson would lose his equilibrium. "No more," vowed Richmond Pearson. As he reached Denver, the last leg of his trip, the train station nearly collapsed from the more than 1,000 women who vied and fought for spots on the platform. The hero rushed off without one kiss.

As the famed lips became inactive, the kissing fever traveled through the world—and it continued without his kisser. Chicago, which took credit for introducing the kissing spree, now turned its lips to a minor hero from the battleship *Iowa*, who supposedly was smooched by 43 lasses in the Windy City.

Lancashire, England, sponsored a kissing contest. The unnamed winner was said to have kissed 1,800 lips—people that is—in one hour—or 30 a minute.

Not to be outdone, a German youth, madly in love, grabbed his lover for a ten-hour affair. He told all who would listen that he kissed his paramour 10,000 times in 10 hours—17 times a minute. Sadly, his affair ended when he fainted and developed paralysis. Of course, reflected the *New York World* soberly, all this kissing might breed lunacy.

Still, Hobson was big business, as one candy manufacturer originated "Hobson's Kisses." And the concerned *New York World* published this delightful verse, with apologies to the Rondeau of James Leigh Hunt:

> Say that I am old and sad,
> Say that health and wealth have missed me,
> Say I'm poor but also add—
> Hobson kissed me.

As the kissing craze subsided, Hobson family and other supporters geared up to defend Richmond Pearson. One of the naval constructor's friends, Robert Underwood Johnson, related the uproar to the English writer, Rudyard Kipling.

"Do you mean Hobson was actually criticized for kissing these women?" a stunned Kipling gasped. "How utterly absurd! Don't Americans know that heroes have always been kissed down the ages? If Hobson had refused, he would have been a cad!"

Kipling was a wonderful authority on kissing. But was he an appropriate source? After all, he had penned some very memorable lines in *England's Answer*: "Deeper than speech our love, stronger than life our tether/But we do not fall on the neck or kiss when we come together."

The family of Richmond Pearson Hobson took the approach that traditionally American heroes have been pursued by idolizers who merely wanted a kiss. When Hobson finally escaped the kissing ambushes and arrived in San Francisco, the family had obviously gotten the message to the press. On December 24, 1898, the *Examiner* carried a feature by Wells Drury titled "Hobson Justified by Precedent." The theme of the story was that Hobson's kissing of patriotic lasses has historical precedent. From the beginnings of our republic, gallantry and bravery have been interchangeable. For example, one venerable dame of three score and ten boasted of having smooched George Washington. Of course, the kissing was done when she was an attractive belle of twenty.

The kissing tradition would not be complete without a story of Abraham Lincoln. While enroute to Washington to assume the Presidency, Abe Lincoln was greeted at a reception by a very persistent matron who urged her charming daughter to kiss America's hero. "Yes, Ma," she agreed, "but first he will have to agree to shave off his beard."

"I accept," said an accommodating President. Those who know insist the President actually shaved his meager beard. His friends will tell you, observed Drury, that Abraham Lincoln was a gentleman who kept his word, and as a gentleman he could only accede to the request for a kiss.

Drury also cited the kissing privileges of other heroes like General Lafayette and General Grant. Of the latter, wrote Drury, "General Grant was another magnificent hero, whose example Hobson has a right to follow in this all-engrossing matter. It is within the memory of the people of San Francisco that Grant kissed many a bevy of pretty girls at his receptions. One of these performances came under my personal observation. A sweet-faced girl, half-frightened and half-laughing, advanced and gave the old general her hand, and as the Western sunbeams gleamed on tresses as bright as Berenice [alluding to the wife of Ptolemy III, whose hair is fabled to have formed the constellation Coma Berenice], she archly said, 'General, my mother has given permission for you to kiss me.' A gentle smile lighted on the illustrious veteran's countenance, as with exquisite gallantry he bent to the upturned rosebud lips, 'I'll kiss you twice,' he said, and he did."

In short, concluded Drury, the fashion for America's poets, fighters, and other heroes, to appreciate—rightly—the charms of maiden's lips that

> Pouting most of bland persuasion,
> Sweetly voicing love's invasion.

While no one could deny these kissing heroes, the problem for the Hobson argument was that his forebears, aside from President Lincoln, were all elderly generals: George Washington, Andrew Jackson, Winfield Scott, William Sherman, Phil Sheridan, Ulysses S. Grant, and Robert E. Lee. Richmond Pearson Hobson, however, was a mere babe of twenty-eight.

Nevertheless, Hobson enjoyed support from many newspaper editors, including William Randolph Hearst, who called the Alabaman's accommodating the lips of the fair "... genius of the highest order." Not surprisingly, Hobson's mother was perturbed by the uproar. He was never a girl chaser, nor womanizer, she told interviewers. "If Richmond ever had a sweetheart in Greensboro, I don't know it," she asserted. "In fact, he never spent time with the fair sex when he was a boy and since then has been at home only on brief visits." Other folks in Greensboro were frankly disgusted—not with Hobson, of course, but with the idolizing maidens.

In a letter to the editor of the *Greensboro Watchman*, an unsigned reader titled his complaint "Disgusting Affections." The writer employed a story of an aged Duke of Wellington that the Greensboro citizens felt applicable to Richmond Pearson Hobson. As the Duke of Wellington prepared to cross a crowded street, a young man approached with a lifted hat and led the Duke across the street. "Your grace," said the cavalier gentleman. "This is the proudest moment of my life. I had the honor of serving the hero of Waterloo and Conqueror of Napoleon."

Snapped the irritated Duke, "Young man, don't make a d—n fool of yourself."

Argued the man from Greensboro, "This with the profanity omitted is what Hobson might say to dames and maids."

Of course, Hobson was convinced that the matter would be closed once he left San Francisco for Hong Kong. How mistaken he was! While he occupied himself with reconstructing Spanish gunboats, "Shame," whispered his fellow officers. They refused to talk with him, not to speak of socializing with him. In fact, they even took apartments to be physically distant from Hobson. Hobson's supporters attacked these self-righteous critics as "jealous," both of Richmond's good looks and wartime achievements. Just as Hobson ignored those who shunned him at the Naval Academy, so did he take no notice of his Far East ostracizers.

Wrote the *New York Times* on June 2, 1899, "Hobson found no difficulty in taking a prominent part in the social life of Hong Kong, and [was] getting many favors beyond the reach of his less prominent comrades."

When Hobson himself tried to explain the saga to a friend, it boomeranged on him. He sent a letter to a friend in Baltimore, but he had no idea his confidante would peddle the letter to the *Baltimore Sun*.

"As to those wretched reports," he wrote his unnamed pal, "they were the grossest forms of exaggeration and misrepresentation ... . [A]ll those interviews with me were pure fabrication. I gave out but a few lines in Denver and San Francisco to testify to the pure and patriotic impulse of the schoolgirls and ladies who were concerned, and as for myself I would have cut off my right arm rather than to offend one of them." As for the criticism, he continued, "... criticism based on error and misrepresentation and the drawing of conclusions that I know to be at utter variance with fact can never endure ... . They shall interfere in no wise with my own steadfast purpose for future service."

The *New York Times* of August 15, 1899, wished Hobson had maintained total silence on the kissing craze, "... a wretched work of sensationalism helped out by jealous malice." Concludes the *Times*, the bravery of Hero Hobson "... was not affected by it in the slightest degree."

But for many of Hobson's contemporaries, the name of the hero of the *Merrimac* had lost its idealism, its luster. As the *Times* observed on April 29, "There is something distinctly tragical to the fact that the name of Hobson now brings to the minds of a considerable part of this country's inhabitants, not the recollection of a heroic act rarely paralleled in military history, but the image of a fatuous youth submitting to or seeking the cheap caresses of a lot of foolish and vulgar women."

The Peace Jubilee in Philadelphia, November 1898.
Lieutenant Hobson and his crew pass through
the court of honor.
Courtesy: Stan Cohen.

7

SALVAGING A CAREER

Richmond Pearson Hobson had achieved special heroic status with the bravado of the *Merrimac*. His face—and lips—had charmed American households afterwards. While the kissing craze whirled about Hobson, he sought to build a professional reputation. However, he failed to achieve any success with his glorious project of raising and repairing the sunken Spanish ships off Santiago harbor.

At the peak of idol worship, he promised Americans upon his return to Cuba, "I shall return to Santiago and shall not come back to the United States until the *Colon* comes with me. I recognize the difficulty attendant upon the execution of this project—that it is an engineering achievement of great magnitude to float the vessel—but I am sure that my plan will work successfully."

Indeed, Hobson returned to the United States, but the *Colon* remained behind, mark of a project that failed. Merritt & Chapman, the wrecking group, had visited the *Colon* and found her in very bad condition, not worthy of salvage.

Perhaps the project was never feasible. At a meeting in the White House with President McKinley and Navy Secretary John D. Long in the summer of '98, the young naval constructor was able to convince the Chief Executive of the plan's feasibility. However, the Merritt and Chapman Wrecking Company of New York had preceded Hobson's White House visit with its counsel that the Spanish wrecks were beyond hope.

Hobson was convincing. He worked out a thorough and systematical method. It was his chance to do what many thought impossible. Without delay, he went to New York to procure wrecking tugs, pontoons, and all needed equipment. Specially constructed apparatus was made for *Cristobal Colon* from Hobson's plans. The mission was organized and America's hero was off to Cuba.

Santiago de Cuba . . . Fall 1898

The *Reina Mercedes* was raised and later was the station ship at the U.S. Naval Academy, but the salvaging operations for *Colon* and *Maria Teresa* were total disasters. After landing in Santiago, Hobson was greeted by news that the experts in charge of the wrecking crew had given up hope and abandoned the *Colon* operation.

A similar fate awaited the *Teresa*. Hobson intimidated the workers into not giving up the plan and he took full direction of the operation. His plan was to set up air pumps that would empty a single compartment of water to make the compartment airtight. While each compartment was made airtight, it would once more be filled with water so that the *Teresa* would not drift on the floor of the ocean. The next step was to make all compartments airtight. This being realized, water would be pumped out for a final time. Finally, the ship full of air would rise to the surface.

Hobson had meticulously worked out all the details. But he did not foresee the health risks involved and the obstinacy of the workers. Many of the compartments were filled with parts of decomposed cadavers. Many Cuban workers became ill, and they were replaced by unskilled laborers.

The wretched conditions were described by Hobson years later when he appeared in Washington before being named Rear-Admiral: "Down in those compartments where I had to go, the provisions, stores, bodies, and amputated limbs were decaying. It reeked with infection. I went down into the compartments by candle light and directed the work of making them tight. We put Cubans at work, and as they would get sick, we turned them off and got new Cubans. The wreckers got sick, and finally I got sick. The wreckers would lay off. Sometimes we had a third and sometimes less than that who were able to go down to this work. We were fighting against the coming of the first hurricane, which would have ended it all, and I could not leave the work.

"I did do this much: I thought it was my duty to find out whether it was yellow fever. The head of the military hospital himself came off and said, 'Get off this ship.'"

Hobson was afflicted with fever and returned to shore for medical attention. "We do not know what your fever is," doctors told him, "but we are certain it is not yellow fever."

Satisfied with the diagnosis, Hobson returned to work. However, he was confronted with workers ready to leave and disgruntled supervisors who insisted that Hobson's methods would not succeed. Hobson came up with new methods, but the supervisors were still not satisfied. "Get me new officers," Hobson wired the Navy, "and tell them they must follow my plans." The Navy agreed, but the new men worked with little optimism and enthusiasm. "It will be at least five weeks before this ship will haul off, assuming that it can," a despairing captain told Hobson. To complicate matters, a cyclone struck the shore while work was proceeding.

"One more cyclone," thought Hobson, "and the operation will certainly be ruined." Unfazed, Hobson vowed, "Providence will protect our work because it has been faithfully performed. We will leave on Friday after the autumnal equinox."

The American fleet came from Guantanamo to see if Richmond Pearson would make good on his promise. "Hobson is only a visionary projector," sneered the captain of the wrecking crew. However, as an astonished audience watched, *Teresa* trembled, shook, rose, and floated phoenix-like on the ocean. Hobson hoisted to her mainmast the Stars and Stripes. Fully convinced, each vessel in the fleet fired a salute of congratulations. The naval constructor steered her, towed by two tugs along the coast, and reached Guantanamo at dusk.

Sadly, all Hobson's hard work came to nought. Details have never been fully and satisfactorily explained about this disaster—Hobson himself, for no explained reason, was not aboard the vessel as it sailed for the United States—but the captain in charge, an unenthusiastic participant, set out for Norfolk, Virginia, via the stormy route by the Bahama Islands rather than the sensible path via Florida.

A second mistake was devastating. Facing a storm, captain and sailors abandoned the *Teresa*. Although leaderless and sailorless, the vessel did not sink during the storm. In fact, the *Teresa* was strong enough to weather the gale without any guidance. "By some mysterious impulse," a saddened Hobson related afterwards, "she sought the shore of the first spot of land that Spain had claimed in the New World, the little island where Columbus first placed his foot and which with his reverent heart he had called San Salvador." *Teresa* was pounded into scrap metal amid the rocks and waves. A never-say-die Hobson implored the Navy, "Can I go and rescue her?" Their refusal ended all future plans for *Teresa*.

Hobson next sought to resume the *Colon* operation. Once again came a rebuff, this time from the U.S. Board of Construction.

Hong Kong and the Philippines, 1899-1900

For the next two years, Hobson was assigned to repair and reconstruction work in the Far East and in the United States. After the *Teresa* failure, he was summoned to Washington and ordered to Hong Kong to help in the repair operations of the ships sunk in the battle of Manila. Salvaged from the bottom of Manila Bay, three Spanish gunboats awaited rebuilding. In particular, he was assigned the rebuilding of the *Don Juan de Austria*, *Isla de Cuba*, and *Isla de Luzon*. While not dramatic successes, he experienced positive results during some sixteen months from 1899-1900. Reconstruction made the vessels faster than when they were new. The vessels were valuable in American Far East operations.

The next stop for the *Merrimac* hero was Manila. He was ordered to Manila in May 1900, to head the repair division of the Cavite Navy yard. During his three-month stay he oversaw the refitting of Spanish cruisers and the docking of the *Brooklyn*. His work in Manila brought him contact with the ships destroyed during the Manila battle led by Admiral Dewey. It was the substance of an interview that clearly demonstrated the openness of Hobson which attracted admirers but also drew a horde of detractors during his later public career. In an interview published in Vancouver, Hobson maintained that the Spanish ships were sunk because the plugs were drawn by the Spanish. Critics quickly assailed Hobson for seeking to minimize Dewey's glory. "They sunk the ships themselves. Our shell fire did very little damage," Hobson attested.

Under attack Hobson recanted, claiming that he was misunderstood. Dewey had "compelled the Spaniards to sink their ships," he said, "and that was just as effective [as] sinking them."

It was at Manila that recurrent eye problems made it impossible for Hobson to carry on his duties. He believed these troubles began while working inside the Spanish wrecks in Santiago. As a naval constructor, he spent days focusing on blueprints or overseeing construction in the dim lights of shipyards. The condition was aggravated under the burning sun of Hong Kong.

Although his vision was still "adequate," Hobson feared that without treatment and reassignment, he might go blind. That never happened, but he always related his later illnesses of eye, nose, and throat, and spinal arthritis to his naval experiences.

The condition so worsened in Manila that an eye specialist was consulted and reported that congestion of the retina had set in. Unless medical procedures were immediately taken, warned the doctor, the hero would be totally blind. Four operations did not produce the desired results, so he was sent to the Navy Hospital at Yokohama, Japan in July. He was assigned to limited duty in Kure, in connection with the docking of the *U.S.S. Oregon* in Puget Sound, in Washington State.

Home Again . . . Fall, 1900

After a board of surgeons was convened, Hobson was ordered to leave the Far East for the United States in September. Actually, friends in hometown Greensboro anticipated his return. According to a front page *New York Times* story of August 10, a reception was being readied, probably in early September, as a testimonial to the hero, who would receive a silver service with etchings illustrating the sinking of the *Merrimac*.

In October, Hobson was assigned to the Brooklyn Navy Yard. He quickly consulted an ophthalmologist, who suggested six months leave so that the constructor could rest his eyes and brain. As Hobson prepared to return home, the American press recalled the hero's past exploits. Papers like the *Knoxville Sentinel* spoke of his unfair treatment by the American public, a consequence of the perils of hero worship: "Poor Hobson! Sympathy for him will be created by the news that he is coming home sick. Hobson did a really brilliant deed at Santiago and bore himself modestly during the first stage of hero worship. But he was led astray by the sirens and he acted in such a ridiculous manner that the country was disgusted.

"We have contended that the indiscretions should not have injured his reputation, as it seems to have done. Our people are too mercurial in their judgment of men. They do not treat them fairly.

"The American people are too like Parisians in regard to their heroes ... . We soon tire of a sensation after going wild for a short time ... . Perhaps if we do not overdo the hero-worship business, we would be more fair and just to those who have done great deeds. As to Hobson, his exploit in the *Merrimac* was one of the most daring in the annals of naval warfare. The country was justified in enthusing over it, but it was not justified in pursuing a course to turn the head of the young man a little, and in lampooning him and driving him out of the country."

Hobson visited his mother's home in Greensboro. Before touching down in his hometown, he aroused controversy during a public reception in Atlanta, where he attacked Commodore Winfield S. Schley for his "selfishness" in seeking to claim all credit for the Naval successes in Cuba. Hobson felt Schley had belittled the achievements of Rear Admiral William Sampson. The Alabaman compared Sampson at Santiago to George Washington at Valley Forge.

"As his junior officer serving under him," said Hobson, "I express the deliberate opinion that Admiral Sampson is the colossal figure of the Spanish-American War, the genius of the naval victory of Santiago ... . In the clamor of calumny and detraction, he holds his peace, though his great heart be rent with this unkind cut. He suffers in silence."

After leaving Alabama, Hobson went to Washington, where signs of typhus first appeared. Physicians told him that he was in the first stages of typhoid and advised immediate hospitalization. He went to New York during the last week of November to prepare for hospitalization and meet with his close friend J. G. Bertron.

"Will you stand by me through this siege of typhoid?" Hobson asked his friend as they met at the Army and Navy Club in Manhattan.

"You are my best friend." Bertron agreed.

"I am a bit sick," Hobson wrote his mother, "but there is no need to worry." His last public appearance before hospitalization was at Manhattan's West Side branch of the Young Men's Christian Association, where Lieut. Hobson gave a stirring address. The event also featured an address by another war hero, Gen. 'Joe' Wheeler.

The YMCA speech was notable for its patriotic and religious fervor, the hallmarks of Hobson's public addresses. He praised the late Admiral John Woodward Philip, commander of the Brooklyn Naval Yard and commander of the *Texas* in the Santiago operations. After five full minutes of applause, Hobson eulogized Philip, recalling the commander's words to his crew following the victory: "'Let us give thanks in silent prayer, and I announce here my faith in Almighty God."

Hobson continued praising Philip's genial nature and love of life: "A Christian man has the right to be the happiest man on the face of the earth. And ... his chivalry and gallantry toward women. I think that this ... is a part of the plan of Creation. I think man should cultivate a creed that would say that every man in the presence of every woman in any circumstance should act the part of a cavalier and knight."

"Mail this letter if it really turns out to be typhoid," Hobson instructed Bertron. "Now I am ready for it. I want to go about this just as if I was planning to sink an enemy's ship. I have not a thing to worry me now, no matter what happens. I'm stripped for action."

Presbyterian Hospital, New York, NY
... December 1900 - January 1901

Richmond Pearson Hobson was admitted during the first week of December to Manhattan's Presbyterian Hospital with typhoid symptoms. Dr. Russell Bellamy told reporters, "Mr. Hobson is very run down, and his system is weakened as a result of his hard work in tropical climates."

His fever raged for many days, and little hope was given for recovery. Hobson quickly learned that while he had endured criticism during the past two years, the world had not forgotten his heroics and he still had scores of friends and admirers. Newspapers carried daily health bulletins.

One-time foe Admiral Cervera sent a cable to the *New York Journal*: "Greatly afflicted to hear of valiant Hobson's unhealthy state. Pray God to restore him to health, if not to take him into His presence."

Elizabeth Sampson, the wife of the Rear Admiral, wrote Hobson, "You can believe with what regret and distress of mind we learn that you are ill in New York. I wish it might have happened in our home so that we could take care of you ... . The Admiral sends his love and best wishes. I wish you have not started out on a prolonged illness."

One of his first visitors— though Hobson did not receive him—was Nicola Tesla, the discoverer of the principle of the rotary magnetic field.

Beyond the wirings and calling of VIP's, an avalanche of phone calls and flowers reached Presbyterian from concerned citizens from across the country. On the second day of hospitalization, the *New York World* ran a large story complete with pre-*Merrimac* photo and a drawing of Hobson in bed, awaiting deliveries of flowers and gifts.

"The hero of the *Merrimac*," read the cartoon, "is very ill and that he still holds his popularity in feminine hearts is shown by the many gifts and messages sent him by women young and old."

The theme was continued in the lead: "That Lieutenant Richmond Pearson Hobson is no less a hero than when he first set foot upon American soil, after he had sunk the *Merrimac* in Santiago Harbor is evidenced by the fact that since he has been at the Presbyterian Hospital, suffering from typhoid, hundreds of persons have called to inquire about him, and great quantities of flowers have been sent to him."

Even before 7 a.m. two large boxes of American Beauty roses had been delivered at the hospital. Many worried Americans came to the office to inquire about his health. The usual reply: "Mr. Hobson passed a good night and his physicians say that his condition this morning is as good as could be expected."

Not all were satisfied with the report. "Well, there is no apparent change," said an attendant. "His temperature is slightly above the normal, but there is no cause for alarm."

Smiling, a sweet-faced little girl, with a satchel of books, obviously schoolbound, chirped, "Then, he will get well."

Hobson's service friends learned of Richmond Pearson's status through a bulletin board at the United Service Club on West 31st Street.

The next day the *New York World* cited attendants, who observed that the hospital had never received as many calls about a patient. "Many Girls Anxious for Hero Hobson's Recovery," proclaimed the headline. A large cartoon showed a depiction of the sinking of the *Merrimac*, on top of a nurse attending the hero.

No one was permitted to visit with Hobson, and no flowers or letters were shown him. Inquiries were coming from all sections, said the paper, "from nearly every section where the telephone service is in operation."

No change was reported in his condition. At a more favorable time, said the hospital, he would be given the flood of letters and telegrams. According to the hospital's office-manager, "It would take a week to read through all of the letters that arrive for Lieutenant Hobson in a single day. There is no use in trying to see the patient, nor for the present is there any use in sending him flowers or communications of any kind. They will not reach him until such time as his physician permits."

Hero Hobson recovered and was granting interviews after eight weeks. One of the first interviews was a given to a *New York World* reporter, who found a changed lieutenant, not only minus his mustache, but "reduced to a bundle of sinews and bones. Though his face is thinner and his lips sharped, he is still good to look at. His pale face has the same look of determination ... . He is very weak and talks slowly."

However, he was in great spirits and grateful. "It is my hope to get out of here in another week," he said. "I have been held here prisoner for eight weeks, but it is the most delightful prison I ever was in. Aside from the fever which has given me a bad pull, I have enjoyed my stay. You cannot imagine how utterly out of the world these good nurses and doctors can keep you."

Confined for so long, Hobson thirsted for world news: Congressional appropriations, peace in China, etc. He was saddened by the death of Queen Victoria. "Is she dead?" he queried." She has been such a good ruler, a good wife, and a good mother. The whole world respects her."

The outlook for America was optimistic, beamed Hobson, because of America's youth. "The coming race of American boys," he said, "will witness and have a hand in great things. Have you noticed of late how the schoolboys are taking an interest in the national affairs .... I think that it prophecies great things for America. What can menace this country of ours with such things in the hearts of the boys?"

Naval Assignments in Washington, D.C. and Elizabeth, NJ ... 1901-1902

Finally, Richmond Pearson Hobson said farewell to Presbyterian. He was out of danger, for now, but he was not the same person physically as the hero of the *Merrimac*. The Navy also realized this and sought assignments that would not worsen his condition.

In April 1901, Hobson was back at work in Washington with the Bureau of Construction and Repair. In her *Memoirs*, Mrs. Grizelda Hobson noted that Hobson was pleased with the assignment because he had many friends at the Capitol, among them attorney Hilary Herbert, formerly Secretary of the Navy. Herbert "took great pleasure in having the young officer accompany him to various functions and point him out to foreign officers ... as without doubt the greatest naval constructor in the world."

One of Hobson's assignments included special representative at the Pan-American Exposition at Buffalo, New York. While he enjoyed this assignment, he was saddened by the assassination of President McKinley at a public reception of the exposition on September 6.

"The death of the well-beloved President McKinley," wrote Mrs. Grizelda Hobson, "plunged that city and the nation in grief."

In November he was put in charge of the Government Exhibit at Charleston, South Carolina.

What remained unsettled was the possibility of his returning to service as constructor. He appeared before a Retiring Board in January 1902, to resolve the question: Could he resume his career as constructor? "Yes," said Hobson, "for now. But eventual blindness is the probability if I once more take on such assignments." Answered the panel, "Well, then, you are now fit. An officer can only be retired when wholly incapacitated for duty." In May 1902, Hobson was sent as Superintending Constructor to the Crescent Shipyard, in Elizabeth, New Jersey.

The decision to retire was finalized in the fall of 1902 when he received orders from the head of the Department of Construction and Repair to be in charge of construction work at the Puget Sound, Washington Navy Yard, starting in February 1903. Fearing that the duties of constructor could lead to total blindness, Hobson realized that the only avenue of relief was special Congressional legislation.

"While I can perform duty," Hobson wrote to the Navy's Bureau of Construction and Repair, "yet the duty required in the Construction Corps in connection with plans and blueprints and in connection with inspection and supervision in the glare at shipyards and navy yards requires just the kind of use of the eyes that is painful and injurious and would tend to thwart their recovery. Under these circumstances I believe I should not continue such work, and since it appears that relief cannot come through the Retiring Board, I respectfully request the transmission to Congress of the application I hereby make for special legislative authority for such relief."

After a through investigation, Hobson won the endorsements of the Secretary of the Navy, the Chief Naval Constructor, and President Roosevelt, who sent a special message to Congress in support. Hobson now girded for battle in Congress that he would lose in a bitter, protracted struggle.

The opposition, particularly Hobson's representative, Alabama Congressman John Hollis Bankhead, spread word that the handsome hero was planning a Congressional run once out of service. Bankhead had no plans of helping Hobson launch his own career at the expense of his, so he lined up support to block the Hobson bill.

Bereft of his own party's support, Hobson turned to the Republicans. Oregon Congressman Malcolm A. Moody entered the bill in the House while New Hampshire Senator Jacob H. Gallinger did the same in the Senate. The legislation was favorably reported by the Senate Naval Affairs Committee and was entered on the calendar for passage. However, Congress adjourned before it could get out of the House Naval Affairs Committee.

Obviously, Bankhead was exerting his influence. When Congress reconvened in December 1902, Bankhead assembled his troops. With only nine members present—a bare quorum—the House Naval Affairs Committee voted on January 8, 1903. The vote against reporting the bill was five to four—three Democrats joined two Republicans to defeat four Republicans. In short, Hobson did not gain one vote from his own party.

Frustrated by Congress and refusing to jeopardize his eyesight, Richmond Pearson Hobson had only one option: resignation from the U.S. Navy after eighteen years of service that began with arduous study at the Naval Academy, continued with stunning heroism at war, and followed with experiences of idol worship and stinging criticism, assignments throughout the Far East, beset with illness, and ending with rebuff in the halls of Congress.

Hobson formally resigned on January 29, 1903. Navy Secretary William Moody was reluctant to accept the resignation. "Give yourself another chance," pleaded the Secretary. "Think it over."

Hobson did; the answer was the same. So the Secretary accepted the resignation on February 6.

Concurrent Successes on the Home Front ... 1899-1902

The post-*Merrimac* years, indeed, were filled with difficulties and ended on a bitter note. But service to country aside, Hobson had personal triumphs during this period.

While Hobson failed to move Congress to retire him, he had better fortune in the campaign for promotion. As he served in the Far East, Congress was still entangled over a joint resolution introduced by Alabama Congressman Oscar W. Underwood and Senator John Morgan. Introduced on June 17, 1898, while Hobson was in a Spanish prison, the resolution sought not only to congratulate the *Merrimac* hero, but also to advance his status. The bill was complicated by the desire of also rewarding others in the Santiago campaign, and then the battle ignited between the rivalry between Hobson's 'patron,' Admiral Sampson, and Admiral Schley. The latter influenced House Speaker Thomas B. Reed and Pennsylvania Congressman John Dalzell to stall the legislation.

The Sampson bloc prevailed, and the resolution finally passed on February 11, 1901. Hobson was advanced ten numbers, i.e., ahead of ten men above him in the small list of the Construction Corps. He was promoted from assistant Naval Constructor to Naval Constructor. More amazing was the jump of three grades, from Lieutenant to Captain; at thirty-one, he was the youngest ever to achieve that rank.

Ironically, all this brought little material gain to the *Merrimac* hero because naval constructor salaries were determined by longevity, not rank. On the other hand, Hobson earned the 'wages' of resentment and bitterness of other naval men. For example, Richmond Pearson Hobson skipped over such Naval men as David W. Taylor. A fellow alumnus of the Naval Academy, Taylor had graduated four years before Hobson and boasted the highest grade average ever earned at the school.

"I believe he was promoted over the heads of two hundred-odd officers," notes Mrs. Grizelda Hobson in her *Memoirs*. "It can be understood there were a few cases of bad feelings among all those, though nearly everyone, especially those who had served with this young, brave lieutenant, rejoiced at those honors to him. It was a very proud time for his home town."

Certainly, no ill will greeted Hobson's publishing success. The Century Publishing Company had invited him to write his war experiences—appropriately called *The Sinking of the Merrimac*—and rewarded him with a handsome $5,000 advance, an incredible sum in those days.

What did he do with his new-found wealth? "Instead of spending it on himself," his mother told the *Saturday Evening Post*, "it has gone to help his relatives."

His generosity was recorded later by his wife, Grizelda Hobson, in her *Memoirs*: "Richmond's goodness to his mother and sisters, even his brothers, was never ending. In a letter to Mr. Bertron from Hong Kong, on April 23, 1899, he wrote,

> If I remember correctly, June 1 is the date for the first settlement on royalties for my book. I haven't the slightest idea what the amount may be. I have nothing on which to base an idea. If it is adequate, however, please let my mother draw on it as she may see fit, as to which I am writing her ... [my sister] Florence might be able to save something from this towards making visits to friends and going to Europe. As soon as I know what can be depended on, I want to make provision for the matter of education of cousins in Kansas City and wish to begin now a small settlement on my namesake, cousin Mary's little son. Provision is made for cousin Henry Hobson, for tuition, books, etc, clothing, and expenses to go home, if he desires in summer.
>
> In case of further expenses for Henry, let the contingent fund be drawn upon. Your letters thus far do not state total of remaining indebtedness—I allow it for $500. Should it be more, let balance wait till next estimates rather than encroaching on other times.

Hobson's letter continues with promises to help fund plastering and other improvements such as the installment of 'Water Works' at Magnolia Grove.

The constructor then details

> ... extraordinary expenditures for a summer trip for [my brother] Gus, allowing $50 per month ... . Sister Annie's visits during the summer—$40 per month, in addition to allowances. [My sister] Maggie's for going with you for your summer trip, $25. In addition to allowance, Maggie's expenses at college or boarding school, $40 per month.

In addition to above, I include $400 for Sister Annie's trip to Hong Kong, which may remain with contingent fund till needed. I am sorry I did not have a bank deposit to cover such matters, and avoid troubling you.

In short, as his mother told the *Saturday Evening Post*, "I think that I have much to be proud of in my son, but, principally, that as a boy and as an adult, he has been as much of a hero as he has been a man. We are glad that he is brave, but just as glad that he is generous, loving, and upright. People don't know how generous he is."

Mrs. Richmond Pearson Hobson.
Courtesy: Magnolia Grove

8

REUNITING WITH GRIZELDA

In a brochure compiled for Hobson's first political campaign, Greensboro native Julia S. Tutweiler ended her narrative with the adverse action in the House of Representatives: "The hope of relief being totally cut off and his eyesight at stake, Captain Richmond Pearson Hobson was forced to resign from the employment of the United States. Thus, the American Navy lost its noblest hero—one whose name, deeds, and character had added fresh luster to its glory."

Hobson's plight was painted more sternly in Grizelda Hobson's *Memoirs*. "He was now," she wrote, "for the first time since a child without salary of any kind, and this was particularly hard for him, as he had always sent the greater part of his earnings home to his mother and sisters."

"Richmond Pearson had always seemed to be living on the edge of his salary," added Gloria Cole. "He spent all he had on donations, charitable contributions, or sent it home to the family in Greensboro."

Shortly after his resignation, continued Miss Cole, a tornado struck his Alabama county and destroyed the town of Maundo. "Richmond organized a rescue party and used his own money to see that all, black or white, who had lost their property in the storm were safe." Grizelda Hobson recorded Captain Hobson's actions in her *Memoirs*: "A tornado swept through Moundville in Hale County leaving great havoc along its course; the Captain dropped everything and ordered a special railway train and went to the aid of the injured. Irrespective of race and color, he had those removed to places where they would receive the proper medical care and other comforts. Such things endeared him to his fellows always."

Mrs. Hobson observed that Richmond Pearson had been "denied the chance of saving his eyesight, which has been seriously injured in line of duty!" Certainly, he had claim to be hurt and feel "betrayed." Nevertheless, "even then, bitterness never overcame him," insisted Mrs. Hobson.

However, his first actions and later career question that analysis. Hobson was relentless, often vindicative, in his causes. The *Montgomery Advertiser* cleared Congressman Bankhead from any malice towards a future would-be rival. The paper published a letter from Julien Walker, Bankhead's private secretary, whose purpose was to absolve Alabama's Representative. The letter of February 18, 1903, stated in part:

> He [Hobson] was not retired in the ordinary way because two different Medical Boards of the Navy found that he was not physically qualified for retirement, that his eyes were quite good enough for the delicate and difficult work of a Naval Constructor. He was not retired by act of Congress for this reason, in part, of the findings of the Medical Board, but mainly for the reason that a special act in his behalf would establish a precedent extremely dangerous to the well-being of the Navy, in that any young officer could with just as good excuse ask to be retired while the Navy is already gravely underofficered.

Aware that Bankhead was taking his case throughout Alabama and across America, Hobson quickly responded to Walker's letter. His letter of March 15 to the *Advertiser* retold his side of the story, especially his examination by the Medical Board and his appearance before the Retirement Board and its decision. The Board had told him, "They had no power or jurisdiction over matters of the future ... [and at present his] vision was good." However, observed Hobson, "my only chance of recovery lay in avoiding such work as that of the Construction Corps."

Much of the letter is a castigation of Bankhead, who, Hobson claims, has sought refuge behind claims that he never lined up opponents against the bill or that he was absent from Capitol Hill when the vote was taken:

> I find myself entirely severed from the Navy after about 18 years service, in which fierce conditions were encountered in Cuba, China, and the Philippines, that caused permanent injury to my eyes, which are giving me almost continual trouble, preventing me, except at a risk of ultimate blindness from performing the work of my profession, either in the Navy or civil life. In this unhappy plight, I am cut off from the just relief which I had a right to expect from my country and am cut off through the action of my own representative, whose help I had a right to claim as a constituent. A great injustice has been done me, and I charge the responsibility directly and absolutely to J. H. Bankhead, who, in the apprehension of a political danger, grossly neglected the duty of his high office.
>
> Mr. Bankhead cannot escape this responsibility behind the evasions that appeared from his supposedly irresponsible mouthpiece, his private secretary, your correspondent ... . Instead of constituting an alleged dangerous precedent, the case stands unique; there has never been a similar case before, and in all probability there will never be a similar case again, where a naval constructor goes off to war service and in this service and that immediately following incurs eye troubles that cut off the practice of his profession ... .
>
> Neither is there escape in claiming that Mr. Bankhead was not requested to introduce the bill, nor in his being absent from Washington when the final action of the [Congressional] committee was taken ... .

Having fully stated the case, it was time for Hobson to move on. Opportunity in the presence of James B. Pond, noted as lecture impresario and manager extraordinary. "You are the most popular young hero this country ever had at your age, and what is the nicest of it all, it does not seem to enlarge your head in the least." After his release from Santiago prison Pond said, "Why not get a few month's leave from the Navy and tour under my direct supervision?" Now was his opportunity.

On the Lecture Circuit . . . February 1902-July 1904

Pond had promised Hobson an astounding sum of $1,000 a lecture, with thirty to fifty lectures guaranteed. If Hobson chose, Pond would set aside sums for the relief of the wounded and sick servicemen.

A skillful speaker from his school days in Greensboro, Hobson now contacted Pond, who had frequently written him with speaking offers. Actually, Pond had encouraged Hobson to make a brief lecture tour in the summer of 1902 for the Chautauqua Society. The *St. Louis Post-Dispatch* related Hobson's gallantry during that lecture tour: "Lt. Commander Richmond P. Hobson came there ... on a lecture tour, and one storyteller related how a young woman on a boat called to Hobson on his boat, 'If I fall into the water, would you rescue me?' Yes, indeed, she was told. Whereupon she promptly jumped into the river and Hobson, in full uniform, had to make good his gallant promise."

Hobson responded to Pond's urgings and signed a lecture contract for a twenty-two-state tour, in addition to the Oklahoma and Arizona Territories, which the promoter termed a "Pacific Coast Tour."

Before Hobson signed the contract, he had written an article for the *North American Review*, "America Must Be Mistress of the Seas." His lecture tour theme was the message of the article: America's destiny must be shaped through supremacy of the seas.

> The Navy can only give safe convoy or a clear road for passage. The Navy can only insure our rights as a neutral, and permit us to realize the security of our isolation and render us, in fact as in word, independent of European turmoil.
>
> It is imperative that America be the world's greatest power for a number of reasons to maintain her stutus as the world's largest exporter; to ensure that the Open Door of China remains open; and, most important, to guarantee world peace.

Expanding on this point, Hobson reasoned that America as a naval power would "... dictate peace to the world ... wonderfully hasten the reign of beneficence in world policies ... give effect to our general advocacy of free institutions, to our advocacy of peace and of the brotherhood of man."

The inaugural lecture was set for February 2 at Williamsburg, Kentucky, with the tour closing on May 16 at St. Paul, Minnesota. Richmond Pearson Hobson had a new look. He was still slim and handsome, but he was without mustache and was balding. Hobson loved the lectern and became more skilled as he perfected the oratorical talent he showed in the Greensboro schoolhouse. He entranced audiences by his impassioned messages; his extolling of America and Americans; his powerful, resonant voice.

After a talk in Phoenix, the *Arizona Daily Democrat* profiled him as: "[an] impassioned, eloquent, masterful, tender, paying the highest tribute to woman's worth, and her potency in influencing the world for good, and making every man in his audience feel that to be an American meant something grander, nobler, and higher than he had ever felt it to be before."

Underlying—if not at the center—all of Hobson's talks, as well as his writings, was the Christian motif. While the name of God was not always present, the Biblical allusions and message were clear. Hobson appealed to the higher nature, man's spiritual progress. "No man liveth unto himself," he told audiences, "neither does any nation; no individual enjoys a blessing without a concurrent responsibility to his fellows, neither does any nation. With nations as with men, Heaven requires works proportionate to talents and opportunities." America was thrust into world leadership because of its Christian practice. He noted in the *Review* that America had more members of the Young Men's Christians Association than all other nations of the world combined. He used the phrase the "will of God" to explain the mission of America. The *Review* article ends on this note, a note that resounded often in his lecture tour: "The most potential nation in history, standing upon the strategic vantage-ground of the world, with unparalleled equipment, is being called upon by the strongest demands of interest and the most imperative appeals of duty. Like the cumulative processes of nature, the movement will be irresistible ... . America will be the controlling World Power ... . The race will work out its salvation through the rise of America. I believe this is the will of God."

After a successful Pacific Coast tour, Hobson went out on a summer Chautauqua speaking circuit, followed by a series of personal engagements. Richmond Pearson Hobson had built up a large, enthusiastic following, who hailed him as a worthy rival of William Jennings Bryan, the "Great Commoner."

Throughout his activity-filled tour, Hobson did not forget his 'protector,' Admiral Cervera. He was one of the leaders in helping establish a National Memorial honoring the Admiral and Spain for their kind treatment of Hobson and the crew of the *Merrimac*. A framed document expressing the gratitude of the American people, was the brainchild of Arthur Bird, an editor in Sidney, New York. In July 1904, the Memorial was presented by Bird to Cervera, who placed the document at the Spaniard's residence in Puerto Real, Cadiz.

The Admiral thanked Hobson for his "thoughtful act" in establishing the Memorial. In a long letter of July 12, 1904, Cervera said that he "was very touched" by Hobson's act and appreciated his "loyal friendship" and "the esteem" in which the Captain held him. As for the award, he did not "merit" it. "I should be thankful to the United States," he wrote "for their generous treatment of me. I did not do anything special. I acted the way any civilized man, any man of conscience would have acted."

Courting Grizelda . . . 1901 - 1905

Hobson never forgot Cervera, and he never forgot the beautiful Grizelda Hull he had met briefly during the female rush on- stage following his post-*Merrimac* performance at the Metropolitan Opera House. Their relationship resumed, unexpectedly, while he was on assignment in the fall of 1901 at the Charleston Government Exhibit. Hobson was often entertained by the socialites, Mr. and Mrs. Simonds, in the beautiful Villa Marguerita. "Why not join us for the Annual Autumn Ball in Tuxedo?" they asked the Captain. Hobson readily consented to take part in the New York ball, which brings out the debutantes who will make their bow in the winter.

Grizelda Hobson recreates those moments of October, 1901, in her *Memoirs*: "I had grown up attending most of these dances ... in the beautiful circular ballroom with the velvet seats all around for dowagers and parents, all so gala looking, the room always festooned in autumn leaves and evergreens fresh and redolent from the hills ... .

"When Captain Hobson entered the ballroom that October evening, he created a sensation. Everything came to a full stop for a moment—then every woman present hoped in her heart that she would meet him and waltz to the strains of the Blue Danube or the Vienna Woods."

Sadly, the impression that the Captain made was not experienced first-hand by Miss Hull. She received a report on the Captain from her friends. Miss Hull was not at the ball. Instead, she spent that evening with a young French naval officer she had met while making her debut in Cannes. Rather than going to the ball, they decided on a quiet evening since the officer was leaving the next morning.

Fate was kind to Grizelda Hull. Mrs. Simonds was preparing to take Captain Hobson to his late train to New York, for his return to Charleston. "We still have a few hours," said Mrs. Simonds. "Let us look in at the annual tea party of Mr. and Mrs. Kent. This is always a festive occasion. We might even find Miss Hull there. I am still so disappointed that she did not come to the ball last night."

So the carriage changed direction and headed toward the driveway of the Chastellux home of the Kents.

Miss Hull was glum after her French admirer had left and was dressing for the Kents' party. "I put on my best bib and tucker," she writes in her *Memoirs*, "a quite lovely black velvet gown with a hat of the same with a sweeping white plume, and arrived at the tea party just a few minutes after the entrance of Captain Hobson. As I came in, I instantly recognized him, standing with his back to the door, and looking very tall and athletic. As I came up, Mrs. Simonds seized my hand and exclaimed, 'Miss Hull, allow me to present Captain Hobson.'

"I looked up at him and said, 'I have met you before.' Quite promptly, he replied, 'Yes! It was at the Metropolitan Opera House, after my speech ... . I have always remembered you, and the beautiful thing you said to me—that you were proud to be a Southern girl.'

"A disbelieving Grizelda Hull wondered, 'How would you have remembered me out of the hundreds who shook hands with you that night?'

"His blue-grey eyes glowed [as he responded,] 'You wore a dress with little rosebuds on it!' By then my heart was going so fast that I hardly heard Mrs. Simonds, who said, 'Captain, we must hurry if you are to catch that train to New York.' He bent over me, and I whispered, 'I am still proud.'"

The Captain said farewell, but the long courtship had begun. Several days later, Mrs. Simonds received a letter, which she shared with Grizelda and her mother: "You asked me to come out again as soon as I could. Would it be agreeable to have me again next Sunday, and if so, would you be good enough to ask Miss Hull if I may have the honor of taking her to church?"

Miss Hull accepted. "We went to church that October day," she reminisced, "with the leaves all turning red and gold, and the lake sparkling in sunlight, warm and brilliant."

Not surprisingly, her parents, George—president of the American Pig Iron Warrant Storage Company—and Lucia Hull, were very receptive to the Captain when he visited them after church. "My parents were most cordial naturally to this young and distinguished Southerner," observed Miss Hull, "as we sat talking before a log fire." Besides their Southern roots, the Hulls and Hobsons had commonality. Mrs. Hull's uncle, George S. Houston, had appointed Captain Hobson's father, Judge James Hobson, as Probate Judge of Hale County, Alabama.

The Captain's forefathers—the Hobsons, Pearsons, Moreheads, Whites, and Williamses—were prominent in the history of North Carolina, and Tennessee. The Hulls were descended from the Polks, Houstons, Longs, Jones, and Eatons, who were noteworthy in the story of Kentucky and Alabama. Moreover, both families traced their lineage to New England: the Saltenstals and Brewsters on the Hobson side, and the Strongs, Farnhams, and Doolittles, the roots of the Hull family.

Captain Hobson's visits increased upon his leaving Charleston for the Crescent Shipyard in Elizabeth, New Jersey. "Sometimes he would bring along a big sheaf of letters from friends or admirers all over the country," related Miss Hull. "Many of them were very funny, especially from people he had never seen, but whose patriotic ardor had been aroused by his heroic exploit at Santiago. He was so young and so handsome and had a courtly manner innate with him, which drew people to him with irresistible force."

Grizelda Hull had spent much of her teen years in Paris, Brittany, and Cannes, France and had lived with relatives, the Baron and Baroness de Charette, during her girlhood, so the Captain's manner was new and delightful. Grizelda Hull, for example, spoke of her skating abilities. "I was a fancy figure skater in those days, when it was more of a rarity," she said. "He used to watch me go through intricate steps, and would say admiringly, 'How did you ever learn all those twists and pirouettes.'"

She had been taught by a handsome Frenchman, but "very fast the Frenchman who taught me was fading in my memories. This elegance of Captain Hobson's manner attracted me tremendously, for a good deal of my girlhood up to then had been passed in France."

The romance was blossoming, but the engagement did not come until May 6, 1905. Perhaps this could be explained by Hobson's protracted dealings with the government until his medical condition forced resignation in 1903. Without career, he sought to carve out a new life, which took him on an extended lecture trip across America.

Grizelda Hull does not deal with the extended courtship in her *Memoirs*. Gloria Cole commented about reports that there were other suitors, perhaps the Frenchman mentioned in Grizelda's writing. However, Miss Cole points out that Richmond and Grizelda corresponded often. "In fact," she said, "there is one long love letter from Richmond to Grizelda included in her *Memoirs*. It was the tornado in Hale County that made Richmond recall a conversation they once had. Richmond fantasizes being with Grizelda during a storm both at land and at sea."

Mrs. Hobson presents this long love missive in her *Memoirs*:

> The papers say you are having a fierce storm in New York. I wish I were with you to enjoy it. Didn't you once promise that you would take care of me on land if I would take care of you on the sea? Well, we must have a storm together, both on land and sea. You must get your

plans ready for the storm on land. Mine are all ready for the storm at sea ... .

All the afternoon we watch the rising fury of wind and sea. You say the green curlers are so cruel as they strike and pound the staggering ship. I tell you that it is not cruelty, only the manifestation of power. You tremble a little as the huge waves crash over the bow and sweep aft. I press your hand and assure you it is all right ... .

A solid wall of water sweeps over the bow and bears us down. I stand out over you to break the force. We cling to the stanchion and the rail and to each other. Emerging from the deluge, a lightning flash reveals your face, blanched, but in the eye I see the conquering spirit. 'Do you still trust me on the sea?' I ask. You nod 'Yes' and I rise and fling a defiance to the sea and the wind ... .

Prof. Houston Stokes, grandson of Richmond and Grizelda, is very much aware of their courtship and sees nothing unusual in the long relationship. "In those days long courtships were not uncommon," he said. "More important, once they were married, they had a very happy life together."

Tuxedo, New York . . . May 1905

All thoughts of a lavish wedding for Richmond Pearson Hobson, 35, and Grizelda Hull, 27, were put aside when Judge Hobson died. It was a small, simple wedding; no formal invitations were sent. Only close relatives and a few intimate friends attended ceremonies at the Tuxedo home of the Hulls. The bridesmaids were her sister Lucia and Carolina Astor Drayton, later wife of America's Ambassador to Italy William Phillips. Recently graduated from West Point, Lieutenant James Marcellus Hobson served as his brother's best man. Among those waiting on the groom was his Congressional campaign manager L.B. Musgrove. The ceremony was performed by the Rev. William Fitzsimmon, the rector of St. Mary's Church in Tuxedo Park.

Among the guests were war heros Rear Admiral French E. Chadwick and Lieutenant General Nelson A. Miles; Massachusetts

Governor Curtis Guild and Mrs. Guild; inventor Nicola Tesla; Robert Underwood Johnson, editor of *Century;* and the daughters of the Civil War and Spanish-American War hero, General Joseph A. Wheeler, who was a cousin of Mr. Hull. General Wheeler was himself too ill to attend, but he sent his congratulations to the newlyweds. Referring to the Hull's Eastern roots, the General rejoiced, "If anything was needed to bind the North and the South more closely, such weddings as these would do it!"

Another invitee, Spanish-American War naval hero George Dewey, wired his regrets and complimented Richmond Pearson's choice: "I know of her, and am sure that you have won a prize, and equally sure that you deserve the prize."

The couple were delighted with the gifts, but nothing gave the bride more pleasure than the groom presenting her with the key to his prison cell at Morro Castle, Santiago.

Nothing would have completed the Hobson story more than for Admiral Cervera to be at the ceremonies. He was unable to attend but sent his warm congratulations from his home in Porto Real, on May 20.

The couple honeymooned in a picturesque camp in the Adirondack Mountains, owned by Mr. and Mr. John Dunlap, editor of *Engineering Magazine.* They then made their home at the old Hobson homestead, Magnolia Grove, in Greensboro.

9

INITIATION INTO POLITICS

Richmond Pearson Hobson left Navy service in 1903, went on tour in 1904, and was married in 1905. What happened in between was his entry into political life: a loss in a primary campaign that was one of the bitterest and most vicious in Alabama history.

His foe was sixty-one-year-old John Hollis Bankhead, who had been the Congressman in the Sixth Alabama District for eighteen years. Hobson had targeted Bankhead ever since the Representative had led the opposition to Richmond's naval retirement. The battle was the first under the state's new Democratic primary system.

As soon as Hobson opened the campaign on January 25 at the courthouse in Greensboro, he was challenged by state committee members on the grounds that he was not a registered voter when the books were last open in 1902. Hobson agreed, but sought to excuse himself because he had been in the Navy—out of state—at that time. Surprisingly, Bankhead asked the state committee to allow Hobson to remain on the ballot. "I would love the opportunity to beat him myself, and I will," Bankhead assured the committee.

Hobson's campaign manager was Lycurgus Breckenridge Musgrove, who was most eager to unseat Bankhead and establish a power base in the state. Publisher of the weekly *Mountain Eagle*, he had also earned repute as banker, coal miner, and philanthropist. The novice Hobson had little chance of winning, according to the *Birmingham Age-Herald*. Aside from his lack of political experience, Hobson had to contend with the state committee, whose newly elected chairman was the Congressman's son, William Bankhead, Jr. The younger Bankhead had been a member of the Democratic

Executive Committee of Walker County, the most heavily populated of the district's nine counties.

Hobson gave his first major speech at the county seat in Jasper. He told an interested audience that creation of a stronger Navy would be the focus of his campaign. To the delight of Musgrove, a foe of the railroad industry, Hobson assailed Bankhead as a "railroad Representative." Bankhead, Jr., jumped up to respond, but Hobson paid him no attention.

Hobson's most popular campaign forum was the church, especially the Episcopal Church of Alabama—under the charge of the Rev. R.H. Hobbs— where he was a lay leader. He also did not miss opportunities to speak at a Baptist Sunday school or the Epworth League. He combined the themes of naval supremacy with missionary duties in China under the theme of "America's Mighty Mission."

At first Bankhead paid no attention to the challenger. However, the fiery campaigner had excited audiences. The *Montgomery Advertiser* was impressed with the campaign, which was "such as has not been seen before or since." They agreed to a first debate in Hamilton. Although the town was some sixteen miles from the nearest railroad, the *Advertiser* reported that a large turnout came by "wagons, buggies, and various sorts of vehicles."

The debate was more of a marathon—four and one-half hours long. Most observers called it a draw. Hobson's thrust was the need for a strong Navy and criticism of Bankhead as a puppet of the railroads and corporations. While Hobson stressed the importance of China as a cotton market, Bankhead countered with racist appeals.

"I have always voted to keep these Chinamen away from America," boasted the Congressman, "and I will continue to do so. The black peril in Alabama is ten fold worse than the much-talked of yellow peril in the Orient."

How did the second debate go? No one seemed to know because it was in Boxar, a town even more inaccessible than Hamilton. The third debate, however, was well publicized and well attended in Jasper. A large contingent even traveled by train from Birmingham, sixty miles away. It was a battle, proclaimed the press, between the "tireless veteran" and the "new political sensation."

Hobson continued his past approaches of attacking Bankhead for his railroad favoritism and stressing the importance of a strong Navy. His presentation ended, said the *Birmingham Age-Herald*, with "an eloquent peroration on the advantages of a great Navy."

After defending his Congressional record, Bankhead delivered a volley of low punches. "My opponent," said the portly Congressman, "has set his campaign on the lowest level. What kind of Democrat is he? He has never voted, which is easy to understand because he is not registered to vote. If voters do not like me, I can accept that, but, please, if you beat me, for God's sake, don't beat me with a man not of our party.

"My opponent claims he could not vote because he was in the Navy. Why didn't he vote while he was on leave? ... He was in Atlantic City or some other place in New England in a blue silk swimming suit ... . He danced and had a good time with the girls ... . Yes, one day he preaches in the church and the next day he leads a dancing party." As for spending money for a strong Navy, Bankhead preferred more accessible roads throughout the state.

Hobson had the last word, and, according to the press reports, had won the audience. The Naval hero did not refute the Congressman on the issues, but delivered a ringing emotional half-hour response, interwoven with Biblical allusion. "I have to apologize to all those here today," said Hobson, "especially the women and children who are witnessing such an inappropriate exhibition by my opponent ... . Verily, The Scriptures have been repeated of the swine and his wallow, the dog that returns to his vomit ... . You cannot overcome God's eternal truth."

Hobson stopped after the audience answered with, "Amen, amen." He then described the horrendous conditions in China, as women openly wept. "You cannot imagine the lowly conditions of the people in China. They are God's people as much as we are, and they deserve our Christian sympathy and help. I will not stop preaching sermons on behalf of these souls until they receive the proper help."

The end of the response was targeted at his opponent: "Let me tell you, a cyclone is after you, and that oak tree will be blown to fragments in April. Pieces of it will be found as far away as China ... . It is not because he loves his party less, but because he loves his railroads more."

Several additional debates were held the first weeks of March. The media, for example, the *Washington Post* and *New York Times*, were taking the Hobson candidacy seriously. The *Times* predicted Bankhead winning by a small margin, citing figures by a "shrewd politician," later identified as a Bankhead Congressional crony.

One serious local issue emerged. Bankhead claimed credit for the series of locks on the Warrior River that extended throughout the nine counties of the Sixth District. Realizing the difficulty of challenging Bankhead on this issue, Hobson could only counter—with little success —that the locks would be insufficient if river traffic were expanded.

Bankhead did not let up on the personal attacks and tried to draw himself as the simple country boy, a simple "Alabama hill billy," compared to his opponent, "a dude, a city slicker, who danced and made merry in the pleasure spots of the North."

Never known as an skillful speaker, Bankhead had played into Hobson's hand by agreeing to debate the charming orator. But Bankhead and supporters played down his debating success. "Most of my opponent's success," he claimed. "came from women, children, and Republicans. The Republicans and some of the small boys can do a lot of yelling, but they don't do the voting."

However, Hobson seemed to be making inroads into Bankhead's rural support. The Captain averaged about three speeches a day, including church appearances on Sundays, and the campaign trail stretched close to thirty miles daily. Part of that distance was often on foot, when Hobson decided to alight from the carriage and walk. In addition, he kept his name before the public by writing a series on the Russo-Japanese War for the Hearst Syndicate. The *Birmingham Age-Herald* gave the series front-page treatment.

While not supporting him, the media praised his abilities. "Verily, the Captain is a man of many parts," wrote the *New York Times*. Even when he seemed to be praising himself, Hobson was adroit in not seeming the braggart. When one reporter questioned his Navy service, Hobson responded with the words of Admiral Sampson: "The world will never know the valuable work this young man has performed for his country."

"Hobson has a way of saying these things about himself," noted a reporter for the *Montgomery Advertiser*, "that robs them of the appearance of egotism and invariably awakens immense enthusiasm."

Of his speaking skills, continued the reporter, "Hobson reaches his argument speaking faster and faster, and with an intensity that is thrilling. Deducting the conclusion from the argument, he fires his climax, like the climax of a thirteen-inch gun, and one does not to have to go around and wake up the claquers. The applause is awaiting the discharge, and it is invariably long drawn out."

Although minimizing Hobson's popularity, Bankhead knew he was in a race, and he was forced to extend himself to try to counter the energy of the younger candidate. They both became ill during the campaign. Bankhead had already given his approval for Hobson's place on the ballot although the challenger was unregistered. When the state committee met in March, Bankhead still gave his nod—not because of noblesse, but because he simply did not want to create additional sympathy for Hobson, who, then, could have been a write-in candidate. Taking its cue from Bankhead, the State Executive Committee allowed Hobson's name to remain on the ballot.

As the campaign came down to the final weeks, Bankhead—not wanting to be vengeful or worried—treated his opponent with guarded respect. In one debate Bankhead described the *Merrimac* incident as being "as brave and heroic an act as was ever performed in ancient or modern warfare." The Congressman then proceeded to speak of his own 'heroism' in the Civil War.

Hobson was a relentless campaigner and was not swayed by Bankhead's 'good will.' He hammered at his opponent's legislative record, alluding to Shakespeare's *Henry VIII*: "Had I but served my God with half the zeal I have served my king, he would not in mine age have left me naked to mine enemies ... . [A]nd had my honorable opponent but served his constituents with half the zeal he did himself he would not now be left."

Were the Alabama papers favoring Bankhead? The Buffalo *Illustrated Times* said, yes: "In this campaign Bankhead had every important influence behind him, including the leading daily papers of the state." However, a closer analysis revealed that neither candidate had any media advantage, endorsement-wise. Not endorsing either candidate, the *Montgomery Advertiser* said the race had received "more attention than any other Congressional fight in the State." Most experts called the contest a horse race.

Richmond Pearson Hobson, unregistered, went to Magnolia Grove on April 10, awaiting the returns the following day. Hobson lost, and the margin was not as close as most expected. Bankhead won 1,466 to 676. The Congressman won the primary with more than 68 percent of the vote and won six of the nine counties. More than half of Hobson's votes came in his own Hale County, which he carried along with Walker and Pickens Counties.

Musgrove charged the Bankhead forces with dishonest election practices. Hobson's campaign manager said that the outcome was an "outrage," especially in Walker County, where Bankhead's son was in charge of the voting, and where "only red headed democrats" were granted the vote. Musgrove's charges seemed absurd since final tallies showed Hobson carrying the county by 30 votes. Without explanation, the victorious Bankhead forces cried "irregularities."

Since it was Alabama's first general primary, continued charges and recriminations could have destroyed the experiment in political democracy. Hobson stepped forward to accept the voters' decision "without complaint" and was ready to endorse Bankhead without reservation in the fall election.

"Captain Hobson Accepts Defeat in Good Spirits," read the headline in the *Greensboro Record*:

> Sufficient information has been received to indicate that Hon. John Hollis Bankhead has received a majority of the votes cast at the recent primary election. I beg to state that I accept this verdict without complaint and will give Mr. Bankhead, along with the other nominees, my hearty support in the November election.
>
> I beg also to express my deep gratitude to all who honored me with their support. It is a source of keen gratification to know that this support came voluntarily and spontaneously without any promises of any kind. Indeed, the wonderful enthusiasm and disinterested devotion of my friends in this uneven fight deepens my admiration and love for mankind and will make this, my first political campaign, a source of inspiration for me as long as I live, an inspiration to a higher consecration to the services of our state, our southland, our country, and the world.
>
> I feel the keenest sympathy for my friends in their sore disappointment, but I beg leave to tell them that I believe ere long we shall all see that the result was for the best. Certainly no noble effort in the cause of right can ever be lost. This universe is so organized that right will conquer and frequently the later the day the greater the victory.

Even in defeat, Hobson could count his gains. He was a novice taking on the dean of the Alabama delegation in the House of Representatives.

He had shown himself a tough campaigner and skilled debater. His stance on a large Navy, while not accepted everywhere, attracted much attention in the media and won many followers. Less than a month after his loss, the state committee asked him to serve as presidential elector-at-large at the State Democratic Convention in Montgomery.

His popularity was evident at the Democratic National Convention, held in St. Louis that July. Hobson was at the convention only as a visitor. However, before the nominations began, Alabama's G. W. Pratt moved that Hobson be allowed to address the convention. He was introduced by Convention Chairman Champ Clark and was greeted with applause. Yet, a few jokesters smacked their lips to mock the Hobson kissing episode.

The large hall was filled with 15,000 people; listeners were surprised that Hobson had enough power to reach the extremities of the hall, a feat that had seemed reserved only for William Jennings Bryan. In proper form, Hobson attacked the administration of President Roosevelt. He continued to attack Roosevelt's policy as being too pro-labor, but not all cheered when he added, "It has been ten years since a Democratic President was brave enough to enforce the law against a labor-union violator." His call for strict enforcement against "corporation law breakers" was more readily accepted.

Hobson's words on Roosevelt's racial 'tone' perhaps played well to the convention and found receptive ears in the Alabama delegation. However, Hobson was 'irregular' on the racial issue. As in many other instances in his life, Hobson himself was a complex personality, full of contradictions and paradoxes.

Hobson was critical of Roosevelt's appointment of Southern Negroes, for example in South Carolina. He also chided Roosevelt for considering Booker T. Washington a "social equal." Of course, Hobson insisted that he was proud of the achievements of Tuskegee educator Washington. But, reasoned Hobson, Washington understood the "fundamental principle" that the races must be segregated.

Yet, these remarks were not fully in line with Hobson's personal views, which were more "progressive" than those of his fellow Southerners. As Sheldon writes in the 1972 *Alabama Review:*

> By Southern standards, Hobson was 'soft' on the race question: He could criticize President Theodore Roosevelt for appointing a Negro to a position in South

Carolina, while at the same time he urged that whites be allowed to teach in Alabama's Black schools .... He could scold Roosevelt for putting ideas of social equality into the head of Booker T. Washington, yet advise fellow Alabamian J. Thomas Heflin to abandon his race for Congress because of the extremity of the statements on the same subject.

The *St. Louis Republic* recorded Hobson's closing remarks comparing Roosevelt to Napoleon and also the response of the audience: "Aye, he comes from victories in the peninsula. I see Wellington take up the standard of Democracy, (loud applause). Yes, ... the great battle line is extended. There it lies. Here are the armies. My friends, let us make the Republicans give the name to that battlefield, and on the ides of November, let us make them call it Waterloo. (Prolonged cheering and applause.)"

The Democratic National Committee was suitably convinced that Hobson was the man to campaign through the North. Indeed, one West Virginian lauded Hobson for coming to his state because "there was no national speaker who came into our state who did us so much good as did Captain Hobson." On the other hand, Hobson was reluctant to give up campaigning in Alabama, where his political future rested. Therefore, he readily listened to local leaders and spent the last two weeks of the campaign in Alabama.

Having completed a vigorous season of campaigning for Congress and for his party, Richmond Pearson Hobson clearly outlined his political profile for his party. He was a dynamic, charismatic personality, but there were distinct negatives. He was persevering and not willing to compromise his principles—a quality not suited for political survival. For that reason, he showed no diplomacy in asking veteran Alabama Congressman J. Thomas Heflin to withdraw from the race because Hobson thought his public statements were damaging to the Democratic Party.

As for issues, he at times would become too immersed in great international issues, e.g., naval supremacy, and shunted aside vital issues of importance to the average American. Hobson was so obsessed with the Naval issue that he spent months chasing William Jennings Bryan to debate on American supremacy of the seas. Grizelda Hobson noted in her *Memoirs*: "Hobson devoted practically all his thought to the popularizing of the question of our Naval supremacy before the people of the land."

The naval supremacist wrote to his "warm personal friend," William Jennings Bryan, about debating the issue. "A great Democratic leader," Hobson wrote Bryan, "ought not to stand out against an important and urgent policy, saddling this party with the responsibility for opposition, unless he can maintain his position from the facts and truth."

Hobson suggested the Chautauqua assemblies in the summer as the proper forum for the debates. Politely but firmly, Bryan rebuffed Hobson's call for debate. For one thing, his summer was filled already. For another, he had no desire to debate "what ought to be considered a Democratic policy." And thirdly, the Convention committee had rejected the plank with Hobson's position, "and as the platform was unanimously adopted by the convention, I hardly think that it is a debatable question."

Bryan concluded with wishing Hobson "well" and felt the Captain would not fail to raise the issue in public: "You doubtless have abundant opportunity to present your views and if, as you say, the policy which you represent is 'an important and urgent one,' you do not need anyone to assist you in bringing it before the public. I might add that I am not trying to 'saddle' my party with responsibility for opposition as you intimate, for while I refer to the Navy question whenever occasion requires, I am not devoting anything like as much time to the defense of the Democratic position as you are in assailing it."

Having been beaten in his political debut, Richmond Pearson Hobson vowed to succeed next time. William Jennings Bryan would not debate him, so the Captain took his case on Naval supremacy to the country. He enlisted the support of Alabaman legislators, Congressman A.A. Wiley and U.S. Senator E.W. Pottus, to introduce bills in both chambers.

He went on a whirlwind speaking marathon that would reach some one million listeners in forty-two states. His theme ... . "A powerful Navy would preserve American peace and world peace."

He elaborated:

> I am not a dreamer. I have not had the utopian version of universal peace, but the time has come for a new era on the face of the earth. Man now controls the forces of nature. The cry is for men. We don't have to kill men now as they did in the devastating wars of the past.
> Institutions that are oppressive to mankind in this age will be crushed into dust. Birds, beasts, and men of

prey are going to the wall. If we can only restrain the cruel march of war; if we can only restrain the strong over the weak and allow the economic forces to supplant the art of war. If our nation can keep the forces of war down for one century, militarism will be destroyed.

America should go forth and keep the peace of the world. We should be the balance of power, so when the yellow and white races face each other, or when the great markets of China threaten to override the world, we can as peacemaker make the races friends. We should be the arbiter of the world. The way to do these things is to give a powerful Navy to the peace nation. Let us then make effort to bring about this consummation.

After hearing these words, audiences were asked to sign a petition in the form of resolutions endorsing the Treaties of Arbitration and International Parliament.

Richmond was joined by his bride in late May, in time for a number of commencement addresses, including Washington and Lee in Lexington, Virginia. In the summer, the duo covered the Chautauqua lecture circuit in Illinois, Indiana, Iowa, Kansas, Minnesota, Wisconsin, Nebraska, Missouri, and the Indian Territory, later Oklahoma. The same routes were covered, but in more urban centers, during the winter season in the Lyceum circuit.

They came across 'big name' speakers on these tours, among them Julia Ward Howe, American social reformer; the Rev. Lyman Abbot; William Dean Howells, novelist and editor; Robert E. Peary, who reached the North Pole; Henry Van Dyke, American clergyman, author, and educator; and William Jennings Bryan.

The lectures, the contacts made, and the fees earned were stimulating and rewarding. Grizelda Hobson described these tours in her *Memoirs*:

We swung around these vast areas in one-night stands, like a theatrical company would, sometimes having others on the same trains, who were on the program in the same day ... . Neither the screen nor the radio were as yet known, and the country farmers and small business people journeyed many miles in their conveyances of all sorts, to attend these gatherings that had three sessions a day and lasted in each place seven days ... . Little cottages or cabins grouped under cool groves of trees, afforded shelter, and in the center was the great canvas tent where the 'meetings' were held.

However, all amenities were not ideal, continued the new bride.

> Day coach travel, largely on branch lines, was accompanied in those days by much inconveniences, often even hardship. Sometimes we changed trains three or four times in a night, or we snatched a few hours' sleep in some hotel beside the railroad tracks, or even in a freight yard.
> When daylight came, we generally ate a quick breakfast and were off again, through the fresh morning air, the car windows wide open and the perfume of the fields in our nostrils. Usually late in the afternoon, we reached the small town, where we might be met by the mayor and leading citizens and even a town band! We were then escorted either to a hotel, or in a case there was no hotel, then to some private house. I remember at one of these, at luncheon, we all used a common fingerbowl, passed around the table, with especial formality.

Aside from speaking on Naval supremacy, Hobson was thinking hard and 'reassessing' his political approach. Sheldon in his study of Hobson's thought and ideology places the Captain in the tradition of "The Southerner as Progressive." In fact, the Southern Democrats, particularly in the House of Representatives, were the leaders in reform legislation. "The omission of the South from the annals of the progressive movement has been one of the glaring oversights of American historians," writes C. Van Woodward in *The Strange Career of Jim Crow*.

According to Sheldon, Hobson shared many of the qualities of the Progressives. Like them, "[he] held a romantically idealistic concept of American nationalism ... proud of ... American racial superiority ... devoted to the principles of a classless society ... suspicious, if not hostile, to labor unions because the unions emphasized class differences."

Hobson set out to not place all his campaign time on Naval supremacy but to give serious consideration to Progressive issues such as railroads, trusts, and tariffs. In Alabama, nothing mattered more to reformers than railroads. For that reason he hitched his wagon to a new star: Braxton Bragg Comer, a Progressive railroad commissioner who was a candidate for Governor.

On the Campaign Trail . . . 1906

The State Democratic Executive Committee set the Congressional primary for April 23, 1906. All other primary races had been set for August 27, forcing Hobson to cancel all speaking tour dates, starting in February. He was unsuccessful in appealing to the committee to fix the Congressional date for August. In fact, William Bankhead, the incumbent's son, belittled the Captain's chances. "He fought his best fight last time, and we don't anticipate any such struggle."

Apart from a wizened campaigner, Hobson went into this battle with an invaluable asset: his wife, Grizelda. She relished being on the campaign trail and added a touch of glamor to a charismatic speaker. While Magnolia Grove was their home, Hobson had hardly spent time in Greensboro before their marriage. Thus, the taunts of 'carpetbagger' were not to be taken lightly. The issue became somewhat defused with the presence of Zelda, as she was known. George S. Houston, her great-uncle, was governor of Alabama from 1874-79; cousin 'Fighting Joe' Wheeler was an Alabaman Civil War and Spanish-American War hero; the wife of former President Benjamin Harrison was a relative.

Still dogging Hobson was the criticism—justified—that he was an unregistered voter. During the last primary, Hobson maintained that his Naval service prevented his registration; now he asserted that his campaigning for fellow Democrats had kept him back.

The 1906 campaign opened with both Hobson and Bankhead in attendance at a speech of gubernatorial candidate Comer. "I support Braxton Comer," Hobson announced enthusiastically at the end of Comer's talk. "Mr. Bankhead, who will you support?" The Congressman gave his challenger a cold stare: "Mr. Hobson, no man who has never voted a Democratic ticket in his entire life has the right to ask me how I propose to cast my ballot."

Hobson identified himself fully with Comer, who would win the nomination in August. He publicly announced his support of the railroad commissioner and appeared at nearly every speech Comer gave in the Sixth District.

The Hobson strategy was carried out as planned: hammer away at the need for a strong Navy and attack his opponent's positions on railroads, trusts, and tariffs. "Three evils pervade our government and economic system," Hobson stressed. "The railroad interests have become too powerful. They do not serve the people faithfully. We can rectify this by proper legislation. Trusts also control the government and severely harm our economic system at the expense of the general public. The high tariffs only serve to overprotect big business and only damage and oppress America's farmers."

While supporting Comer, Hobson blasted Bankhead as a "railroad Congressman." The incumbent's defense was that he had supported regulation under the Hepburn Bill; furthermore, Congress had no regulatory power for railroads that were intrastate.

Hobson struck a popular note in calling for railroad legislation. He told voters, "On all legitimate grounds, I am a friends of the railroads ... [but they] have no place in the politics of a free people ... . They have bought newspapers ... . They back the dominant party."

The most serious obstacle that Hobson faced in the primary was the opposition of labor, who would neither forget nor forgive his anti-union remarks at the 1904 Democratic National Convention. The President of the United Mine Workers of America in Alabama, Ed Flinn, said that he had long been an admirer of Hobson, but could no longer support him because of those remarks. That statement was featured in a broadside that was distributed throughout the Sixth District. It was titled "Communication From Birmingham to *Montgomery Advertiser*, July 10, 1904, Relating to an Interview With President Ed Flinn, United Mine Workers of America in Alabama."

The opposition did not prove fatal, for on April 23 Richmond Pearson Hobson won, even carrying Bankhead's home county, although the majority was a slim 344.

Why did Hobson succeed this time? Undoubtedly, he had few equals as a debater. Bankhead had no answers for his rival's youth, handsomeness, and for an opponent who still retained his aura of charismatic national hero. Richmond and Grizelda were an irresistible couple. "He and his bride," wrote Sheldon, "seemed to symbolize the promise of a wonderful and glorious future, about which he often spoke with such intense belief."

In recalling those campaign trips, Mrs. Hobson noted how well Richmond made his case for a large Navy to those so far removed from the seaboard. "His contention that such a Navy would be a potent factor in preserving the peace of the world and in protecting our growing trade in foreign lands was gradually producing its effect upon his audiences all over the district. These plain people in the little isolated towns had time to think and they had time to appraise this young man who had come down here to talk to them, who wanted to know them, and who wanted to go to the halls of Congress to serve their interests."

The campaign trail did not offer Mrs. Hobson the day-to-day living she gloried in at Tuxedo Park. "For six weeks," she wrote, "we campaigned over roads filled with deep ruts, which shook me nearly to pieces, sometimes. We used bathrooms, with only a rubber tub, which was filled with pitchers of water, hot and cold."

However, the satisfaction of convincing voters to vote for Richmond outweighed any inconveniences experienced. "It was gratifying to see men rally to Captain Hobson, not having met him and heard him speak," she said.

Grizelda Hobson proved a very persuasive campaigner herself. She related that many uncompromising Civil War veterans lived in the district, had voted twenty years for Bankhead, and refused to come to Richmond's talks. "One day," she narrated, "we passed a little house perched on a cliff, at the side of the road. An old man with a very long white beard sat rocking on the front porch. I asked to stop.

"'There is no point, darling,' said my husband. 'That's old Sartain. He is one of Bankhead's staunchest supporters.'

"'Nevertheless, I would like to shake hands with him,' I persisted.

"So the surrey was stopped, and Captain Hobson with a lenient smile got out and called up, 'Oh, Captain Sartain, I have my wife here and she is anxious to meet you. Won't you come down?'

"The old man did so. He had a superb head and looked up searchingly at me, as I said to him, 'Captain Sartain, you look like a good man. My husband is a good man. Won't you vote for him?' He was rather taken aback, but gallantly responded that he 'would think about it.' But he seemed much more impressed when told I was a cousin of Gen. Joe Wheeler and a great niece of Governor Houston. When the election was over, I received a letter from him telling me that not only had he voted himself for my husband but had also brought in the votes of other family members and friends. I was a 'good judge of human nature,' he said, that I was right that I put him down for the Captain—that my right name should have been Wheeler Houston Hobson and that he wished us both a long, happy life."

While Grizelda Hobson secured the votes of Sartain and others, her role in Richmond's election is but one factor. So, too, was the Captain's endorsement of Comer, who won his contest four weeks later.

The *Birmingham Age-Herald* left no doubt that Hobson won because he had skillfully and "deceivingly" portrayed himself as a farmer like many of his electorate. In fact, the paper featured a cartoon of Hobson as an unkempt farmer in overalls, in need of a shave, kissing a woman identified as the 'Sixth District.' In the corner of the cartoon was a Negro saying, "Dem ole farmer clo'se is whut done hit." Hobson was joined in the drawing by campaign advisor Musgrove, also in overalls, rejoicing, "Whoop la! He can shave now!"

More sophisticated analyses were offered by the *New York Tribune* and Hobson himself. President Roosevelt, said the paper, had strongly supported a large Navy, so candidate Hobson had identified himself with a popular national cause.

"I got my message across to the people," reasoned the winning candidate. "It was a campaign of education. The people accepted my position of 'new ideals in politics.'" The Captain spent $6,000 on campaign literature alone. As recorded in the *Alabama Official Register*, Hobson outspent Bankhead in the campaign $6,945 to $1,696.

Whatever the reasons, no one could argue with the results. The loser was gracious in defeat and sent a congratulatory telegram: "Accept congratulations on your splendid victory. If I can assist you in making your majority in November the largest ever given the party in this district, please command me."

In response, Hobson wired Bankhead, "Many thanks for your thoughtful and generous telegram just received. The loyal spirit manifested by you and your supporters testifies to the unity and strength of our party in the Sixth."

Greensboro, November 6, 1906

Victory in the Sixth District primary was tantamount to election, and on November 6, 1906, Richmond Pearson Hobson was elected to the Sixtieth Congress, running unopposed and amassing 8303 votes.

Greensboro readied a gala celebration for their hometown hero. The night after the election the Hobsons were greeted at the depot by hundreds of fellow townsmen and neighbors throughout the county. "There were over a thousand who cheered and waved flags," recalled Mrs. Hobson,

> ... while the handsomest carriage in the town, with four coal black horses, decked in flowers, was provided for us. We drove at a walk through the little street from the depot to Magnolia Grove, with a torchlight escort on both sides of us, singing and cheering, A number of carriages and transparencies followed and I remember one bore on its side a flight of steps, the bottom one having inscribed on it 'Magnolia Grove,' the next 'Southern University,' and in regular order, 'Annapolis,' 'France,' 'Santiago,' 'Mrs. Hobson,' and 'Congress.'
>
> The two top steps were left vacant, but the imagination of the crowd soon had those filled with 'Senate,' then 'President.' Then we arrived before the gates of the old homestead, and they swung open to receive us. The scene down the long driveway and the lawns was enchanting, all lighted within with candles, and the lace curtains stirring gently with a cool night breeze, and music on all sides. Rockets soared, anvils boomed, college boys from his alma mater yelled, and Captain Hobson, after the address of welcome, was escorted to the front amid renewed enthusiasm.
>
> Then amid admiring silence, he spoke to his people. He told them he was touched to the heart by their welcome, that he was grateful for their share in winning the victory. He came to them, hostile to no man, under promise to none, ready to work with all possible zeal to do his best for his home district, for nation, for humanity.

10

CONGRESSMAN RICHMOND PEARSON HOBSON

The newly elected Congressman was anxious to take his seat in the Sixtieth Congress. It would not convene until December 2, 1907, but the former naval constructor was not idle. He had long coveted a seat on the House Naval Affairs Committee. In fact, his running for Congress was born out of a mission to advance his Naval values for America. On March 2, 1907, he wrote House Speaker Joseph G. Cannon requesting that seat. Hobson's application had the approval of the other ten Alabama Congressmen. After conferring with other Democratic Congressional leaders, House Minority Leader John Sharp Williams of Mississippi agreed to recommend the freshman Alabama Congressman.

The Sixth District . . . 1907

While a strong American Navy, according to Hobson, would save America and the world, Hobson did not forget his home base. He organized a visit of specialists to Alabama under sponsorship of the U.S. Department of Agriculture. For twelve days during May, 1907, he joined them in a tour of the Sixth Alabama District. The experts told the farmers about the boll weevil, crop rotation, soil fertility, and other relevant concerns. At first, the farmers resisted using cattle dipping—immersion in a disinfectant solution. But they were won over.

Hobson's initiative proved so popular that the press applauded the 'Hobson idea.' The farmers were so turned on to scientific

This photograph of Congressman Hobson appeared
on a flyer announcing an address by him. c. 1914.
Source: Magnolia Grove.

agriculture that during 1907-08 they requested and received much more Federal assistance than in previous years. In fact, Hobson's district received more than one-third of farm subsidies set aside for Alabama. The visits led to other stopovers in 1908 and 1909 dealing with livestock as they related to the animal and plant industries, and health and sanitary conditions.

The incumbent also made solo tours of his district to tell his constituents about his legislative agenda: Federal aid for filling farm ponds and lakes with fish; building schoolhouses and roads in rural areas; expanding education, especially agricultural instruction in rural areas; extending Rural Free Delivery; strengthening Alabama's regulatory railroad laws.

The farmland of Carollton had been devastated by rains and flood. To alleviate their plight, Hobson collected the names and addresses of the hard-hit farmers so that they would receive free cotton seed from the Department of Agriculture. According to Walter Pittman, "The tour was as well organized and efficiently run as a military expedition. It captured the national imagination and was regarded as one of the shrewdest political tricks of the recent past. Some newspapers predicted all Congressmen would have to follow suit in order to survive politically."

Hobson also invited road experts on three separate expeditions into his district. The first two dealt with plant life, followed by meetings and gatherings on animal life and human health, respectively. The final visit had been long in the making and featured lectures by Dr. Charles Wardell Stiles, discoverer of the hook worm. He also spoke on typhoid fever and other diseases endemic in the South, primarily because of poor sanitation. Dr. Stiles was joined by Dr. Von Exdorf, malaria specialist; Dr. Julia C. Lathrop, chief of the U.S. Children's Bureau; and Fannie Nesbitt of the Red Cross, who spoke on practical nursing. Dr. Lathrop's presentations were so popular that Hobson was overwhelmed with hundreds of requests about baby care. Pamphlets were prepared under sponsorship of the Russell Sage Foundation.

The Hobsons Move to Washington, D.C. . . . 1907

Grizelda and Richmond Pearson Hobson were becoming acclimatized to their surroundings—and their growing family. They bought a house at 2117 S. Street Northwest, off Connecticut Avenue. Their first son, Richmond Pearson Hobson, Jr., was born there in November. "Oklahoma had just been added to the states at this time," recalled Mrs. Hobson, "so when a newspaper spoke of 'the new baby,' it sometime became difficult for us to know whether the reference was to Oklahoma or young Hobson.

"This happy event made life very complete and wonderful for us. He was a most adorable little fellow, radiant from the start and hardly ever crying." Serving as his Godfather at baptism was Rear Admiral Washington Lee Capps, who headed the Bureau of Construction and Repair. The bearded Admiral "nearly frightened him to death," said Mrs. Hobson, "patting him at close range, as a dutiful Godfather should do."

The Hobsons also celebrated the arrival of a new book, *Buck Jones at Annapolis*, an account of Richmond Pearson Hobson's experiences at the Naval Academy. The autobiographical nature of the work was discussed in Chapter 1. Those days had a very strong effect on his thoughts of the dangers of liquor, as will be noted later. The volume was dedicated to Little Richmond.

On Sundays and holidays, Congressman Hobson often delivered the sermon in a nearby church. His themes were "Patriotism and Character Building" and "The Urgency of a Great Navy and Merchant Marines." On this latter theme Hobson authored a series for a number of dailies, in particular for the Hearst Syndicate. His recurrent message was: America must be able to defend its vast coastline against any possible combinations of European or Asiatic powers.

"A large number of these articles," said Mrs. Hobson, "pointed out the danger of Japan in the Far East. Many of the elements across the country scoffed constantly at my husband's attitude on the Japanese menace. Nevertheless, he went on pounding away."

Hobson critics and mockers were quick in forming once the Alabaman went to Washington. After thirteen days in the Capitol, he announced preparation of a bill for a new official weekly journal for the American people "which shall contain brief notices of the work of the various executive departments and the independent bureaus of the Government, of the Supreme Court, and of the proceedings of Congress, so far as the same may be of general interest."

The *New York Times* poked fun at the freshman legislator on December 30, in its headlines and story. "Hobson Wants Publicity, Congressional Record Not Enough—He Plans a New Government Journal"—proclaimed the headlines. The story began with a Washington Dec. 29 dateline: "The Congressional Record, that brazen old chronicler of uttered and unuttered eloquence and market of political capital, is in danger of meeting competition at last. For decades this publication has occupied a field alone, but now danger threatens from an unlooked-for source. Capt. Richmond Pearson Hobson, hero of the collier *Merrimac*, having served thirteen legislative days of his term in Congress, has discovered that The Record is insufficient to meet his demands."

"'Insufficient!' exclaimed Representative Robert Minor Wallace of Arkansas, who in one minute of time inserted three long speeches in *The Record*. 'Insufficient! Why, Hobson doesn't know how to use The Record.'"

Although Hobson's thoughts on replacing *The Record* were taken lightly, his maiden speech of April 11, 1908, was eagerly awaited. After all, only William Jennings Bryan was his equal as public orator. But there was more at stake than Hobson's debut. The House was immersed in a Naval bill debate. Ironically, Hobson was leading the fight for the position of the President—a Republican. Roosevelt looked to Hobson and other Democrats to get the Administration measure through. The Naval Affairs Committee called for two new battleships. Hobson, with the President's encouragement, introduced an amendment, asking for four.

"When the 'Hero of the *Merrimac*,' rose to speak," wrote Grizelda Hobson, "the cloak room was quickly vacated and members poured into the rostrum, taking their seats with unusual show of interest. As a general rule, when a member gets up to make his maiden speech, most of the members leave the chamber. Today on all sides one heard the remark, 'Hobson is going to speak.'"

A silenced house awaited Hobson's words on House business, especially, on that day, the Naval Appropriations Bill. The freshman legislator began with an urgent call to meet America's great need for four battleships. A Texas Congressman interrupted: "Does not the Congressman know?" he asked, "[that]our Navy has not been able to man the vessels already in our possession?"

Hobson responded, shouting, springing forward with clenched fists. "The gentleman does not know anything of the sort." The other Congressmen caught the fire of Hobson and cheered him lustily. The galleries, jammed to the doors with Hobson admirers, welcomed the opportunity to roar their approval. Observed Mrs. Hobson, "Here was a Democratic defender of the Roosevelt Navy policy! His knowledge of his subject made the membership forget that this was his maiden effort ... . His resonant voice reached the far recesses of the Hall ... every seat was filled ... the galleries were tense."

Hobson's message was clear—American supremacy on the ocean was necessary for the preservation of world peace: "The penalty for being unprepared for war would stagger the imagination ... . The only rational basis for proper national defense is for us to proceed to guarantee control of the sea against any nation of Asia in the Pacific and against any nation of Europe in the Atlantic, both at the same time.

"I here proclaim, whether we realize this policy or not, as inevitable for our national defense, or whether we shall have to learn the lesson that for the elemental purpose of self-preservation, the very first duty that we owe ourselves, in keeping with the first law of nature, is that America must be supreme on the ocean."

Hobson strengthened his arguments by telling his listeners that he had already given more than 1,700 speeches for peace throughout America and read a partial list of the cities that had adopted his resolutions for peace and a strong Navy.

His maiden speech received rave reviews in the media. "If ever a speech in Congress made votes," wrote the *Boston Transcript*, "this speech of Hobson made them." Commented the *Washington Times*, it was "one of the most powerful speeches delivered in the House this session." The *Times* continued its praise: "Seldom has a new Member ... attracted such attention. Where disorder had reigned when some 'old timers' had been talking on the Naval appropriations bill, the hero of the *Merrimac* was able to secure a death-like silence ... . Republicans and Democrats alike, caught by the spirit of the speaker, cheered him, and the galleries, jammed to the doors with admirers of the young Representative, accepted the opportunity to express a roaring approval of the Democratic defender of the Rooseveltian Naval policy."

The Alabaman's eloquence notwithstanding, the amendment was defeated 199-83 after a long and acrimonious debate; Hobson had promised the President fifty-eight Democratic votes. Only twenty-six voted for the measure. Other amendments for one battleship and three battleships were also defeated. A compromise, however, was finally reached, for two battleships and $1 million for construction of a naval station at Pearl Harbor in Hawaii. The funding for naval construction exceeded by twenty-three percent the expenditures of the previous year. For Hobson, this was a mere beginning.

The Literary Digest of May 2, 1908, revealed that eighty percent of the country's newspapers were in favor of four battleships. Now, he must rally the public, reasoned the Congressman. In three articles for *Cosmopolitan*—May, June, and September, 1908—Hobson sought to activate the public sentiment for a larger, more powerful Navy.

The focus of the articles was that America and Japan, because of historical reasons, were now bitter antagonists fighting for control of the Pacific and power in the Far East. Hobson was convinced that Japan had the resources to invade America's Pacific Coast. The first strikes would be at the Philippines and Hawaii; the next targets would be Washington, Oregon, and California. If Japan succeeded, Hobson warned, it could "lead to great exhausting wars between the nations of the white race and pave the way for the supremacy of the yellow race."

In the end, however, Hobson predicted that America would win and Japan's expansionism would be checked, leaving Asia for the Asian peoples. As he stated in the final *Cosmopolitan* article: "Whether America and the world are to go through fire on the way will depend on whether America will take time enough from her absorbing business and domestic problems to recognize in advance the necessity for her supremacy on the sea, and whether the European nations, in their scramble for empires in the East and spheres in China, will see the handwriting on the wall and withdraw from continental Asia without the struggle that now seems inevitable."

America must, therefore, strengthen its Pacific fleet, he told the Naval Training Station and War College in Newport, R.I., in June, 1908: "The fleet of Japan has given that nation complete control of the sea in the Pacific and a great standing army in readiness behind that fleet has made Japanese power supreme ... .

"The only practical programme left for the United States is to have our fleet in the Pacific and to proceed with all dispatch to unite a new fleet for the Atlantic. We have become a two-ocean Nation and must now go on to a two-fleet basis of defense."

Hobson's energies for advancing America's Navy were diverted somewhat by three personal battles in 1908: one with Connecticut Congressman George L. Lilley; a second with Populist Tom Watson; and a third, surprisingly, with President Roosevelt.

No sooner had Hobson gained his place on the Naval Committee than Republican Connecticut Congressman Lilley charged that the Alabaman's cause had been promoted by the Electric Boat Company. That company, according to Lilley, was being granted government contracts through pressuring members of the Naval Committee.

A special committee conducted a lengthy investigation. Hobson readily admitted he had been in constant touch with Lawrence Y. Spear, construction officer of the boat company, and Hobson's classmate at the Naval Academy. "Spear was a classmate of mine at Annapolis," said Hobson "and we kept up our cordial relations for a number of years after we were in active service. I got a letter from him last November in which he said he wanted to see me in regard to a matter which would be for our mutual benefit. This did not surprise me, as he had already spoken to my secretary." Hobson continued his testimony: "I was ill with the grippe at this time and did not answer the letter. He then telephoned to me. He said that if he was assured that if I was in favor of the submarine for which the Electric Boat Company is a contractor, he would see to it that I got a place on the Naval Committee. I told him that I did not want anybody's influence, and that I would not disclose my position."

Queried the head of the investigative committee, Congressman Olmsted, "In what direction did he say that his influence lay?"

Hobson responded with shocking candor, implicating the man he had approached for committee assignment. "Through the Speaker [Congressman Cannon]."

Several days later, Spear, technical head of Electrical Boat, challenged his classmate's testimony:

> I told Mr. Hobson on one occasion that I had heard a man, whose name I think is Lynch, tell Elihu B. Frost, Vice President of the Boat Company, that he had influence over Mr. Hobson, which he was willing to exert in behalf of submarine legislation. Mr. Frost rejected the offer with scorn.
>
> Later, I called Mr. Hobson up on the phone, and asked how he was getting on with his race for the Naval Committee and offered to help him if I could. He refused, saying, it would not be proper for him to accept any favors in such a matter.
>
> As to my alleged remarks about having influence over the speaker, Mr. Hobson must have confused my talk with him over the phone with such conversation I had during his illness with his secretary. I told his secretary that I supposed John Sharp Williams would recommend him and that the speaker would appoint him.

As for Congressman Lilley, he spent three hours giving testimony, with little value and even less integrity. Most of the testimony was read from typewritten notes that did not substantiate any charges against Hobson or other Committee members. In fact, under cross examination Lilley identified Hobson as the Navy Committee member who spurned Spear's offer to use his influence with Speaker Cannon if Hobson "was straight on submarines." Lilley also admitted that his own statements came through advisement by former U.S. Senator John M. Thurston, who was an attorney for Lake Torpedo Company, an Electric Boat rival.

After lengthy hearings and two volumes of testimony, the investigative committee vindicated Hobson and all other members of the Naval Committee. The charges were concocted by Lilley as a means of aiding the Lake Torpedo Boat Company. A disgraced Lilley never won another election.

Having been identified as the leading proponent of a larger Navy and merchant marine, Hobson then found himself, in May, 1908, under attack by the *Jeffersonian*, a combative weekly, edited by Tom Watson, onetime Populist leader. In a May 14 article, Hobson was accused of being in the employ of the 'Steel Trust.' Richmond Pearson's brother, Samuel Augustus, challenged Watson's facts. His brother, he informed, had limited financial resources, in part because "he helped support family members, and had endured financial and social setbacks in the 1890's because the family had worked for Populist causes!" Watson promised a public apology.

Preparing for the Denver Convention ... 1908

Richmond Pearson Hobson had come through two 'episodes' in his freshman year in Congress and now looked forward to an idyllic late spring and early summer at Bateman's Point in Newport, Rhode Island. The Democratic Convention in Denver was eagerly awaited. Grizelda Hobson recalled those days in her *Memoirs*: "Our first-born learned to toddle about. It was most pleasant seeing my husband's many Navy friends of former days, and one never-to-forget day we spent at the Training Station. Admiral Fullam sent his barge to Agassiz's landing place for us, and the jackies placed our baby carriage on the small deck, where the American flag flew over it, caressingly, as we crossed from the mainland."

Before proceeding to Denver, Hobson left for a brief Chautauqua tour. Grizelda Hobson presents her husband's letter, marked by love for family and faith in God: "I watched the lights of the lightship till they sank low and the light of Judith Point. The night was very, very beautiful and the sea spoke to me of my wife and little boy left behind and reminded me that God is with me, and I know He will take care of you both ... . [W]hen I awakened [I] wondered if it was time for the little boy to come in with his mouth wide open singing. Kiss him a thousand times and tell him that when his father slipped off in night, he left good-bye blessings and will soon return. Give ear to the ocean as it tells you that your husband loves you with an infinite boundless love."

Richmond Pearson Hobson, hero of the *Merrimac*, had made an impression—both positive and negative—in the First Session of the 60th Congress. For a brief while he was being considered a Vice-Presidential candidate. However, that quickly cooled because he was not very supportive of William Jennings Bryan, especially not of Bryan's views on the Navy. Hobson, in fact, openly favored Minnesota Governor John A. Johnson.

On losing the potential Vice-Presidential candidacy, Hobson let it be known that he intended to be a Presidential candidate on the Democratic ticket in 1912. That news thrilled the *New York Times*—not because it awaited his Presidential bid, but because it removed him from 'making trouble' in this year's election. In a sarcastic editorial page article titled "The Patience of Hobson," the *Times* wrote: "This announcement is welcome for two reasons. In the first place, it removes any lingering fear that Mr. Hobson will be a candidate, on any ticket, in this troublesome year ... . The country would survive the running of Hobson this year, but it might be a disturbing factor.

> The announcement is reassuring, too, because it indicates Mr. Hobson's belief that the United States of America and the Democratic Party will both be in existence in 1912. We had feared, from some of Mr. Hobson's remarks, that the Nation, at least, was in danger of early dissolution. What with the threat of the yellow peril, an inefficient Navy, and the lack of a really purposeful hand, at the helm of State, we had gathered that Mr. Hobson thought things were going speedily to the bow-wows. If we are to survive until 1912, there is hope that we may, in time, live down many of our troubles, including Hobson. Meanwhile the Alabama states-man is to be congratulated on his unexpected prudence and his patience.

The media criticism could not dampen Hobson's euphoria as he arrived in Denver. However, the Convention would quickly prove Hobson's undoing. More than anything else, the Convention set the tone for Hobson's political behavior. He refused to "play the game."

Richmond and Grizelda Hobson
Painting by O. Bigelow.
Courtesy: Magnolia Grove

11

TAKING ON TEDDY

As soon as he arrived in Denver on July 7, Hobson appeared before the Committee on Resolutions and detailed the 'Yellow Peril' and the urgency of a two-ocean Navy. Although some skeptics felt America could handle Japan with minimal preparation, the Congressman left the committee room in an upbeat mood.

Overjoyed, he wrote a letter to his wife, a letter filled with love and happiness in his progress: "I have been walking on air all day. I gave them a lecture that swept everything. The chances are good that something will be done ... . It makes me humble in my great joy that I can be worthy of such a wife! I could go on through fire and floods this minute ... . What work I am going to do to show my gratitude to Heaven for giving me such a mate ... . Precious, it is so glorious to be alive. God is very, very good. You ought to be very happy at the thought of the supreme happiness you bring to a mortal, transforming earth into a paradise."

According to reports in the Denver *Rocky Mountain News*, Hobson was scheduled to address the convention on day two on the need for a larger Navy. His speech would create "hot shot and broadsides enough to delight any lover of a fight on sea or land," forecast the paper.

Hobson was announced as the second speaker for the session, to follow Oklahoma Senator Thomas P. Gore. The Oklahoman set off a demonstration of an hour and a half simply by mentioning William Jennings Bryan. Everyone on the platform stood up in unison to join the celebration of Bryan—everyone except Hobson!

"C'mon, Richmond, stand up!" pleaded audience celebrants. Hobson remained seated. Frankly, he did not approve of Bryan's policies, so why stand up, he reasoned. Nevertheless, many at the convention read his act as a statement of disrespect.

That was not forgotten when Temporary Chairman Theodore Bell of California went to the podium to introduce Hobson as the first speaker of the evening. When Hobson spoke at the 1904 Convention, he was preceded by great musical fanfare and much anticipation. Four years later, his presence at first created disinterest. Convention delegates seemed more interested in talking among themselves than listening to Hobson.

"Please give the speaker your full attention," M.T. Ormond of Florida stood up and pleaded. "No!" came a chorus. "If he enjoys sitting on the platform, let him sit," came an irate response. Bell called for a vote. Many "noes" were registered. "I have a very sensitive ear," said Chairman Bell, "and I hear a tie. It is the privilege of the chair to cast the deciding vote. I cast it in the affirmative, and Congressman Hobson is invited to address the convention." According to the *Los Angeles Examiner*, Bryan had instructed Bell to let Hobson speak.

Hobson was permitted to speak, but the circumstances were humiliating. Nevertheless, believing he had an important message to deliver, Hobson tossed the personal insults aside. Basically, his speech was a rehash of the message he delivered to the Resolutions Committee, but this audience was not receptive. They roared with laughter when he warned of an impending war with Japan.

Aware that his audience was hostile, he begged, "My countrymen, my message is nearly through." "Amen," said a pleased delegate, and laughter erupted once more.

Hobson went for what he thought was the knockout punch. "Not so very long ago," he shouted, "the President of the United States said in my presence, 'There exists the greatest possibility of a war with Japan.'"

That remark exhausted the patience of the galleries. "Sit, down!" "Come off!" "You're crazy." Hobson endured the anti-Hobson outbursts for five minutes. "Come to order," demanded Chairman Bell, "or I will clear this hall." Bell succeeded, and Hobson was able to finish his remarks and leave, with no more outbursts.

After Hobson ended, a voice in a back row shouted, "Hurrah for the *Merrimac!*" Not to miss out on the laughter, Chair Bell remarked, "The chair hails from the Pacific Coast and up to the present moment he has seen no occasion to enlist." And to end the proceedings on an upbeat mood, Bell told the cheering audience: "If we have our way out on the Pacific Coast we will have a big enough Navy to protect our coast."

Although humiliated, Hobson felt he had won the victory. Referring to the strong Naval plank, he wrote his wife, "Bryan has consented, so it's going in."

Perhaps it was not the all-mighty Navy Hobson wished for, but the 1908 platform gave the Alabaman satisfaction: "The Constitutional provision that a Navy shall be provided and maintained means an adequate Navy, and we believe that the interests of this country would be best served by having a Navy sufficient to defend the coasts of this country and protect American citizens whenever their rights may be in jeopardy."

Hobson did not lie about the President's warning. In 1906, Hobson was present at the White House when Roosevelt told Indiana Congressman Tom Watson, "Today, there is the greatest probability of trouble with Japan." But why did the Alabaman expose the President to embarrassment? "I spoke very frankly," Hobson wrote to his wife, "but of course could not bring up the facts and arguments as when before the Committee of Platform ... . The situation [impending war with Japan] is desperate. And I decided to state the cold facts regardless of personal consequences. This decision led to my making a remark in the course of my speech which from all sides was not the good of the country and would appear indiscreet ... . [A]nything is warranted to awaken the people to our danger." The media gave Hobson mixed reviews.

In its report, the *New York Times* could not hide its 'dislike' of Hobson. Whatever one thought of Hobson's ideas, the Alabaman was still considered a premiere, charismatic orator. "Hobson is an earnest but not a magnetic speaker," said the *Times*, "and after five minutes he seemed to have lost his crowd, and there were occasional jeers from the galleries."

Southern journalist John Temple Graves told the *Los Angeles Examiner* that Hobson had courage in telling the truth, and the delegates' insults to Hobson would damage Democrats. The *Independent*, a pacifist journal, termed the Congressman "a public nuisance and a national disgrace ... rabid, foaming, and frothing."

The President wasted little time and expended much effort in responding. At Oyster Bay, New York, Roosevelt huddled with his private secretary, William Loeb, Jr. What emerged was a statement that the President was misquoted. "Emphatic Denial," read the headline on page one of the *New York Times*. What the President had actually said was that with the proper Navy, America would never be led into war with Japan.

In its comment, the *Times* noted that the 'gentle' tone of denial was uncharacteristically tame for the President, so there must be some truth in Hobson's attribution. "This is something new," said the *Times* editorial page column titled "Contradicted but Very Mildly: "[T]here is not one chance in a thousand that there was any essential inaccuracy in the repetition of Mr. Hobson's words."

Perhaps this 'tameness' was the diplomatic opportunity for Hobson to retract the quote. But Roosevelt went beyond a hint in writing on July 9 to the Congressman: "I assume of course that you were misquoted when you were reported to have made the statement in your speech in Denver that you heard the President call war a 'probability.' I never made any such statement, and do not believe it either as regards Japan or any other nation. On the contrary, as I have repeatedly told you and as you have agreed with me, all that we need to do is to build a sufficient Navy, and we shall make war a practical impossibility.

"In addition, my dear Mr. Hobson, I know you realize that if I found that you tried to quote in public our private conversations, it would mean that I could hold no private conversation with you whatsoever. The obligation of not quoting private conversations between gentlemen is ten-fold stronger when they occupy official positions, and when one of them is President.

"My experience has always been that if anyone so far forgot himself as to try to quote what I had said to him in private, it actually turned out that his memory was too defective to enable him to quote it correctly."

From the Midst of a Chautauqua Tour . . . July-August 1908

Perhaps Hobson was naive, simply too honest, didn't know how to play the game, or didn't want to play the game. On July 21, the Alabaman responded with a five-page letter from Cedar Rapids, Iowa, in the midst of a Chautauqua tour. Most of the letter deals with Hobson's thoughts on American Naval expansion. As for "L'Affair Quote," Hobson was friendly, innocently reminding the President that the meeting with Hobson obviously slipped the President's busy mind. In any event, argued Hobson, it is understandable that the President would publicly deny the quote, but he was surprised that the President would deny it in a private communication.

As for 'violating' the President's trust in revealing the conversation, Hobson sought to excuse himself by his desperate position at the Convention:

> I assume of course that you have forgotten the conference at which Mr. Watson of Indiana was present, but you will recall it when I mention the circumstances. We were considering the outlook for getting four battleships in the Naval Appropriations Bill .... You remember you told us right here two years ago that one battleship a year was enough. [We said] we are going to take you at your word. You replied in these words: 'Yes, at that time, there was not the remotest probability of trouble; *Today there is the greatest probability of trouble with Japan ... .*'
>
> The convention was hostile from the outset, thinking that I was antagonistic to Mr. Bryan, and it took me forty minutes to make a ten-minute statement. As the antagonism grew, I determined to give my warning and drive it home at any cost to myself, and I took the responsibility of violating the confidence of your private conversation and quoted you as reported. I expected you to deny the statement officially, but I confess it is in the nature of a surprise to receive your private denial.
>
> Now, Mr. President, each man must determine for himself what his own duty is. I pray Heaven that I may be wrong, but believing that war is inevitable, I am trying to do my part.

Roosevelt had read enough, and he told Hobson as much in a July 24 letter. There would be no more private conversations. Indeed, Roosevelt said that he remembered the conversation with Watson, but he still insisted that he never spoke of the "probability" of war with Japan. The President charged Hobson with "a breach of honorable confidence." Concerning Hobson's surprise that the President would repudiate Hobson privately, Roosevelt said that this was an "extraordinary proposition." In effect, according to the President, Hobson was saying, "In effect, you expected me to lie publicly—and that is fine and understandable—only as long as I do not deny it privately."

The President wrote: "When a man is guilty of such a breach of honorable confidence, he cannot be expected to repeat accurately what he has heard. You in effect state that having determined to violate the confidence necessary for intercourse among gentlemen, if such intercourse is to continue, you expected me to tell an untruth in public and apparently would have approved of it so long as I did not confirm my public statement by a private statement."

The gloves were off as far as Hobson was concerned. Roosevelt was no longer addressed as President, but as "Theodore Roosevelt, Esq.," in the letter of August 1. He was angered that Roosevelt had charged him with "dishonor and false nature." Perhaps, suggested Hobson, heads of state indulge in public lying, as he had intimated Roosevelt had previously done [in July 1907], "when you denied that the fleet would go to the Pacific. You have no warrant for bringing in this ugly word [untruth] and absolutely no justification in intimating that I would approve any man's telling an untruth."

Warming to the attack, Hobson continued to assault Roosevelt's patriotism: "The nearest thing to treason I can conceive of is for an American citizen with knowledge of our danger to withhold that knowledge from the people." Continued Hobson, "When a man is not loyal to the truth, he could scarcely be expected when self-interest conflicts to be loyal to his fellow man or loyal to his country." The most vituperative commentary closed the letter: "I agree with you in your conclusion that our personal relations must end; not, however, because I wish to 'protect myself' [quoting Roosevelt's words] but simply because I cannot possibly help having feelings for you of unutterable scorn and loathing, akin no doubt to the feelings General Grant must have had when he said, 'I hate a liar, and I hate a coward.'"

Having reflected a bit, Hobson wrote Roosevelt a week later from Sword, Nebraska, still addressing the President as Esq. and still not budging on the truth of the quote. However he asked to "withdraw" the last paragraph and other comments on the President's loyalty to country. "I have come to realize," said Hobson, "that in writing them I was in the wrong."

Roosevelt had nothing further to write Hobson, but he wrote to his own friend, American Secretary of State Elihu Root, that Hobson was a "blackguard" and a "cad."

The political 'friendship' had ended. Years later, in 1928, Hobson met with Watson, who corroborated the content of the private conversation with the President. However, Roosevelt came to admire Hobson over the years. As Mrs. Hobson wrote in her *Memoirs*: "Years later, after his retirement [and shortly before his death], Theodore Roosevelt sent to Hobson by Reading Bertron, their mutual friend, his kind greetings and his hopes that Hobson would come to see him in Oyster Bay. He spoke of Richmond in the highest of terms. It was always regretted by my husband that we did not have an opportunity to comply with this cordial message."

However, several years after the President's death, Bertron and Richmond Pearson Hobson visited Mrs. Roosevelt in Oyster Bay and "had a most delightful visit."

The Roosevelt battle, in effect, precluded any future high-office aspirations for Hobson. He refused to play the game, and he was not to be trusted. However, Hobson would still accomplish a great deal in Congress and afterward.

He persevered in his battle for American supremacy on the seas. Ironically, several weeks after the Convention controversy, Roosevelt addressed the Naval War College and basically sustained Hobson's thesis for the urgency of Naval supremacy. The echoes of Hobson so worried the *Army and Navy Register* that it lamented the President's words which "somehow sustains Mr. Hobson's political hysteria."

But no war was imminent. The Root-Takahira Agreement of November 30, 1908, put to rest all war hysteria. Yet, Hobson was not satisfied, and still seeking to maintain an American fleet in the Pacific. He initiated a campaign with a lengthy letter—later a sixteen-page pamphlet—detailing his position. He sent the letter to the President and later the pamphlet to Congressmen, Cabinet members, and the media. All this met with little success.

12
CRUSADING CONGRESSMAN

As soon as Richmond Pearson Hobson had entered Congress, he had involved himself in progressive—or reform—legislation. In his study of the Alabaman's progressivism, Sheldon speaks of the qualities of the Progressives, citing the historian George Mowry in *The Era of Theodore Roosevelt 1900-1912.*

The reformers, according to Mowry, were "strong good men ... the protectors of morality, the originators of progress. They were ambitious men and ruthless, but only ruthless in their zeal for human advancement. They were supremely alone, the causative individuals."

Hobson had informed voters of his concerns when he ran for office. Although the issues that interested him were national, they were still of much concern to his constituents. They included such issues as railroad abuse, monopolies, protective tariff, labor benefits, government democratization, race relations, and woman's suffrage. He had a great interest in Prohibition, which would play a major part in his later life.

While running for office in 1906, Hobson issued a five-part platform. Planks four and five dealt with these Progressive issues. Plank Four included the improvement of waterways, the erection of public buildings, extension of rural deliveries and soil surveys, and the allotment and homesteading of public lands. Plank Five concerned the questions of tariffs, trusts, and railroads. "In doing my duty as Representative of the District and State," Hobson pledged, "I will throw myself into the fight of the people against the Tariff, Trust, and Railroad Tyranny, which the men now in office have permitted to fasten itself against the country. These men are joining in the cry for a remedy, hoping to satisfy the people with words, instead of deeds. The people cannot be deceived in this way. They know that relief cannot come till the men who caused the evil are turned out."

Progressive Legislation . . . 1908-1914

Hobson's position for the railroads was government regulation rather than government ownership. While the Hepburn Act of 1906 fixed railroad rates and strengthened the Interstate Commerce Commission, Hobson sought to further extend the powers of the Commission.

The Mann-Elkins Act of 1910 called for establishment of a special commerce court. Hobson objected to the provision that centralized the court, thereby removing localities from questions that affected them directly. He also wanted to broaden the act to cover telegraph and telephone rates. The telegraph and telephone, Hobson argued, have become, like books and music, "fundamental parts of the system of distribution." To his dismay, Hobson and other Progressives were unsuccessful in seeking to defeat the bill's passage.

Hobson favored passage of the Physical Valuation Bill of 1912 which tied determination of fair rates and profits to physical valuation of the railroads. "We can not proceed to an orderly system of development unless we can have transportation properly systematized and regulated," Hobson stated. The bill passed at the end of President Taft's term.

The Clayton Antitrust Bill and the Federal Trade Commission Bill were the most important legislation passed during Hobson's Congressional years. Both were enacted during Wilson's term, in 1914. The Alabaman favored both, believing that monopolies hindered reform by promoting radicalism. As an opponent of the "money trust," he also voted for the Postal Savings and Federal Reserve Bills.

Hobson was an aggressive foe of the protective tariff. He saw the tariff as engendering one evil after another. The tariff created big bucks for the corporations, which then bought off the government, undermined "the will of the people," and wrecked "legitimate reforms."

With agrarian and rural Alabama in mind, Hobson charged that these tariffs were responsible for "an abnormal growth of city life."

He focused his energies on the proposed protectionist Payne-Aldrich Tariff Bill of 1909. Arguing that his naval constructor background gave him unique expertise, Hobson told the House that the iron market was the "barometer of trade." He cited facts from an unpublished manuscript written by George H. Hull. What he cleverly did not tell his colleagues was that Hull, president of the Pig Iron Storage Warrant Company, was his father-in-law.

Hobson's thesis was that a stable price for iron was essential for a stable American economy. The institution of a sliding tariff would prevent the danger of a fluctuating business cycle. In short, this would guarantee a steady supply of iron at an acceptable cost. The arguments failed to convince the legislators, as did his motion to reduce certain duties and place other items on a duty-free list.

The Payne-Aldrich Tariff Bill was enacted, but Hobson and others continued to press for tariff reform. These activities facilitated passage of the Underwood Tariff in 1913, which reduced import duties. It also incorporated Hobson's proposal for tariff reduction for items brought in on American-owned ships.

Hobson stressed that the tariffs were especially harmful to the American worker. America's lowest wages, he charged, were caused by the tariffs and monopolies, most notoriously the steel trust. Such companies championed immigration so as to create a labor surplus; they would force men out of work by shutting down factories and then raise prices to make up for lost sales.

Government had a responsibility to the American laborer, so he proposed a bill that would set up a commission to study work-related injuries. While the proposal failed in 1912, his amendment was incorporated four years later in a bill that set up a commission on industrial relations. The amendment authorized the commission to look "into the conditions of sanitation and safety of employees, and the provisions for protecting the life, limbs, and health of the employees." In the introduction to the amendment, Hobson attributed the unhappiness among workers "to the conditions—the actual physical conditions—of labor, particularly those bearing upon sanitation and the danger and exposure to life and limb."

Hobson also fully endorsed legislation for the Department of Labor and a bill that limited injunction in labor conflicts. He also threw his support for a Constitutional Amendment imposing a graduated income tax, ratified in 1913. An income tax was preferable to onerous tariffs and would be in the interest of workers, in harmony with "the Democratic doctrine of equal burdens ... the least burdensome of all taxes on wealth."

In the spirit of the Progressives, Hobson also dedicated himself to the democratization of government and its institutions. He served as a member of the Committee on the Election of President, Vice President, and Members of Congress and chaired the special subcommittee on the popular nomination of President and Vice President.

Ahead of his time, Hobson advocated the public announcement of campaign contributions in national elections. He proposed the elimination of national nominating conventions and the Electoral College and called for a Constitutional Amendment for the nomination and election of the President and Vice President directly by the people in its place.

The proposal was never reported out of the House Committee on Elections; however, unfortunately, it had a devastating effect on Hobson's career and was possibly crucial in his defeat by Oscar W. Underwood in the 1914 U.S. Senatorial primary. The Underwood campaign pointed out that the proposal would have diminished Alabama's strength—as well as that of other Southern states—because its popular vote was proportionately much smaller than its electoral college vote. One of Underwood's campaign themes hammered away at the Hobson proposal as "the most dangerous blow at the Southern Democracy that could be devised." Seeking to alarm voters, Underwood saw the proposal as an opening for Negro suffrage. What received little comment was that Alabama, and the rest of the South, had low vote totals because they were virtually one-party states—Democratic—and few Negroes voted.

Southern politicians were also worried about his stand on the direct election of U.S. Senators who were at that time chosen by the state legislatures. Hobson spoke out vigorously on behalf of the proposed amendment. Reform legislation was being stalled, according to Hobson, because of the nature of the Senate's conservative makeup. Hobson assailed the Southern critics who feared, without justification, Federal intervention in, and supervision of, local elections.

"I am not in favor of the Government having such power," Hobson told Congress on May 13, 1912. "I do not even like the thought of the Government holding the power of imposing Federal restrictions of any kind upon the election machinery or upon the local institutions of the States ... . The very surest way to prevent the exercise of such power is to accept the Senate amendment and place the Senate in the hands of the people."

Hobson and other Progressives helped carry the vote, with only 39 nays registered. The Seventeenth Amendment went into effect in 1913.

Education was yet one more of Hobson's progressive concerns. According to Hobson, education was, naturally, a key to America's development. An educated America would advocate reform. As a member of the Education Committee during the Sixty-second Congress, he strongly favored Federal aid to education. Costs, including construction, would be shared equally by Federal, state, and county governments. His bill for a Federal survey of education failed because Southern opponents lobbied strongly against the measure. They feared that Federal aid would mean Federal control and desegregation of the schools.

As a member of the House Committee on Education, Hobson took a special interest in using the resources of the Departments of Agriculture, Commerce, and Labor.

> I am trying to bring about a condition where the Agricultural Department will not only issue the technical bulletins ... but will also conduct correspondence courses in scientific agriculture, so that any poor boy or poor man, without paying a cent ... can carry on a course of instruction and equip himself to become a scientific farmer.
> ... the Department of Commerce would conduct a business course so that any poor boy or man could take a business course of instruction. And I would have the Department of Labor conduct courses in the trades and

mechanic arts, so that any wage earner, any poor man engaged in a trade could learn from the hands of his Government, without cost, how to become skilled and expert.

In seeking to achieve visionary reforms, Hobson was throttled by narrow-minded opponents, especially in the South. He was quite proud of his Southern heritage, but he always saw himself as a Congressman who represented the best interests of America.

This was clearly seen in his dealings with the Southern Society, comprised of expatriate Southerners who now made their homes in the nation's capital. Once elected to the presidency of the society, he sought to push through an amendment in 1913, opening up membership beyond Southerners. When the amendment failed, he resigned the office and blasted the sectionalism of the society.

Civil Rights and Women's Rights . . . 1908-1914

In his article on Hobson's Progressivism, Sheldon comments that most reformers of Hobson's day paid little attention to racial questions. Hobson had a somewhat 'mixed' position in this area. As Sheldon notes in the *Alabama Review*, "Hobson's views on race were typical of the progressive attitude. The superiority of the Anglo-Saxon civilization, he asserted, was demonstrated by the fact of its position of world dominance, its 'free institutions,' and its representative form of government."

Such statements aside, Hobson's position on the race issue was exceedingly liberal for his day and not in tune with other Progressives. He was criticized in Alabama for being "soft" on race relations or for being "irregular" in these matters. No doubt, his record on race relations contributed greatly to his not winning the U.S. Senate election in 1914.

As early as 1904, long before taking his seat in Congress, he called for white teachers in Alabama's black schools. On the other hand, he criticized President Roosevelt for naming a Negro to a position in South Carolina. Although he had a large Negro constituency in his district, he firmly told fellow Congressmen that his district was "ninety-nine per cent American and Anglo-Saxon."

However, his opponents readily seized on his record, which was for the most part highly liberal for the South. Hobson advised fellow Alabaman, J. Thomas Heflin, to abandon his Congressional run because Heflin's views were too negative and too extreme on racial questions.

In no issue—racial or otherwise—did Hobson stand up more forcefully for his moral principles, at the risk of his political career, than on the Brownsville Bill. On August 13, 1906, one man was killed and two others injured when 250 rounds of ammunition were fired into several buildings in Brownsville, Texas. Townspeople blamed the all-colored Companies B, C, and D of the First Battalion, United States 25th Infantry. These soldiers were stationed at Fort Brown, near the site of the incident.

The soldiers and their white commander insisted they had no knowledge of the raid. The townspeople did not believe them, and an investigation condemned the soldiers. President Roosevelt also set up an investigation, which placed responsibility on the soldiers, but not on the white officers. The President recommended that "all enlisted men" be discharged from the army. By the end of November 1906, all soldiers in the battalions were dishonorably discharged.

The issue would not die. The Constitution League, an interracial civil rights group, reported to Congress that the soldiers were innocent. Angered community activists were referring to the episode as "The Black Dreyfus Affair." By 1908 the ugliness of the affair was especially worrisome to an outgoing President Roosevelt—whose life was saved and whose political career rose when black soldiers rescued his Rough Riders at San Juan Hill in 1898—and to his successor, William Howard Taft, Roosevelt's Secretary of War, who discharged the members of the regiments.

Led by Ohio's U.S. Senator Joseph Benson Foraker—whose career would be wrecked before the affair was resolved—a vigorous campaign fought for a tribunal to enable the soldiers to answer the vicious charges. Foraker and the others settled for a court of inquiry made up of high-ranking Army officers that would decide whether any of the men "qualified for reenlistment."

In short, the direction of the court would be, "We feel you are guilty; prove your innocence." Yet, the vote for the court was not unanimous. Voting was almost strictly on party lines—211 for, 111 against, 72 not voting—the bill passed in January, 1909, and was signed by Roosevelt before leaving office.

Richmond Pearson Hobson was the only Southern Democrat to vote for the bill. He was loudly applauded for his emotional oratory on the House floor. The issue of racial supremacy was not the issue here, he told the House. It was a question of justice, which "links man to the Divine." Emotionally, he told his listeners that blacks had been brave in America's defense and had saved his father in the Civil War.

Senator Foraker praises the Alabaman in his biography: "Richmond Pearson Hobson of Alabama, although a Democrat and although party lines were rather tightly drawn in the House, as they had been in the Senate, yet supported the measure not only with his vote, but also with some able and eloquent remarks."

Foraker goes on to quote these remarks in full: "'When these crimes were committed at Brownsville, the President of the United States could have ordered all officers and men to remain within barracks and could have ordered a Court of Inquiry, followed by a court martial, which ... would no doubt have established the guilt or innocence of all the men, and would have given a regular legal opportunity to every innocent man to establish the fact of his innocence ... . But the President did not proceed in this regular, legal way. He scattered the men, guilty and innocent alike, to the four winds and thus prevented the ends of justice ... . These men have never had a chance to appear before a Court of Inquiry; never before a court martial; have never been under oath. This bill provides the least that can be done for the cause of justice.

"'Mr. Speaker, I saw black men, carrying our flag on San Juan Hill; I have seen them before Manila. A black man took my father, wounded, from the field of Chancellorsville. Black men remained on the plantation after the proclamation of emancipation and took care of my mother and grandmother. The white man is supreme in this country; he will remain supreme. That makes it only the more sacred that he should give absolute justice to the black man who is in our midst (loud applause). I submit it to the conscience of my colleagues. This ought not to be made a party measure. We are standing here on the field of eternal justice, where all men are the same. It is justice that links man to the Divine. Whether the heavens fall or the earth melt away, while we live let us be just (loud applause)."'

Mrs. Hobson was present during her husband's speech, and her pride in her husband is evident in the *Memoirs*: "His eyes glowed—his voice vibrated with emotion. From a seat in the gallery, I watched him. Someone whispered near me, 'Catch Hobson's eyes.'" She further writes that with her husband it was more than a moral cause. "He loved the colored folks, whom he knew so well, and they loved him, and were well aware that he was really their friend, with their best interests always at heart. Even the most humble had admiration for him."

She quotes from a letter he received from an old hometown barber, Ed Huckabee: "Dear Old Friend:/I hoped you received the package all right. I am sending it to one of the best men in my judgment that is living. Your father and your mother always sent you children to me to do good work, and your father went nowhere else while he lived. Heap of people says that my race cannot love white people, but I do, as I want to go to heaven, and the Bible says we must love everybody ... . May God be with you always. With love from your old friend."

Unfortunately, few shared Hobson's consuming passion for justice. The bill passed and the inquiry came back in 1910 with a majority report concluding that some soldiers, unidentified, were responsible for the shootings. Since no identification could be made, the full discharge of the battalion was upheld, even though one minority report did find that no soldiers took part in the shootings. The affair, sadly, lapsed into history and forgetfulness—until 1973, when the Brownsville battalion were granted honorary discharges. Only one of the 167 men had survived.

Hobson's defection on the Brownsville vote was another signal to his political enemies to attack him for his "irregularity" on race issues. A day after the Brownsville vote, three candidates announced their candidacy for his seat. Hobson did not wind up losing any Congressional elections, but it was not for lack of enemy effort. When one such enemy, Frank Moody, went after Hobson in the 1912 primary, focusing his attack on the Brownsville vote, Hobson told the House how the Moody campaign had enlisted twenty-five speakers to march through the district vilifying the incumbent: "They were 'flying squadrons,' but before we got through with them we called them the 'fleeing squadrons.'"

The attacks would be more forceful and prove more effective when Hobson later left his House seat to run in the Senate primary against Oscar W. Underwood, the popular Democratic Senate floor leader. Although other issues, especially Prohibition, would contribute to Hobson's defeat for the Senate, Hobson was undoubtedly damaged mostly by his race record and Underwood's strategy would be to keep the race issue at the fore: Voters would be reminded that Hobson was "the only Southerner in Congress to stab his people on the great issue;" Hobson would be accused of "Negro-philandering," a Congressman who "consistently legislated for Negro equality," who undermined the cause of white supremacy even with such seemingly innocuous issues as direct election of the President. Underwood campaign literature would maintain that national Prohibition would bring about "the national enfranchisement of the Negro."

The opposition would also seek to extend the 'damage' of Hobson's race record by citing his support of legislation for Filipinos which included enrolling Filipinos at West Point and the Naval Academy. Underwood campaign material would depict Filipinos as "Moros, Igarettoes, bushmen, stranglers, fast-blacks, and Chinese mixtures ... Negroes, negritos, and negorillas. "The Underwood people gasped at the thought of Filipinos dining at the Academy with white students "in the same rooms! at the same table with our boys!"

Suffrage laws in the South were then 'sacrosanct.' Negroes, of course, were to be excluded, and Southerners wanted no part of a Federal government telling them who to include—and this included women. But Hobson saw women's suffrage as more than a matter of equality. Women were valued allies in his drive for reform in such areas as public health, child welfare, and public morals, especially Prohibition.

"We find ample provisions of law," he addressed Congress, "for dealing with cholera in hogs or foot-and-mouth disease in cattle, but there is nothing to reach infant mortality and little to reach child labor, debauchery, and moral obliquity. To get these questions properly dealt with ... we must invoke the political aid of that part of humanity that gives daily attention to such matters."

No sooner did Hobson take up the cause than he was the subject of ridicule. New York Congressman Michael E. Driscoll coupled his aversion to Hobson's expanded Navy proposal with his unhappiness with woman's suffrage. "Does the gentleman expect," Driscoll asked, "if ladies were elected to Congress that they would vote for battleships?"

Responded the Alabaman with a satiric barb at the New Yorker, "I believe as compared with the gentleman from New York that they would show a commendable intelligence and patriotism on such questions."

Aside from enlisting the political participation of women in such matters in which they had special interest and expertise, Hobson saw women in an "evolutionary" way, that is that the human race is elevated by women. As he told the House on April 24, 1912:

> Self-government is a trait that is evolved in humanity. Humanity does not escape the great law of heredity that governs the rest of creation. If you want to create a great pacer, you look to the development of the mother of the pacer as much as and even more than to the development of the father. If we wish to produce a race of men of the highest capacity for self-government, of the highest wisdom in politics, we must see that these faculties involved in government and politics are developed in the women of the race ... .
>
> We are weak in the development of our men whenever we are weak in the development of our women.

But Hobson's greatest critics, not unexpectedly, were his fellow Alabama Congressmen. In defiance of logic, Congressman Oscar Underwood stated that he unequivocally would give women the right to vote, but only when the majority of white women wanted the vote. This position, he said, is "in accordance with the Democratic principle of local self-government ... when a majority of the white women of Alabama desired the vote he would be willing for them to have it." But how do you vote for suffrage when you can't vote? No one queried Underwood.

Long-time foe Congressman J. Thomas Heflin waited anxiously for March 1, 1913. Woodrow Wilson was to be inaugurated on March 3, so the suffragettes planned a parade for their cause simultaneously in Washington. Richmond Pearson Hobson was named to be one of the parade leaders.

Frenzied activity took place March 1 on Capitol Hill. The debate was on: Could the marchers parade down Pennsylvania Avenue? "No!" argued Congressman Heflin. "Why cause traffic problems? Let the women only have the fringes of Pennsylvania Avenue."

Heflin was enjoying his performance, which was received with applause and laughter. Then he focused on his fellow Alabaman: "It is rumored that he will command a portion of the suffragette paraders. If he does, I want him to march clad in the paraphernalia of a woman. And now I suggest that he don a bonnet and wear a dress on that occasion."

Sharpening his wit, Heflin recited satiric poetry and narratives:

> The lark was up to meet the sun
> The bee was on the wing;
> And soon the sufferin'-yetss begun
> To make the 'welkin ring.'

Most of the gallery howled when he related the words of writer Yad Potter from the make-believe "Squash Center:"

> Don't be alarmed men, this here crazy movement among certain women will soon disappear. There are bound to be a few female cranks along man's pathway.
>
> I remember when I was a boy my daddy put 25 settin's of eggs under 25 different hens, an' when they hatched out the entire hill was covered with little chikhens and most of 'em wus hens, and, by golly, there weren't but one crowin' hen in the whole bunch.
>
> Yet she caused more confusion in the barnyard than ever you saw in your lifetime.
>
> Whenever she crowed the roosters charged at her and when they got there and found she wus not a rooster they wus pestered powerful.

Unruffled by the derision—certainly not his first such experience—Hobson replied firmly to Heflin. He began by praising Heflin's mother: "The admirable traits of my friend from Alabama are largely inherited from his mother." Hobson proceeded to call women's suffrage "one of the great, evolutionary questions of our age. It can not be laughed out of court ... . If the capacity for political government is as low in women as my friend [Heflin] intimates, then he ought to develop that capacity by giving women political activities ... .

"It is only when men and women join together in their activities that the highest sympathy and happiest lives can be attained in the House."

The parade proceeded. Some 5,000 marchers drew an audience of 500,000 in what the *New York Times* called "the greatest parade of women in history ... . Scattered throughout the parade were the standards of nearly every state in the union ... . It was an astonishing demonstration."

So much for the positive. The parade began peacefully but quickly turned ugly. The unfriendly spectators heckled, taunted, harassed, pushed, and "mobbed" the marchers. Some drunks tried to climb aboard the floats. A group of hoodlums gathered around a reviewing stand near Mrs. Taft and Miss Helen Taft. The Rev. Anna Howard Shaw, National Suffrage President, who had previously marched in New York, California, and London, "had never seen such a disgraceful exhibition."

Where were the police? Well, they stood by and laughed heartily. One woman was struck in the face as one policeman watched. "Some of the women were punched black and blue [as policeman turned away]," reported the *Times*. Mrs. Genevieve Stone, wife of an Illinois Congressman, complained to a policeman, who snapped: "If my wife were where you are I'd break her head." Harriet Stanton Blatch telegramed the President for the Women's Political Union to protest that peaceful women were left "at the mercy of a howling mob on the very streets which are being at this moment so efficiently officered for the protection of men."

A member of The Suffrage Association's Congressional Committee sounded off in the Washington office: "Here, politically, we have long been treated as criminals and imbeciles, but what shall we say of the treatment we received ... . They would have taken better care of a drove of pigs being driven through the streets by some farmer than they did of us."

Anticipating the potential for a riot, Hobson had asked the War Department for cavalry protection. The request was refused. Angered, Hobson went on the Congressional floor to blast the attitude of law enforcement. "One woman called me," reported Hobson, "that her young daughter had been riding on one of the floats when a ruffian climbed on the float and insulted her daughter."

"Her daughter ought to have been at home," interrupted Illinois Congressman James R. Mann.

California Congressman John R. Raker was piqued. "She had as much right there as anyone. The gentleman ought to be ashamed of himself to make such a remark."

For Hobson, the issue was clear. Women had as much right to protection as anybody else had. And he closed the exchange by challenging Mann: "The gentleman from Illinois does not mean that he would not give protection to this woman." Hobson charged the Federal and municipal authorities "were grossly and willfully negligent" in performing their duties as directed by the Congressional resolution on the parade. Hobson wanted three more minutes on the issues, but the Speaker refused the request. It was time to go back to the important issue on the floor: a pension for a Boston fire official.

Women's suffrage was not resolved until 1920, when the Nineteenth Amendment was written into the Constitution of the United States. Hobson continued as a most outspoken advocate. On January 12, 1915, when a resolution was introduced to enfranchise women, he gave an impassioned 13-minute speech in the House. First, he sought to reassure the South that the resolutions refers only to sex. "It does not inject any new problems into the franchise problems of the states." Secondly, women were men's equal, perhaps even superior. "If anyone should be disqualified from voting, it should be men. The character of women on the average, was at least the equal of men, and probably was even higher ... ."

He concluded with a familiar Hobson theme: Placing women in the political process would be the proper direction along the natural course of human evolution:

Several times today I have been ashamed of my sex. Can anyone conceive of a woman saying such things as have been said here today apparently with gusto and selfish gratulation, things that show an utter materialistic view of life where the relation of sexes was regarded as one of lust, not of the spiritual relationship, of true inspiring love ... . Man has an immortal soul. It is this spiritual part of man that gives dignity to human life above the life of the brute. In the differentiation of occupation, the women in the homes, in the schools, in the churches, in the charities and tender ministries of hospitals and philanthropy, the women of the race have conserved and developed the spiritual nature of man ... . The great need of our day is to project women's sphere, women's activities, and women's influence into government, so that questions affecting the home, the protection of the children, and good morals of society would share with business, the attention of public servants, the efforts and aims of public policy.

The only really effective way to accomplish this result is to give the ballot to women ... . All government exists to promote the evolution and uplift of the Nation and the race. If women had the ballot, it would broaden her views and make her better equipped to be the companion of her husband. It would make her better equipped in heredity to be the mother of men. At the same time it would project woman's life more and more into the life of her husband and not only make a better foundation for a true home but develop more the spiritual side of her husband. Our institutions need woman's suffrage. The home needs woman's suffrage. Woman needs woman's suffrage. Man needs woman's suffrage. Woman suffrage is now a crying need for the evolution of the race.

Hobson was most anxious to involve women in the process because they were his strongest allies on Prohibition. However, the time for woman's suffrage would not come for another five years, and the resolution was defeated—204 to 174—in 1915.

The Alabaman had not given up his demand for for naval supremacy and for protection against the 'Yellow Peril.' In February, 1911, he predicted that within twenty months America would be at war with Japan. "Whether we agree as to the date, that time is going to come. This nation is not going to prepare, and the day is going to come, when it will be struck by a nation that is prepared."

He was right, but not time-wise. That was enough for the acerbic *Independent*, which labeled the Congressman "a national nuisance" and offered—with abstract allusions—appropriate criticisms of Hobson, in its January 1913 issue: "Even so Wali Dad 'carried the curse of the unstanched speech' to the Red Chief Gholum Hyder, and cried, 'The Russ is upon us!' And the Red Chief put him up a peach tree with a score of bayonet points under it to watch until the Russians came, or to fall on the bayonet points. It would not be courteous for Congressmen to point Hobson to a Washington peach tree."

With the threat of war diminishing, Hobson made little headway for an expanded Navy while a four-term Congressman. The first substantial increases in expenditures for Naval preparedness came during the Wilson Administration in 1916, after Hobson was out of Washington.

When enlarging the Navy did not find acceptance, Hobson turned to another plan: maximizing the efficiency of the Navy. Hobson's contributions to the development of the U.S. Navy are detailed in Rear-Admiral Bradley A. Fiske's *From Midshipman to Rear-Admiral*. Fiske had served as Aid for Operations of the Fleet and had invented the naval telescope sight, the stadimeter, and the horizmeter among others. As World War I opened, concerned about American preparedness, he proposed to the Secretary of the Navy that it use a new invention simply because Hobson, whom he considered "a very brilliant man," was convinced it would work. The newly invented diving shell he proposed was designed so that if it missed a direct hit on its target and hit the water, it would dive and either strike the underbody of, or explode very near, its target.

What was even more important to Fiske, according to his book, was Hobson's input in reorganizing naval operations. Fiske called for a general staff to "direct the Navy as a whole," covering both the military and engineering phases. In his diary, Fiske noted that on December 27, 1914, he called on Hobson and they agreed not to discard the present system but rather to add a Chief of Naval Operations with fifteen assistants. In his book, Fiske writes: "The entries of December 27 and January 3 give the outlines of a good deal of work that Hobson and I did on those days and in the intervening week. The plan ... was drawn up in the light of my knowledge of strategical requirements and Hobson's knowledge of Congressional requirements." The bill passed one subcommittee on January 4; the full House Naval Committee agreed on January 6 to incorporate in a naval appropriations bill provisions for a 'Chief of Naval Operations.' The provision for fifteen assistants was stricken from the final bill even though it had passed the Senate Naval Committe. Nevertheless, a very pleased Fiske added to his diary that the measure achieved "a greater advance than any other naval legislation has accomplished in many years."

"Most officers said that it was as great a boon to the Navy as the act of Congress, in 1890, which authorized the 'new Navy' in the shape of the steel ships *Chicago, Atlanta, Boston,* and the *Dolphin,*" Fiske continued. The newly created system, he said, "is the organization by which the Navy Department handled the Navy throughout the war. The excellence of the system is now admitted by everybody, including the Secretary." In cooperation with Fiske, Hobson helped obtain authorization for a Bureau of Naval Operations. After some legislative setbacks, the office of Chief of Naval Operations was created in 1915.

It did not come into being until he left Congress, but Hobson worked hard for the establishment of a Council of National Defense. It would be composed of the President; Secretaries of State, War, and Navy; the Chiefs of Staff of the Army and Navy; chairmen of appropriate House and Senate committees; and presidents of the Army and Naval Colleges. Frustrated by Wilson's inaction, Hobson, before leaving Congress, assailed the President and the Secretary of State as America's "greatest obstacles" to attaining the proper national defense.

In her *Memoirs*, Mrs. Hobson called the creation of the Office of Chief of Naval Operations her husband's "most important piece of legislation." Citing from Fiske's book *From Midshipman to Rear Admiral* and from a letter to Richmond Pearson, Mrs. Hobson notes that Admiral Fiske considered that office as being responsible for preventing chaos in World War I:

> Admiral Mayo, when in command of the United States Fleet, stated under oath before the Senate Committee investigating the Navy Department, following the armistice, that but for the Office of Chief of Naval Operations, the conditions in our Navy when we entered the war would have been 'chaotic.' That was a correct and unexaggerated statement and means that our Navy Department would have been unable even to start to get our troops across to Europe until after a long delay ... .
>
> This means that if our Navy Department had not already the machinery of the Office of Naval Operations, the legislation for which you alone initiated, our troops could not possibly have reached Europe in time and we would infallibly have lost the war. I yield to no one in admiration for your splendid feat with the *Merrimac* and realize that from the standpoint of enduring fame that has been the outstanding act of all your life. But from the standpoint of service to the Navy and the Nation, your action in initiating the establishment of the office of Chief of Naval Operations was immeasurably more important and beneficent.

Years later, on the 36th anniversary of the sinking of the *Merrimac* and 15 years after World War I, Georgia Congressman Carl Vinson added his praise for Hobson's "tireless work" in the House Committee on Naval Affairs which led to the creation of the Office of the Chief of Naval Operations and which was accomplished, in Vinson's words, "in the face of the disapproval" of the Secretary of the Navy.

Vinson detailed the importance of the Office: "High authorities have testifed that this office alone produced the efficiency that enabled us to get our armies overseas in time to save the World

War for the Allies. It is realized now in all responsible quarters that in this Office of Naval Operations is bound up the efficiency of our Navy in the wars that the future has in turn for America."

Having been defeated in a Senate bid in 1914, Hobson served out his final Congressional term with decreased power. As the war heated up in Europe, however, he took to 'advising' the Government by way of letters and articles in the media. Always the keen military mind, he properly analyzed Germany's surprising action of bombing select Britain's coastal towns in December 1914. While some sought to explain the action as a German technique of terrorizing civilians, Hobson reasoned: "Unless the attack by German naval forces on the British coast develops further, it would appear to be in the nature of a decoy. Evidently, in addition to the moral effects to be gained by the impression created in the mind of the British public by the attack, it has the purpose of drawing away the British battle fleet from its present position in order to lay it open to attacks by submarines."

Hobson's goals were to end the war or, that failing, keep America out. He called for the convening of a peace conference in San Francisco. His resolutions died in committee. Once out of Congress, he wrote a long article, in the May 5, 1915, *New York Evening Journal,* accusing the government of being militarily unprepared. America was becoming dependent on Great Britain and her allies because of the former's naval supremacy. For that reason, commented Hobson, America was aiding Britain, not Germany. In fact, American foreign policy, argued the former Congressman, was being directed by London.

Commentary on Hobson's analysis came to a halt on May 7 when the *Lusitania* was sunk with 128 American victims aboard. President Wilson sent a sharply worded note to Germany and America awaited war.

Hobson had his own response. He spent May sending a series of letters and telegrams to the President, basically advising Wilson to balance his warnings to Germany with 'suggestions' that he tell Britain to rescind its order for merchant ships to strike German submarines. Moreover, said Hobson, Britain must be asked to halt the "illegal and inhumane" blockade which was responsible for the "starvation of civilian populations of enemy countries."

In his final telegram of May, on May 31, 1915, Hobson warned the President that if America entered the war, "[it] would throw away [its] manifest destiny as a non-military nation, the common friend of all nations, the peacemaker of the world."

The President noted the telegrams and acted as he saw fit. Hobson coupled these telegrams to Wilson by sending copies to the German Ambassador and advising him that American public opinion had been victimized by propaganda from London.

How strange were the actions of Hobson! Yes, Hobson received many letters of praise, but most were signed by writers with German names. Was Hobson simply pro-German? According to Sheldon, "It seems that Hobson's actions at the time were motivated by a desire to keep the United States out of the war rather than by a pro-German bias. He was not unaware of the threat Germany posed to America." Indeed, after America entered the war, Hobson came out unequivocally for the defeat of Germany, but asked that the German people be spared.

It did not happen in peacetime, but sizable increases in naval spending were realized during war. The figure was $1 billion in 1917; $2 billion in 1918. Unquestionably, Hobson was not satisfied. The rationale for a large Navy was to preclude war. By being forced into war, Hobson rightly feared, American would become a militaristic power. And while he favored international organizations, he insisted that such bodies do not guarantee peace. In short, only the threat of force would prevent force and ensure peace.

Obviously, Richmond Pearson Hobson had widespread opposition to his calls for force, i.e., American Naval supremacy. His first were before the 1908 Convention, and he had many other adversaries after that gathering. But nowhere did Hobson's views receive a more unsympathetic hearing than in his own Alabama turf.

Writing after his death, the *Tuscaloosa News* called Hobson a prophet and, "like all other prophets, he ended up with less honor at home than almost anywhere else." Specifically, said the *News*, the call for Naval supremacy to meet the challenge of Japan—"the Yellow Peril"—"that was the straw that broke the camel's back." People mocked him when no war came and one citizen told another, "'Aren't you glad that you laughed at Hobson when he warned you of the wrath to come?'"

Also reflecting after Hobson's death, the *Birmingham News* moaned his espousal of certain "causes," especially Naval supremacy: "Hobson's unfortunate ventures into politics a few years after his heroics," said the paper, "dimmed somewhat the glory of his heroism, as did his overzealous espousal of certain causes ... [his] staggering accounts of Oriental evil lurking in wait for them at every school corner [an allusion to the San Francisco school riot of 1907]."

But Hobson did have his believers and disciples. A lieutenant commander in the Naval Reserves, Arthur S. Postle, called Hobson "the American Nostradamus" in a 1949 feature article for the Louisville *Courier-Journal*. In the prophecy about Japanese danger, wrote Postle,

> [Hobson predicted] the attack would come at the moment America would least be able to meet it, and we would not know of the assault until it was too late. The seizure of the Philippines and the Hawaiian Islands would be the first move. All this he wrote more than 40 years ago!
>
> Hobson did not live to see the fulfillment of these predictions, for he died in 1937. Yet, he had calculated with uncanny exactness the strategy of the war 33 years before the first gun was fired. He said: 'The Japanese plan ... to lure our fleet to the relief of Manila. The siege would be planned to stir the American people ... . Should we make the blunder of attempting the relief ... the annihilation of our fleet would be practically assured.'
>
> In the early part of 1942 we came close to making this very error ... . In the end he prophesied, 'America that opened Japan will shut her up again.'

The espousal of wide-ranging visionary causes never brought enduring fame to Richmond Pearson Hobson. It was not only that the issues were most controversial. It was more. It was his flamboyant personality, his unconventional tactics, his not working within the 'system'—he simply did not 'play the game'—the way politicians ought to.

All this became more evident in his crusade for Prohibition.

13

LIQUOR:
THE "GREAT AND POWERFUL ENEMY"

> I know there is danger in confronting this great and powerful enemy, but in time of war the good soldier does not stop because of danger. It may be I am politically dead. My political life [may be] destroyed by the liquor interests, but I would rather hold my head up and fight like a man, though I had to die a hundred political deaths. I would rather do a man's part in the struggle to cut the millstone of a degeneracy from the neck of humanity. I would rather do that than be United States Senator from Alabama, and if I know my own mind, I would rather do that than be President of the United States.

The above remarks of Richmond Pearson Hobson concluded the Congressional debate on the resolution for the Constitutional Amendment on Prohibition. During his four Congressional terms, Hobson embraced a variety of progressive causes, e.g., women's suffrage, direct election of U.S. Senators, and Federal aid to education. However, no one issue so totally consumed him as did his crusade against Prohibition. It brought him great benefits, economically and in national attention, but it crushed him politically and nearly ruined his idyllic family life.

It was a Christian crusade for Hobson, rooted in his upbringing. His family were abstainers, and early in life he was told to avoid alcohol. According to his sister, Margaret, Richmond never tasted alcohol.

The physical and moral destruction wreaked by alcohol was described by Hobson in *Buck Jones at Annapolis*. The young Hobson recalled one of his fellow midshipmen, Casey, who was ruined morally by liquor and who came close to death. The midshipman ('Buck Jones') spoke bitterly about alcohol: "'It's all due to the liquor Malone smuggled on board. I'd like to see every drop of liquor in the world poured into the sea.'"

It was only when Casey nearly lost his life that he awakened: "Casey probably would not come up with so much liquor in his stomach ... .

"'Mr. 'Jones,' do you believe in God? I had given up the belief long ago.'"

"'There is a God,' said 'Jones,' 'and God is good, and we must try to do our part.'"

When he first entered Congress, his home state was still embattled in the conflict between drys and wets which had begun in 1702. This conflict is detailed in the monograph by James Benson Sellers, *The Prohibition Movement In Alabama, 1702-1943*. As a pragmatic freshman legislator, Hobson decided to research the issue in the Library of Congress. He came to the task with certain preconceived ideas, especially that alcohol was harmful to America's economy due to all the work hours lost to the effects of drink. Always thinking of Naval supremacy, he argued that peace would come with America's developing the strongest Navy in the world. And the funding would be easy: just siphon off five percent of America's annual liquor expenditures.

He became actively involved in the successful 1909 Alabama campaign of a Prohibition Amendment to the state Constitution. The campaign pitted politicians and liquor dealers against the ministry. One Congressman charged, "I love preachers, but a number of them have descended from the pulpit to the dirty mire of politics."

Responded the editor of the *Alabama Christian Advocate*: "We do not accept orders from those men, and put them now on notice that the preachers propose to stand always for the best interests of the people. If that calls them to take the stump in any moral issue, they will go out in that service to the people, conscious that they still represent their Lord and the church in service to their state and in the fight against liquor."

Reflecting on the campaign in later years, the president of the Anti-Saloon League, commented that one of the most beneficial byproducts of the 1909 campaign "was the development of men to fight our battles."

Hobson came out of the campaign convinced more than ever that prohibition of liquor traffic was the "only way to preserve the nation from destruction." Added Professor Sellers, "[Hobson] spoke with the zeal of a new convert."

With added fervor, Hobson returned to his research. The emerging thesis was that alcohol caused degeneracy in all organisms. Three conclusions were drawn, all of which formed the major portion of Hobson's *Alcohol and the Human Race* (1919): "First, alcohol is a protoplasm; second, alcohol is a narcotic; third alcohol is a specific cause of degeneracy."

Hobson's stand on alcohol was very much tied in to human evolution. He was not a Darwinian; rather, he believed that individuals and nations survived because of moral and spiritual development. As he wrote in his book: "Nature ... is trying to produce a race of God-fearing men, living in the spirit of brotherly love, controlled and directed by moral and spiritual forces [that] reign supreme in the hearts of men. Interpreted through Scriptures and through nature, God's purpose is the development of the 'perfect man' of Christlike attributes in the true image of his Maker."

According to Hobson, alcohol impeded the proper course of evolution by weakening sensitive parts of the brain.

On a national level, Hobson determined that America was experiencing a loss of 25 percent in the production of goods—all attributable to alcohol. Standing in the way of progress, said Hobson, were the liquor interests, who wielded enormous power in both the Democratic and Republican Parties. To win the battle, Hobson called for an intensive program of education and prohibition legislation.

Before publication of his book, he carried his message to America, in condensed form, in a speech called "The Great Destroyer." The speech was delivered in Congress in 1911. More than two million copies of the speech had been distributed by 1914, according to Hobson. In addition to distributing the speech,

Hobson went out on an extensive lecture circuit and sent out 1.5 million letters on the dangers of alcohol.

In "The Great Destroyer," he cited the dangers of alcohol, as stated by the U.S. Supreme Court in *Mugler vs. Kansas*: "The train of evils which marks the progress of intemperance is too obvious to require comment. It brings with it degradation of character, impairs the moral and physical energies, wastes the health, increases the number of paupers and criminals, undermines the morals, and sinks its victims to the lowest depths of vice and profligacy."

While Hobson had been derided by opponents at the 1908 Convention for his lack of speaking skills, those who heard the Alabaman on the Chautauqua circuit felt differently. According to reports from towns where he spoke, neither William Jennings Bryan nor Robert G. Ingersoll compared with the *Merrimac* hero. Hobson was "the greatest lecturer with the greatest lecture."

On the legislative front, Hobson was the first to introduce, on December 4, 1911, a Constitutional Amendment "prohibiting the sale, manufacture for sale, and importation for sale of beverages containing alcohol." The resolution died in committee. He persisted through 1914, but to no avail; only one resolution was brought to a vote, but it did not receive the requisite two-thirds.

However, Prohibition was gaining advocates. In fact, the Webb-Kenyon Act of 1913 prohibited the importation of liquor into states that already had state laws banning such import.

Hobson experienced success on the Congressional floor with his Prohibition battle, but he lost the war when the issue helped defeat him and take him out of Congress in the U.S. Senatorial contest of 1914. A seat opened up when Joseph F. Johnston died in 1913. Hobson announced his candidacy six months before the April 7, 1914, primary. Interestingly, it would be the first primary under the Seventeenth Amendment, whose passage he had championed. Congressman Henry Clayton had also announced his candidacy, but under the urgings of President Wilson, who said he needed Clayton to guide Trust legislation, he withdrew.

When Clayton dropped out and the third candidate, House Majority Leader and chair of the Ways and Means Committee, Oscar Underwood, became Hobson's only opposition, it became a battle of the 'wets' and 'drys.' Underwood was for state or local option while Hobson was the leader of the fight for a Constitutional Amendment.

The liquor forces vowed to defeat Hobson and determined to use all means. Connecticut Congressman Jeremiah Donovan assailed the attendance record of Hobson, who obviously was away from the House to speak for Prohibition and on his Senatorial campaign.

Hobson made a lengthy defense of his Congressional record. In response to Donovan, Hobson said his absences were spent in his district conducting "expeditions" dealing with plant life, animal life, and human life. "The last expedition," Hobson told Donovan and friends, invited "the greatest experts in the world, and this expedition demonstrated how, by the simple precaution of providing for the disposal of human waste—human excreta—we could save 1,100 to 1,500 deaths from typhoid alone in the rural districts of Alabama every year, and we could save thousands and thousands of babies who die in infancy. By simple precautions against the mosquito, we can practically eliminate malaria, chills, and fever.

"This will be of great value to my people. I mention this incidentally, because I want the gentleman from Connecticut ... to realize that even though I am not here answering roll calls on unimportant matters, I am not necessarily neglecting my duties or defrauding the Government."

Hobson counterattacked, calling Underwood's campaign manager, Senator John Hollis Bankhead, the "tool" or "dummy" of Wall Street. While Underwood was a man of integrity, he was being exploited by liquor interests, especially Thomas Fortune Ryan. Underwood responded, and the popular Congressman received much more applause than did rival Hobson. Never a consummate politician, Hobson did not act wisely in opening up a campaign by slandering the well-liked Speaker.

Not a favorite of the *New York Times*, Hobson was rebuffed for attacking Underwood "without proof." Also Ryan, as the *Washington Evening Star* noted, had been for years a heavy contributor to the Democratic Party.

On the other hand, Hobson was not lacking strong support. He was heartily endorsed by the Anti-Saloon League and the

Women's Christian Temperance Union, whose support included campaign contributions. Their D-date was December 11, 1913, when Hobson would address the House on the Prohibition Amendment. With voices raised to the tunes of "Onward Christian Soldiers" and "America," the groups—2,000 strong—marched to the Capitol. They packed the House galleries for Hobson's address.

Hobson articulated his well-known arguments for Prohibition, including "a just government exists for the purpose of promoting the highest welfare of its people." The Amendment, later called the Hobson Amendment, was only directed at the liquor trade. "There is no desire," insisted Hobson, "to invade either the individual right or inherent liberties of a citizen."

Hobson presented his arguments forcefully, but he resumed the personal attacks on Underwood, which were first made on the floor three months prior. He alleged that his opposition had warned that Prohibition as a campaign issue would destroy the Democratic Party.

Said Hobson: "My friends, I do not take second place to any man in love of his party; certainly not to any man who thinks that his party's life lies in the hands of the liquor interests. But let me tell you—for we might as well draw the line—if the Democratic Party can only live by joining the liquor's interests, to debauch the American people, then in God's name, let it die."

Reported the *New York Times*, "Mr. Hobson fairly shouted these words as he reached the climax. With arms waving in the air, and shaking his head almost literally, in the face of members who sat near him ... he drew from the packed galleries prolonged cheering and even the stamping of feet to increase the pandemonium."

Underwood protested that Congress should not be a place for political campaigning. As for the charges, he would answer them at an appropriate time and place. Hobson called his opponent a morally decent man. "That only makes him the more dangerous and makes it more pitiful that we should find such interests as the deadly liquor interests trying to capture the State of Alabama behind such a high-class reactionary leader as my opponent."

Hobson was enthusiastically cheered by his packed house of supporters; however, all came to nought when the amendment was not voted on.

Back on the Campaign Trail . . . 1914

Underwood kept his word; he answered Hobson in the most bitter Alabama campaign in history—to that point—or ever. Forney Johnston, son of the Senator whose passing had opened the Senate seat being fought over, authored a campaign booklet that spoke of "The Issue and the Facts," the way the Underwood people saw it. Their side was simple: They favored local controls over alcohol so as to prevent other Federal intrusions, namely in civil rights.

The booklet was mainly a Hobson diatribe: Hobson was a hypocrite who had not abstained before 1907; Hobson was exploiting the issue to amass large speaking fees; Hobson spent much more time in Washington than he did in Alabama. It targeted Hobson's liberal views: women's suffrage; direct election of the President; and the entry of Filipinos and Puerto Ricans into the service academies. The book stressed—with underlining and in large print—white supremacy.

Underwood's campaign charged that members of the Hobson family had been Republicans or Populists who challenged white supremacy. And Hobson had defined himself, said the booklet on the Brownsville Bill, as discussed earlier.

While conceding Hobson's superior intelligence, the booklet reminded voters "that mere brilliancy and intellectual efficiency are entirely consistent with a fixed and definite mental instability."

Clearly on the defensive, the Hobson campaign did not respond effectively. Their own booklet was a tame recital of Hobson's Congressional record in such areas as Naval expansion, aid to farmers, and, of course, Prohibition. While Hobson had financial support from temperance groups, he could not match the outlays provided by the "establishment" monied people. "The Hobson booklet," said Sheldon, "lacked the verbal artistry needed to make it a persuasive campaign document. In short, it lacked those qualities that Hobson would have brought to it had he written it himself."

Despite all the negativity, Richmond and Grizelda Hobson thoroughly enjoyed the campaign. She offers a delightful review of the campaign in her *Memoirs*: "For weeks we swept from one end of the state to the other—through mountains and valleys—floods and sometimes, almost famine for me, as I simply could not eat some days, any food that was set before me. My husband, though, with his never-failing appetite, always seemed to relish the primitive fare."

There was no shortage of inconveniences. "All day Thursday," Grizelda relates, "we travelled from the extreme north Mobile, which we left Wednesday, at 1 a.m., to Athens, where we arrived at dusk Thursday. Richmond left me over [sic] to speak in Nashville. The parties who were to take care of me failed to receive notice of my coming, so I had a forlorn time in a bleak hotel room opposite the railroad tracks ... .

"Early yesterday we started off with a team and surrey and made three places, all in Limestone County, the extreme north of the state. The first place was O'Neal. It consisted of a small brook flowing right across the road and a way-side candy and hat shop! It was bitterly cold. The audience consisted of four men and about ten women, three babies and some stray dogs. We sat and stood around a little stove, and this was our smallest meeting!"

No doubt, Grizelda had to be a hardy soul on the campaign trail:

> Some talks were made from fallen tree trunks, in pouring rain, with pigs rooting about the ground, and old men and women holding umbrellas and smoking corn cobs, and hushing grandchildren's fretful cries ... . I prayed some times not to falter, myself, from loss of sleep, or all the discomforts, for it was a great experience, and few women had been fortunate enough to have it.
>
> Sometimes we put up for the night at little cabin homes, where the halls were decorated with empty tomato cans, where we were offered the 'parlor' as our sleeping quarters, with the tiny mirror of the family organ as all we had to see ourselves in, and perhaps this was fortunate, as we were sorry-looking much of the time. Weeks went by without seeing a bathroom, and we treasured our large round collapsible rubber tub, which we filled with both hot and then cold water, each taking our turn to get a really soothing bath.

Grizelda endured and perhaps enjoyed the campaign, but she was on the trail because of her Southern roots. "My background, connected as it was with the South, became a very important factor in the Campaign," she related. "In most of his county speeches, in rural districts, my husband at the end would say, to the audience, 'And now, my friends, the Underwood forces are saying that my wife is a Yankee, and I want you to meet her right now, and I want you to know that she is also a great-niece of our former beloved Governor George Houston, and she is a cousin of our beloved soldier General Joseph Wheeler. Many of you know them both. Now come up on this platform and shake Mrs. Hobson's hand. She wants to meet you all.'

"Then these rugged, long-bearded old men advanced like an avalanche toward me, saying as they shook vigorously my hand, 'Why, bless my soul, you don't look like a Yankee, and you are just one of us. Why I fought alongside your cousin Joe against them Yankees, that I did.'"

Perhaps Richmond Pearson Hobson was not an adroit politician, but he was a first-rate campaigner. At least, Grizelda saw it that way:

> He has not only learned some of the tricks of politics, but he is tireless. He is a mental and physical athlete. He never seems to get tired. His throat seems to strengthen with exercise.
>
> On the day he made his entrance and speech at Pratt City last Thursday, Captain Hobson made six speeches between 9:30 o'clock in the morning and 9:45 that night. He made six speeches in practically twelve hours and travelled more than 50 miles over the roughest section of Jefferson County ... . He literally spent four hours in his automobile and eight in speaking, with the exception of about an hour taken for dinner with Superintendent I. R. Perkins, of Sayre Mines. The last speech, delivered at Ensley, was the longest and most vigorous of all. At its close he appeared as fresh and fit for the fight as the moment he emerged from his bath at the Hotel Hillman that morning ... . [He} had to be driven to bed about 1 o'clock ... . The newspaper man who had tried simply to follow him for one day was almost dead on his feet and had long gone to bed.

This was the third day of the most strenuous campaign perhaps that was ever conducted in Jefferson County ... .

The people seemed to be impressed with the energy and tireless purpose of the man. His personality is winning. This is admitted even by his bitterest opponents. He compels attention. He is one of the best speakers in America. He is a master in joint debate. He is quick and keen at repartees. Someone interrupted him at Ensley to shout, 'Oscar Underwood is our man. Oscar is from Possum Hollow and we are for him.' Hobson retorted, 'Yes, and I am from Lickskillet. If you don't watch out, we will have the possum in the skillet.'

Hobson's skills and energies notwithstanding, the campaign could still not best Underwood. He not only enlisted big financial supporters, but also gained wide editorial support. The *New York Times* supported Underwood and derided Hobson, who was "generally on the wrong side of every question that is serious." Not taking anything for granted, Underwood made a furious circuit of the state in the last days of the campaign.

Hobson hoped to counter this effort with a novel approach—read bizarre by Underwood—of campaigning by airplane. "No, it is not safe," objected Grizelda, and the plan was dropped.

L. B. Musgrove, Hobson's campaign manager, predicted victory because his man was well-liked "in every section of America where virtue and integrity predominate." The optimism was clearly unfounded. Hobson lost 89,470 to 54,738.

The reasons for Hobson's defeat were clear. Underwood was a powerful and highly popular personality. In addition, Underwood had cleverly torn apart Hobson's record. Apart from charges of carpetbagging and Congressional absenteeism, the issues of Prohibition and race relations were turned against Hobson. The loser charged that Underwood and the liquor interests sent salaried workers to the state to work for his defeat. Underwood, said Hobson, had secured "an army of workers" from Wall Street to defeat him.

While Underwood garnered big donations, the support Hobson received from temperance groups enabled Hobson to outspend

Underwood $16,785.32 to $12,920.01. For this reason, one must assign the major role for Hobson's defeat to his liberal stance, particularly on race relations.

The *Nation*, indeed, attributed the defeat to the race issue. The editor, Oswald Garrison Villard, called the *Merrimac* hero "[one] of the old Crusader types ... a dramatic guerilla fighter for causes rather than the routine worker for results." While the *Nation* was usually not a friend of Hobson, the editor prophesied that Hobson's career as a reformer still had long life.

Lame Duck on Capitol Hill . . . 1914

The *Nation*'s prophesy was an understatement. The Prohibition issue still had miles to go and Hobson's involvement did not slow down. "Undefeated by defeat" was the description of Hobson by one Alabama weekly.

Hobson issued no congratulatory message to Underwood, but instead issued a ringing call to battle with the liquor interests: "Please say to the liquor interests of America that we have only begun to fight; that the work we have done can never be undone; that we will meet them again on the battlefield of Alabama and on a hundred other battlefields; that we expect under God's providence to be in the battle when the thirty-sixth state ratifies the Hobson Resolution placing national Prohibition in the Constitution of the United States. It will be a fight to the bitter end, and I look for success. The fight has just begun."

The Captain would always carry on, observed Mrs. Hobson in her *Memoirs*, because perseverance was rooted in family. As the Captain said of his family, "We are not men who can be scared. We are of a breed that can be neither scared or bluffed, the grandsons of men who left the bloody footprints of their bare feet on the snow at Valley Forge, and the sons of men, who with muskets still clutched, eager to still fight on till death itself, swallowed their hearts when orders came from Lee at Appomattox." While Hobson had lost, Alabamans did elect a number of Prohibitionists to office.

Though defeated in his run for the Senate, Hobson would remain in office as Congressman until March, 1915, and he solidified his ties with the Anti-Saloon League. Hobson felt very comfortable with the group, which was an organization of Protestant churches. The League, like Hobson, wanted to eradicate alcohol and its byproducts: government corruption, vice, crime, disruption of normal family life.

Hobson gathered his energies for one final attempt to move a Prohibition Amendment through the House. As a lame duck Congressman, he was dismissed by many of his colleagues, notably Speaker Champ Clark who, while in Detroit for an address, was asked for his opinion about Hobson's prediction that Prohibition would be the law of the land in ten years. Clark replied: "[Hobson] is a knight errant. Had he lived in the days of chivalry, he would have been one of those who went in search of the Holy Grail. In our day, confronting our problems, he is a political lunatic. Have you got that? Hobson is a lunatic."

The *Times* agreed and called Clark's words "balanced accusations." According to Walter Pittman, Hobson could have responded to Clark by blasting the Speaker's drinking habits, but he restrained himself because he felt Clark could still be useful for the cause.

Despite the many jibes and opposition from the Wilson Administration, Hobson worked to clear the Prohibition resolution out of the Rules Committee and schedule a debate and vote before the end of December. "The fight that all politicians wished to avoid," lamented the *New York Times*, "will be forced on the House and undoubtedly will be used as an issue in the Presidential election."

The much-anticipated day was December 22. The Prohibitionist forces were energized. They had flooded Congress with one million postcards with their messages and pictures of children. The International Sunday School Association dispatched five hundred demonstrators to Washington, while it enlisted three million people to keep praying and "let Congress know" of their wishes. Sermons and Sunday school lessons were devoted nationwide to Prohibition. Youth delegations from every Congressional district knocked on their Congressmen's doors.

The Hobson family came for the big day from Washington and New York to lend their full support. Wrote Grizelda Hobson in her *Memoirs*, "Directly back of Captain Hobson, I sat, with my parents, who had come from Tuxedo, and our two eldest children, Richmond, Jr., age seven, and Lucia, aged five. These two little ones were much concerned when their father failed to go out for lunch. 'But, Mother, Dad will be hungry. Poor Dad.'"

The debate lasted for thirteen hours, and Richmond Pearson Hobson refused to leave his seat for one moment. "Hobson stuck to his guns throughout the entire day," said his wife. "He waved away those who urged him to leave the House for luncheon. No, he would sit on the firing lines, and so he munched a sandwich and drank in [Illinois Congressman] Jim Mann's words at the same time. When dinner-time rolled around, a cup of hot coffee and a few slices of bread were laid on his desk."

The debate excited attention of a magnitude that had not been seen for years. The Speaker's rostrum was decorated with a display of posters on easels—all advocating Prohibition: "Alcohol has more victims than tuberculosis;" "Crime is caused by drink;" "Liquor fills the asylums;" "Drink and immorality go hand in hand;" "The conservation of human life is more than revenue." Across the gallery was hung a petition of *12,000 Groups Supporting the Amendment.*

As the debate progressed, every seat was taken. "There was a steady stream of argument rarely rising to the standard of eloquence," reported the *New York Times.*

The drama was reserved for the climax. Richmond Pearson Hobson strode to the podium at 11 p.m., the final speaker—in what would be his farewell in the Capitol—in that marathon day. Sixty speeches had already been made. Grizelda Hobson captured the mood: "The air was tense with suppressed excitement. Rarely had such a dramatic scene been witnessed in that historic chamber. With every seat filled, with the doorways to the galleries crowded with chairs, upon which stood more spectators, looking over the heads in front of them ... . People were so tense that they had no time to feel tired, especially those who had labored and hoped and even prayed for this day!"

The *New York Times,* less effusive than Mrs. Hobson, still acknowledged that Richmond Pearson Hobson was once more the hero: "Many of those in the galleries were Prohibition advocates, and to them Representative Hobson was the hero of the occasion.

They applauded when he spoke and some of the women sent flowers to him ... . For the time being there was a revival of the popular acclaim which marked the return from the Spanish war after his sinking of the *Merrimac* in Santiago Harbor."

Hobson acknowledged that he also might have sunk his political career by the espousal of Prohibition. But the battle against alcohol is the correct struggle in excising "the millstone of degeneracy from the neck of humanity." He closed with an exhortation for his colleagues to do the right thing for the sake of their manhood, their country, and their God: "I call on you, my colleagues, to hold your heads up in the face of this enemy and be men. In the name of your manhood, in the name of your patriotism, in the name of all that is held dear by good men, in the name of your fireside, in the name of our institutions, in the name of our country, and in the name of humanity and humanity's God, I call on you to join hands with me and each one to do his full duty."

Before the final vote was taken, amendments to alter the resolution were turned down. The amendment passed 197-189—the first vote ever on the issue—but it failed to get the necessary two-thirds.

It was a defeat for Hobson, certainly, and a victory for the 'wets.' However, one Washington correspondent still considered Captain Hobson a victor. Grizelda Hobson records that writer's words in her *Memoirs*: "'As we went out under the stars, our hearts rejoiced for the 200 men who had stood for the right, and most of all for the brave champion who, in the face of such opposition as few men have encountered, stands with head erect facing the foe. His is a determination such as Paul, the Apostle, had when he cried, 'Having done all, stand.'"

In its analysis, the *Times* was pleased that the amendment did not get the necessary two-thirds vote. However, the "Prohibition sentiment" would continue, spurred on by the majority approval in the House. The *Times* was very concerned that eventual passage might devastate the power of states: "If the sale of liquor is to be prohibited in the Federal Constitution, to what other preposterous ends may not that fundamental law be amended?"

But the vote itself was now an insult to the Constitution, so in a parting shot at Hobson, the *Times* said in its Editorial: "That it should have received a majority is humiliating ... . Many who voted for Hobson's plan, knowing well that the resolution must be defeated, doubtless desired to make themselves strong with the anti-liquor element. But the main issue was not the liquor question at all, but a usurpation by the Federal Government of the rights of the states. Eleven hours of valuable time were wasted and nothing was gained, though doubtless Mr. Hobson is satisfied."

While he was not pleased, yes, Mr. Hobson was, indeed, satisfied. He had "done his part." Although he had "failed" for the moment, the fight would continue. Three years later Congress would pass the resolution and give the vote on the issue to the states. Hobson left Congress, but carried on the battle in other arenas.

Lecturing for Prohibition from Tuxedo, New York . . . 1914-1916

For the first time in nearly a decade, Hobson was back in a 'non-political' life. As a politician, he didn't 'play the game.' Now, in 'private' life, he did the same; however, in his immersion in the Prohibition issue, that plan did not always work.

All his time was now devoted to lecturing for the Anti-Saloon League. His fervor often led to his 'stretching' the 'truth' of the cause. Much of his 'evidence' had been based on the early 1900 experiments of Dr. C.R. Stockard of Cornell Medical College. Using his findings, that on a cellular level alcohol destroyed certain cellular components, Hobson drew the conclusion that whiskey could destroy all life forms. However, Stockard insisted he was "misquoted" and his findings manipulated. In fact, he indicated, alcohol had some positive qualities.

Unfortunately, Hobson was indeed guilty, as were many other Prohibitionists, of exaggeration and misrepresentation of the physical harm of alcohol. Sensitive to that charge, Hobson tried to be careful. "On the margin of an undated speech," writes Pittman, "[Hobson scrawled a note] warning himself not to cite any authorities for his facts and not to exaggerate."

Hobson thoroughly enjoyed being in the service of the Anti-Saloon League. Why not? Except for William Jennings Bryan and House

Speaker Champ Clark, no one commanded a higher lecture fee than he did. Between 1914 and 1922, he was paid $171,250 by the Anti-Saloon League. Between 1916 and 1917, he was salaried at $525 for a six-day week, with provision for extra pay for "additional" lectures.

Despite protests by members that he was being paid excessively, Hobson put in for a raise. The numbers supported him. Monies raised at his lectures averaged $2,348.72 per day; $14,623.32 for a six-day week. "Ask for 50 percent of the receipts," Hobson's father-in-law, George H. Hull, urged him, "instead of the 3 percent you now receive." Hobson and League officials settled for a weekly salary of $700, with $100 for additional lectures.

Hobson's work for the cause went beyond lectures. He designed a Grand Strategy of the Fight for National Prohibition. It was presented at the National Convention of the League in Atlantic City in July, 1915. The document dealt with the harmful effects of alcohol and an approach to national education on the issue.

Richmond Pearson Hobson still made news and he told all, at the League convention, in a "special" to the *New York Times*. He knew Wilson would be renominated, and he knew the President wanted no part of the Amendment. That must not happen, and if the Alabaman was committing "political suicide" by these words, so be it: "I am a Democrat, and I know it. The plan is for the President to be renominated, in spite of the one-term pledge of the party platform ... . I know that the President will put a plank in that platform to leave the question of Prohibition entirely to the States.

"My countrymen, it is probably political suicide for me to tell you the truth from the inside, but if political death is to be the price for telling you I am willing to meet it. I was the original Wilson man in Alabama. But if you want to know it, in our fight on the floor of the House, the whole influence of the President was hurled against us in our attempt to submit a Prohibition Amendment to the people."

He had some advice for the President: "Practice abstinence and banish liquor from the White House as an example to the nation ... . Establish temperance as a requirement for civil service."

Hobson's work did show successes. In particular, he was credited for tipping the advantage to the drys in Maine.

As Hobson remained in the news. he was still sought out as a potential candidate. The Prohibition Party looked anxiously at Hobson as being a better choice than William Jennings Bryan for its 1916 Presidential ticket. As for his old seat, Hobson had no desire to contest the incumbent, now William B. Oliver, a long-time friend.

After his loss in the Senatorial campaign, Hobson had resolved never to run again for political office. While his speaking fees appeared financially impressive, Hobson had assumed major family burdens. When his father died in 1905, Hobson had assumed the mortgage payments at Magnolia Grove. For many years he supported two sisters and a brother, who lived at Magnolia. He was also the major support for the education and medical treatment of other family members. In short, large speaking fees notwithstanding, Hobson himself had to do all he could not to fall into debt. This was not the financial profile of a political candidate.

And yet ... . A fresh opportunity, the newly-created 10th District, beckoned and enticed the Alabaman. The 1910 census had led to creation of the new District which included parts of Hobson's old Sixth District. However, it did not take in Hale County, Hobson's legal residence.

During one of his speaking engagements, Hobson was met by a committee of League members and a delegation of Alabama boosters. "You must run," they pleaded. "We need your leadership as Congressman to get the Prohibition Amendment successfully through the House."

Hobson was firm in his refusal, but Grizelda Hobson came up with a plan. Why couldn't the campaign be run by Hobson's associates and other Prohibition leaders? Meanwhile, he could continue speaking throughout the land. In short, Richmond Pearson Hobson would run, would offer his name, but he would not put in time or money. Everyone agreed; however, not all Prohibition leaders were pleased. If Hobson lost again, it might be disastrous for the cause. They argued that, no matter what arrangements were made, how could he expect to win when he was actually living in Tuxedo Park, New York?

Campaigning for Alabama's New 10th District Seat
... February-May 1916

The Democratic primary was scheduled for May 9, 1916, only three months away. The opposition was William Brockman Bankhead, son of John Hollis Bankhead who had bested Hobson more than ten years earlier in the Captain's first political race. Taking on the son of a popular Alabama figure was bound to be a tough race for Hobson. Young Bankhead himself was a practicing attorney and a former member of the Alabama legislature.

The difficulties increased when the Prohibition issue became a non-issue because Bankhead pledged to vote for the amendment if elected. Angrily, Hobson told Prohibition leaders to make it clear to voters that it was he who had authored the amendment and would be in the best position to shepherd the legislation through the House. He also insisted that L. B. Musgrove, his former campaign manager, direct his campaign.

One of Musgrove's first actions was to convince Hobson to establish residence in the election district, so the candidate acquired an option on a farm near Jasper. When Hobson arrived in mid-March for an Anti-Saloon League lecture tour, he was told by Musgrove's attorney that the campaign manager wanted him to canvass the state.

"I thought it was understood that I would not campaign, " said a puzzled Hobson. "I will only campaign if the League continues paying my salary."

Musgrove settled the matter with the League; however, that was perhaps the only campaign problem solved—and in Hobson's mind only. His marriage was tested as it had never been. The candidate had fashioned this scenario: His family would move to Jasper for the duration of the campaign, and brother Gus would move in with them and care for the children, and for Grizelda when she was not out campaigning.

Grizelda gave an unequivocal "no." She had only agreed to Hobson's campaign if he did not actually campaign. Her interest in politics had soured. Despite the glorious prose about their campaign experiences in the Underwood race, it was no fun losing. She had worked so hard and was confident of victory that the defeat crushed her pride.

She was shocked and irate when her husband decided on his own to canvass the 10th District. She told her father to write the candidate. Mr. Hull told his son-in-law that his great oratory was unappreciated and wasted on Capitol Hill. "The longer you are out of Congress, the more you will be able to perform more valuable service than the whole of Congress put together." As for personal campaigning, "The harder you work for the office, the less the voters will want you."

To no avail. Richmond pleaded with Grizelda, knowing full well that with his family living in New York, voters would not be fooled by his farm. He wrote Grizelda, portraying a very healthy campaign financially: "Let us make a honeymoon out of the [campaign] fight," mused the romantic warrior.

In a series of letters, Mrs. Hobson excused herself by telling her husband that the children would not be receiving the proper care. And she could not tolerate the hot Alabama weather. Clearly, she wanted her husband out of office—permanently.

Hobson relished being controversial and combative for the noble causes. He was fearless against the vested, entrenched interests. However, Mrs. Hobson was fearful of the unsavory politicians and lobbyists who owed their careers and fortunes to whiskey. In one letter of April, 1916, she told her husband that she and her children were warned that they would be killed if Hobson did not give up the cause.

Still, he persisted. He had always thought of himself as an understanding husband, so he was "stunned" and "dazed" by her attitude. "I will not give up my campaign," he wrote. "Destiny is hovering over us. We can not take a personal, not to say selfish, view of events in these troubled, tempestuous times. It would be wrong not to do our parts loyally ... . Please join me for the final five weeks."

She responded firmly. "Our lives in politics have been fruitful, and it has also been costly in personal terms. I thought we had both decided that you leave politics ... . I think that in going into this race, you have given away your happiness; you have given away *my* happiness."

That he should not mistake her resolve, she told the candidate: "You can count upon a telegram of felicitations from me if you should be defeated."

Hobson was saddened by these sentiments and by the realization that voters would be turned off by his family's remaining in the upper class New York community. He realized that the reasons for their remaining behind, i.e., the death threats, would not convince voters.

Grizelda's fears about threats from the whiskey interests were not paranoic. In February 1916, Hobson made headlines by addressing the wine and beer moguls at a Republican Club luncheon in New York. In the audience were the Secretary of the United States Brewers' Association; the President of the Retail Wine, Beer, and Liquor Dealers' Association of New York; and the Counsel for the New York State Wholesale Liquor Dealers' Association. He threatened the "liquor men," and warned them to "be good."

Hobson "warned" that if Congress did not enact nationwide Prohibition, the States would convene a Constitutional Convention. Only if the liquor people acted properly would the government do right by them: "There is no power upon the earth that can stop the coming of this great reform. It is written across the sky. Now that we have the liquor interests against the wall, I tell them for the last time that if they fight this through, they need expect no compensation for the loss they will sustain."

Bad news came to Hobson from the Alabama Superintendent of the Anti-Saloon League. Since both candidates were supportive of Prohibition, he informed Hobson—well into the campaign— that the League would take no sides. Nevertheless, Hobson drove himself with more determination, with a daily five-speech-a-day regimen. He stressed that the two popular issues in the district— Prohibition and national security—had been championed by him longer than any other individual, candidate or no.

As May 9 neared, Hobson gained confidence. On the other hand, Grizelda was just as confident that Richmond Pearson would lose and they then could resume "a new life together in the North" where he was "appreciated."

Grizelda celebrated. Richmond Pearson Hobson lost—by fifty-one votes! His campaign shouted, "Fraud!" and there was some legitimacy to their claims. However, Hobson refused to challenge the results, simply glad that it was all over. William Morgan, campaign secretary, bitterly wrote Grizelda, placing the loss upon her shoulders: "[I am] convinced that your presence here would have meant not less than 100 more votes in Walker County for Captain besides the effect it would have had generally in the district."

More bad news followed the election returns. When he had written to the League for his March salary, he had received an angry response that had been hidden from him by Morgan and then Musgrove until after the election. Representing the League, E. H. Cherrington had told Hobson, "No man connected with this department of the League ever agreed to do anything of this kind and it will not be done."

Hobson was stunned when he learned of the deceit. He demanded that Musgrove pay him $3,792.85 to cover his salary and personal campaign expenses. No record exists that shows Hobson was ever paid. Grizelda Hobson was right!

Back on the Prohibition Lecture Circuit . . . 1916-1921

Hobson left his Jasper farm and resumed his work for the cause. World War I suited the cause well. Hobson wrote articles and lectured on the aggressiveness and degeneracy of Germans, caused by alcohol imbibed by the mothers.

American soldiers were "the best soldiers in the world," he said, "because the American fighting force was the only fighting force which did not issue alcoholic rations. Their psychology was of the highest order. They approached the zero hour without the aid of alcoholic stimulants. The American fought in the knowledge that he was in the right and with a trust in his Father in Heaven."

However, his praise of the American soldier in battle differed from his later accusations that created a furor in the summer of 1917. Hobson lashed out at Army training camps as centers of immorality, with their supplies of liquor. When pressed for proof, he cited Fort Riley in Kansas. When challenged further, he conceded that a few bars existed in Wichita near the camp. After the controversy ended, he wrote to a friend about his crusade, "This is a thankless task I have undertaken," he said.

At the war's end, he moved his family to Chicago because he felt that it was the last stronghold of the wets.

The Presidential election of 1916 brought happy returns for the Prohibitionists. Their candidates did well. They were optimistic about the future and were not disappointed. The Senate passed the resolution—65 to 20—on August 1, 1917. The House followed—232 to 128—on December 17, 1917. There were two disappointments for Hobson, however. After he left Congress the name of the amendment had been changed—despite his urgings—from the Hobson Amendment to the National Prohibition Amendment, and his wordings and intent had been changed so that the amendment barred personal manufacture and use. Hobson was fully aware that this provision would be unenforceable—and he was right.

Thirty-six states were necessary for ratification. That magic number was reached in a little more than a year, in January 1919. In October 1919, Congress passed—over Wilson's veto—the Prohibition Enforcement Act, the Volstead Act. It defined as "intoxicating liquor" any beverage containing more than one half of one percent of alcohol.

For Hobson, the mission was not over—in America and throughout the world. Hobson turned his attention to the Presidential race of 1920. He wrote to the Democratic frontrunner—and evenutal nominee—Ohio Governor James M. Cox, asking him to spell out his views on Prohibition enforcement. Senator Warren Harding, the Republican nominee and later President, had voted for the Volstead Act.

Hobson was at the Democratic Convention in San Francisco seeking to rally the drys. Bishop James Cannon of the Methodist Episcopal Church, South, set the tone for the drys, as he told the delegates in San Francisco: "We have freed ourselves from the domination of the liquor traffic and we do not intend to stand idly by while any effort is made to restore that traffic to domination."

The Conventions were a disappointment to Hobson. The Democratic Convention defeated his dry plank and went on record as approving the decision of the Resolutions Committee in omitting any reference to the Prohibition issue on the platform. The only success was the rejection of a plank in modifying the Volstead Act. The Republican Convention in Chicago rejected a dry plank. Neither Presidential candidate, Hobson wrote to Anti-Saloon League head Wayne B. Wheeler, is in harmony with the "new righteousness."

Now that Prohibition was law in America, Hobson and the dry forces planned Prohibition worldwide. "Degeneration cannot support the institutions of civilization," Hobson told a meeting at the Cavalry Baptist Church in Manhattan. Delegates came from Canada, Denmark, France, Ireland and Japan. "It is vain to hope for enduring peace," Hobson lamented, "while the world is brutalized by drink ... . I am here in [the Anti-Saloon League's] appeal to all good men and women to join in this last great drive to bring about a sober world."

Armed with his book, *Alcohol and the Human Race*, Captain Hobson had more ammunition for his world crusade. It was translated into several languages and was used as a textbook in several states.

Fighting from Los Angeles . . . 1921-1929

Education was still Hobson's key to ridding the world of the evils of drink. Toward that end, he organized the American Alcohol Education Association in 1921. He was the General Secretary and the only fund-raiser. The organization lasted less than two years, after he led a campaign to strengthen the Prohibition law in California. His goal was $400,000; he had commitments of $3,600; he collected $500.

He involved himself with a number of other projects regarding enforcement of the Eighteenth Amendment. Automobile czar, W.C. Durant, offered $28,000 for an effective plan to enforce Prohibition. Hobson started work to achieve this prize, but he never completed his plan.

"Hobson Quits Dry Work," announced a *New York Times* story, with a February 11, 1930, Balboa dateline. The subhead read: "Says Laws Are Useless Until People Are Ripe for Reform." Hobson had long realized that mere legislation would not be enough to curb alcohol. Asked by the *Panama American* about his opinion on the effectiveness of the Eighteenth Amendment, he responded: "Let the reformer stick to his proper work of molding public opinion. When people are ripe for reform, the laws will take care of themselves. Until then, they are useless. As I originally proposed it, the Eighteenth Amendment was simply an educational measure."

Hobson was headed for an international conference after conferring with President Arossemena and Governor of the Canal Zone, Colonel Harry Burgess. The agenda was set for the next major battle: narcotics control.

14

INTERNATIONAL CRUSADE AGAINST NARCOTICS

"Upon the issue hangs the perpetuation of civilization, the destiny of the world and the future of the human race ... . The whole world is menaced by this appalling foe—marching—to the capture and destruction of the whole world."

The writer was Richmond Pearson Hobson and, having followed his career, one would naturally, and incorrectly, have assigned those words to the alcohol menace. Hobson was talking about heroin and other addictive drugs.

Dr. William H. Tucker of Mobile, whose wife, the former Francis Bernice Quigley, is a distant relative of Hobson, discussed "A History of Attitudes Toward Opiate Addiction" in a 1995 issue of *Alabama Medicine*. It was natural that Hobson as a Progressive would concern himself with addiction control. Said Tucker, "Deviant behavior was considered a medical and social problem of little concern to the government until Theodore Roosevelt and the Progressive Movement started the idea that The Government should be an instrument for social betterment and change."

Tucker notes that Hobson claimed heroin was so addictive that one ounce was powerful enough to addict 1,000 people, the "living dead." Hobson's statements about the dangers of heroin, according to Tucker, prove the intensity of Hobson's commitment to the cause but also "are still used as examples of the use of overblown hyperbole to influence legislation."

Nevertheless, Tucker's article gives a quick review of Hobson's devoted efforts: organization of the International Narcotic

Education Association, the World Conference on Narcotic Education, and the World Narcotic Defence Association; and proclamation of National Narcotic week by radio, in the press, and by the distribution of millions of pamphlets with the message, "The drug menace is more communicable than leprosy."

Certainly, Hobson's crusade against alcohol naturally led to his battle against narcotics, and as the liquor battle produced the Eighteenth Amendment, Hobson immersed himself more in the war to achieve narcotics control. Just as he stressed the education of youth to fight alcohol, so, too, did he stress that education must be utilized in the narcotics crusade.

His first important move on this front was in 1920. He helped publish and distribute a 25-page textbook to help teachers in their instruction on the dangers of drugs.

The anti-narcotics movement became his number one concern in 1923, when he incorporated the International Narcotic Education Association (INEA). At the time, the Hobsons were living in Los Angeles, where they stayed until 1929. He was named president of INEA, which was formed as a non-profit organization dedicated to "educate the human race in the truth about alcohol, opium, morphine, heroin, cocaine, and any other habit-forming drug."

Hobson had proven his skills as a propagandist in the alcohol war; now he planned to get his message to the more than 20 million youth in America's schools. Forty-four state boards of education were ready to cooperate—as long as funds were forthcoming. Soon, Hobson calculated he would like to distribute 50 million copies of his pamphlet "The Perils of Narcotics."

Captain Hobson enlisted the aid of Kansas Senator Arthur Capper, former president of the Board of Regents of Kansas Agricultural College. Capper suggested that Congress print and distribute 50 million copies of the documents—at no cost to INEA.

The plan gained some support on Capitol Hill until the price tag came up: more than $330,000, according to George H. Carter, the Public Printer. The breakdown: $183,771, paper; $147,539, envelopes. And, yes, the mechanical work would tie up the press for 250 days.

Hobson's experience in the Prohibition battle had taught him that government legislation was a vital element. He actively supported the anti-heroin bill of Congressman Stephen Porter in 1924. Hobson spoke with President Coolidge about the importance of a strong anti-drug plank at the Republican Presidential Convention. He contacted delegates at the 1924 Democratic Presidential Convention in Cleveland and urged such a plank. The following proposal was accepted in good part by the Convention: "We call especial attention of the people to the serious menace of narcotic addiction and its secret and alarming growth among our young people of both sexes largely through the active, illicit exploitation of the powerful drug poison heroin.

"We are proud of the eminent leadership America holds, and has held for more than eighty years in the struggle against the infamous international opium traffic.

"Recognizing in narcotic addiction a grave peril to America and to the human race, we pledge ourselves regardless of politics, vigorously to take against it all legitimate and honorable measures for education, for control and for suppression at home and abroad."

Captain Hobson also succeeded at the Democratic Convention. He labored, to no avail, to break the nomination deadlock there, but his efforts were appreciated. He gained a strong anti-narcotics plank and also got an agreement from the nominee, John W. Davis, to use the issue in his campaign.

Not everyone, however, appreciated his intensity. INEA was distributing a circular letter with 'literature' to various mayors across America. The letter charged that 17,000 New York schoolchildren were drug addicts. "Hobson is slandering New York City," an enraged Police Commissioner Enright told a Women's City Club. New York was doing fine, Enright said: "The Police Department has made for the past few years a very intensive and active campaign against the Narcotic menace. No single school child addict has come under this observation." The conclusion reached by Enright was that INEA was a "self-appointed organization [which] has for its purpose the sole object of obtaining funds ... . [A] great deal of its literature is puerile and untruthful ... . If this is a sample of educational propaganda, it should be suppressed for it is a slander upon the educational system of this great city."

The international nature of the drug trade made enforcement that much more difficult than the problems faced in enforcing the Eighteenth Amendment. The newly created League of Nations offered some hope under its Opium Advisory Board; however, it was not until 1924 that the United States agreed to take part in the Second International Opium Conference in Geneva. Secretary of State Charles Evan Hughes agreed to American participation, and even though he did not do so with great enthusiasm, it was still a step forward and partly attributable to Hobson and INEA.

The conference, held in late 1924 and early 1925, made few practical gains. America did not succeed in effecting an agreement to limit production, but Hobson had directed more world attention to the narcotics problem, and while the Conference was meeting, citizens across America had read a major full-page article stressing the importance of educating schoolchildren about the dangers.

The November 9 article in the *New York Times* was headlined: "Victims of Drug Habit, Alarming Increase of Addicts Called Menace More Dangerous Than War—U.S. Now Consumes Four Times As Much as All Europe—Youth the Victim."

"What is the remedy?" Hobson pondered. His answer: "Since this question involves the welfare and safety of society, the foundation of our institutions, and the future of civilization, all agencies representing the vitality of society ... whether they are governmental, semi-public or private, including all organizations and all good men and women need to take proper steps for the execution of the necessary education program."

When Geneva produced no results, Hobson reasoned, "Let us convene an international Conference in the United States." He succeeded and organized the First World Conference on Narcotics Education, held in Philadelphia, July 5-10, 1926.

The attendance of more than 5,000 was made up primarily of American and foreign educators and physicians. Representatives attended from the American Legion, the American Red Cross, the American Chemical Society, the American Academy of Political and Social Science, Brown University, Cornell University, and the Rotary International Club. It was described by the *New York Times* as "the largest and most representative conference on the subject ever held."

But Hobson was far from pleased at the 'shape' of the conference. According to Hobson, the House of Representatives had passed a modest appropriation to meet expenses for foreign delegates. On the third day of the conference, however, the measure, charged Hobson, was blocked in the Senate by the Bureau of Public Health Service.

In its report, the *New York Times* called Hobson's vehement attack on the Treasury Department "apparently somewhat unpremeditated ... to give vent to indignation that had been accumulating for some time during the latter part of his five years of activity in the anti-narcotics movement."

Actually, Hobson was incited by remarks of E. G. Hoffman, representing the New York City Chamber of Commerce, who cited a Government publication that fixed 120,000 as the number of drug addicts in America.

Rhetorical fireworks then went off in the post-July 4 gathering. Hobson interrupted:

> Our Government is not represented at this conference. I have had to undergo humiliation ... .
>
> A special subcommittee was appointed by the Treasury Department in 1913 and that committee made the most comprehensive survey of the drug addiction problem that had ever been made. The opinion of that committee was that the number of drug addicts in the United States exceeds 1,000,000.
>
> On June 12, 1924, that report was ordered suppressed. The International Narcotics Education Association introduced in Congress a bill calling for the printing of that report as a public document. A representative of the Public Health Bureau opposed the bill. He incorporated in his remarks at a Congressional hearing a document which put the number of drug addicts at only 110,000.
>
> An Assistant Secretary of the Treasury refused to supply a copy of the report which estimated 1,000,000. The answer was given: 'There is none.' Also it was told us: 'Our only copy has been destroyed.'

But I found a copy in the Library of Congress.
Then we asked a copy from the Public Printer. He answered that the type had been destroyed by the Treasury Department.

The usual resolutions at conference end were passed: more education, better enforcement. Perhaps it was his 'experiences' with the government that changed Hobson's direction. In any event, he resolved to fight the battle on the international level.

Continuing the Fight & The Move to New York City ... 1926-1937

Towards that end, in 1926, he organized the World Conference on Narcotic Education to take place in 1927 and founded the World Narcotic Defense Association, with headquarters in New York— where the Hobson family would move in 1929, to which he was elected Secretary-General. INEA would be the parent organization for the Defense body, which would function regionally. The new body's major work would be to take part in international conferences and work with foreign government officials in imposing American control and regulations on drug traffic. It would also work for the enactment of uniform State laws and hospitalization of addicts.

At its first World Conference, in New York, Hobson said that he would seek to raise $5 million for its work. One of its first projects would be a hospital for addicts in New York City. "This conference," announced Hobson, "proposes to take up for the first time in history the whole question of society's defense against this growing menace, through processes of education, processes of law, processes of salvage, and other processes that may be devised."

He gave a clinical description of narcotics' effects: "The first effects of the drug were to increase in a superlative degree one's sense of ego and to magnify the primitive instincts such as courage while deadening qualities such as judgment, caution, pity and honesty which exist in the upper brain."

Then he described the street operation: "At first it is supplied gratis. Then the peddlers raise their prices for the doses as the craving and capacity of the addict are increased from a fifteenth of a grain to sometimes as much as 100 grains."

Much activity marked 1928. Widespread interest was generated in February during Narcotics Education Week, organized by Hobson to give impetus to pending nationwide legislation and to coalesce support for Congressman Porter's bill establishing two Federal institutions for the reclamation of addicts.

At its second conference, Hobson reviewed the World Narcotic Defense Association's accomplishments, in particular its 10-year goal of a $10 million endowment under the newly formed Narcotic Defense Foundation. An alarmist, he stressed the urgency since conditions had deteriorated: "Fifty thousand young girls disappear annually down the drug road. Drug addiction is now the most serious of all public matters, surpassing in importance even the peace pacts. There are five times as many violations under the drug laws as under the Prohibition laws."

What was the solution? Answered Hobson: "My idea is not so much to prevent smuggling as to crush the sources of supply."

While the drug crusade dealt primarily with the physical devastation of drugs, Prohibition was as much spiritual as physical. However, Hobson at times gave the narcotics issue a religious bent as well. He told a weekly assembly of the New York Biblical Seminary that active religion was often the best cure. "Doctors admit that those cured by various methods do not stay off," he informed the listeners, "but in many cases the addict who acquired an active religion actually did not return to the use of narcotics."

Obviously, none of the goals could be reached without adequate funding. One of Hobson's most reliable and generous sources was Josiah K. Lilly, the wealthy drug manufacturer and the Captain's personal friend. Lilly took an active role in Hobson's anti-narcotics campaign by researching the possibilities of a nonnarcotic anesthetic. Lilly and Hobson joined forces, unsuccessfully, to convince Coca-Cola to cease using cocaine in its product. While the amounts of cocaine were small, Hobson was worried that the intake would carry over to addiction of more devastating drugs.

Hobson did not pass up any potential sources, but not everyone turned out to be a Lilly. For example, he was totally frustrated in dealings with Henry Ford, who never gave the Captain an appointment. Ford insisted that the anti-narcotics campaign must be coupled with a drive against alcohol. Hobson was not interested.

In general, the fund-raising efforts failed. He embarked on a two-month Midwest tour in 1929 and was stymied by the Great Crash. The Hobson Papers reveal shortcomings in the Captain's financial management skills. For example, he spent too much money on telegrams and special delivery letters. And while Richmond's endearing sentiments were a reaffirmation of his love to Grizelda, they were billed to the budgets of the International Narcotics Education Association and World Defense Narcotics Association.

In the early 1930s, Hobson concentrated on efforts to achieve international cooperation in preventing the entry of drugs into America, Toward that end, the Narcotic Defense Association established an auxiliary group in Geneva to coordinate anti-smuggling efforts. The Geneva Center of International Relations, while funded by the Defense Association, was comprised of associates of different nations.

In March 1931, Hobson appeared in Washington before the Wickersham Commission on Law Enforcement which was studying the relationship of narcotic drugs to crime. He told of a new menace, the introduction into the United States and Europe of marijuana, a type of Mexican hemp. "This drug can be grown anywhere," said Hobson, "and when smoked in small quantities produces a feeling of physical exhilaration. In excess, however, it motivates the most atrocious acts." His efforts paid dividends: China and Latin American countries intensified their efforts to control production in their countries.

In the summer of 1931, the 57 assembled countries met in Geneva and reached an accord to limit production under direction of an Opium Control Board. Captain Hobson presided at the historic meeting and it was no easy task to harmoniously bring together so many minds and differing opinions to come up with a satisfactory solution. Mrs. Hobson writes of her husband's achievement in her *Memoirs*: "There was great difficulty in focusing many minds on one subject in a clear enough way to get down to business.

"It took the parliamentary knowledge of many years in Congress for Captain Hobson to wield his gavel just at the proper time.

Suddenly, from my spectator's seat, I noticed that things were getting very tense. My husband's usual placid expression had developed into one of stolid determination. I quietly slipped out of the hall, took a piece of paper out of my bag and hastily scribbled three words underlined, "Smile, Smile, Smile," folded it, and handed it to a page, directing Jim to give it to Captain Hobson as soon as I took my seat again.

> A few seconds later, Captain Hobson took the piece of paper, opened it, and read it. A faint smile instantly lit up his face and over his eyeglasses he glanced quickly at me. In a few seconds more he made some witty remark which instantly caused general merriment and everyone was in a happy mood ... .

> I have often seen him change a whole atmosphere in a few instants by his personal attitude. Gradually, these delegates came to know Captain Hobson and, I really believe, to *love* him. One only finds this quick response where every mind is working for the same object and where the human element is so important.

The accomplishments of the conference chair were later detailed at a tribute written by Dr. E. George Payne, Dean at New York University, as a memorial to Hobson, who by then was an Admiral:

> One of the great periods of my life, and perhaps the most significant, has been the association with Admiral Hobson in the development and promotion of a plan for the elimination, or at least the reduction of the illicit and improper use of narcotic drugs. The Admiral sensed, as no other American, the devastating effects of the improper use of drugs upon the world, and particularly the United States, and set himself to the task of drug elimination with an energy, and with an enthusiasm that commanded loyal support of his efforts. He not only gave himself to the cause, but also by his devotion and sacrifice, commanded the enthusiastic assistance of a host of outstanding men and women who were inspired by his vision and devotion to a noble cause in the interest of humanity.

The climax of the Admiral's efforts in this direction was perhaps reached in his World Conference of Geneva in 1931 in connection with the meeting of the League of Nations, which organized a program which will ultimately control illicit drug traffic. The achievements of this world Conference were momentous, and were the single-handed achievements of the Admiral. I say single-handed because he conceived the conference, he organized it, and he was the central figure in everything that transpired. He amazed everybody with the mastery of his detail, with his inspired leadership, and with his ability to achieve what appeared to others as the impossible ... .

Some of these delegates clearly envisaged this conference as an opportunity of attaining for their country a commercial advantage in drug traffic and were not interested in its control. Many of them were selfish and wholly suspicious of the motives of other delegates. The task of bringing unofficial pressure to bear upon this conglomerate body of delegates so that they would present a plan that would be adopted and achieve lasting results required leadership, vision, and superhuman efforts.

All these the Admiral displayed at every point. No one else could have attempted, or could have done what the Admiral accomplished.

Hobson's work in narcotics control was not unnoticed even while he lived. Before the 1931 conference, Pope Pius XI gave a private audience to the Hobsons. After the conference, the Captain received a cablegram from the Vatican expressing the Pope's commendation of his "noble crusade."

The achievements of the 1931 conference were translated into practicality on July 10, 1933, when the League of Nations treaty convention went into effect worldwide, restricting the manufacture of narcotic drugs. The World Narcotic Defense Association celebrated with a radio broadcast by Hobson from the Waldorf Astoria. President Franklin Delano Roosevelt wired his congratulations to "All those who participated in bringing ... about ... their wonderful achievement."

Ratification required agreement by twenty-five of the fifty-seven nations at Geneva, of which four had to be large manufacturing countries. Nicaragua and the United States were the first to ratify. The United States was joined by other large manufacturers, Great Britain, Turkey, Germany, the Netherlands, and Japan.

Said Hobson,

> The putting of this convention into operation constitutes a signal victory for the forces of good throughout the world in the warfare of humanity against this narcotic evil.
>
> The rising tide of narcotic addiction menaces the very foundation of modern civilization. The narcotic drug racket, since the breaking out of the World War, has been based on the chemical industries of Europe, which are manufacturing many times the amount of high-powered drugs required for the world's legitimate needs.
>
> While aware of the importance of the question of raw materials, leaders studying the problem have sought for the last seven years to gain, first, the strategic objective of striking down this base of supplies through limiting, through international treaty convention, the production of these drugs to the legitimate medicinal and scientific requirements of the world ... . With God overhead we are prepared to serve and to fight.

With the ratification of the convention treaty, Hobson continued the battle with greater optimism abroad and more determination at home. The major danger zone was Manchuria, he told the Sixth Annual Meeting of the World Narcotic Defense Association, held in November, 1933 at the Waldorf-Astoria. Manchuria was "the future Centre of infection for mankind. We might as well recognize now as later that not only is the government there systematically developing the opium traffic proper, but the monopoly, composed of Japanese citizens, is rapidly building factories for morphine, heroin, and the other high-powered drugs."

Hobson had better news at the next annual meeting, reporting "progress at home and abroad." Cobra venom had been substituted for morphine to alleviate pain. By 1934, the world's leading victim nation, China, had signed the Geneva Convention. Forty-one nations had now signed the Convention.

"During the past year," he said, "our battle lines have advanced to the Pacific Ocean, leaping vast continental areas. While consolidating the Western European and Central European sectors captured the year before, our victorious ranks have surged over the sector of Eastern Europe, the Balkans, the Near East, and are now besieging the enemy in the last sector of the Far East."

By 1935, Hobson had succeeded, by working together with State Department officials, to effect a stronger anti-narcotics program in Japan and in its possessions, which now included Korea and Manchuria. The time now demanded more focus on America because it was in the hands of the individual states to pass and enforce narcotics legislation. For several years the Depression had severely weakened the Associations under Hobson's direction. By 1935, the Associations were nearly $40,000 in debt. To keep them afloat, Hobson lent them more than $5,500, even though his resources had dramatically dwindled. Hobson had already taken a forty percent salary cut, while other employees also saw their salaries slashed. Richmond Pearson, Jr., the Captain's son, was hired as fund-raiser, at $250 monthly, but he raised little money and left after four months when his salary had not been paid.

The woeful economic situation hit all family members, recounted Grizelda Hobson in her *Memoirs*:

> We moved out of an expensive apartment into a smaller one. We practiced every possible economy. Bills, for daily living expenses, instead of being paid weekly, were unpaid at the end of the current month, then two months, then three. I began a regular system of calls to our debtors, asking them very courteously to be patient, that they would receive all we owed them in time. Then we moved into an inexpensive hotel apartment house. It was on the second floor, dark, and the delicatessen store under our windows smelt of pickles and cheese 24 hours of the day.
>
> The Madison Avenue Street car made noises on the tracks across the street, and taxis blew their loud blasts, and each morning at eight sharp, the food supply of the day was

unloaded in front of our window. The dirt and the noise poured in. We were awakened and numbed by the din.

I watched the people to and from work along the sidewalk in front of our windows, in rain and snow, and I greeted all of the family each morning with some joke or merriment, for we were all gay despite the inconveniences.

The financial picture brightened a bit after 1935, and the organizations were now solvent as Hobson informed the annual meeting in 1936.

Hobson's last major effort in narcotics control was the campaign for adoption of the Uniform Narcotic Act. Hobson and his staff worked vigorously lobbying on Capitol Hill and in the state legislatures, winning the support of the President and other Federal officials, writing articles for the news media, planning broadcast materials, and enlisting the endorsement of national organizations such as the American Bar Association, the Women's Christian Temperance Union, the General Federation of Women's Clubs, and the National Congress of Parents and Teachers.

By March 1937, thirty-four states had already enacted the Uniform Narcotic Laws. Among the notable successes was the McNaboe Bill in New York, where Hobson's groups offered State Senator J.J. McNaboe money and materials to ensure passage of the measure.

When Hobson died that March, the organizations were bereft of direction. The International Narcotics Education Association and World Narcotics Defense Association quickly plunged into debt. Within a month after its founder's death, both groups and the Geneva Center were heavily in debt and no longer extant.

The widespread use of drugs with its devastating consequences worldwide certainly prove the ineffectiveness of Hobson's "noble crusade." Richmond Pearson Hobson's legacy on narcotics control was described as "negative" by Dr. William Tucker, who spoke to us in 1997 from his home in Mobile.

According to Tucker, "Hobson, like other readers of Sherlock Holmes, were convinced of the criminality of opiate use. The misinformation that Hobson created with his writings and lectures is still with us. When people think of narcotic use, they think of evil and criminality. The medical aspects do not receive the proper attention."

In a 1993 article by Peter McDermott titled "Grassed Up" for *The Face*, the author writes of the narcotics crusader: "The pseudo-scientific myths that Hobson invented have had a remarkable persistence. So successful was Hobson at presenting drug use as a threat to civilization that he was able to convince the U.S. Government to commit to a massive law enforcement programme aimed at eradicating drug use."

One of Hobson's disciples, writes McDermott, was Harry Anslinger, who directed the Bureau of Narcotics and Dangerous Drugs for 30 years. According to McDermott, he "emulated Hobson's rhetoric using marijuana as his focus, in an attempt to expand his organizations' power .... Anslinger used the media cleverly and managed to gull the American public into believing marijuana was just as addictive as heroin—perhaps more so."

Nevertheless, Richmond Pearson Hobson devoted more than fifteen years of his life to spread the word—by lecture and publication—to arouse the people to the menace of narcotics. Even the critical Dr. Tucker writes in a letter to us, in July 1996, "This most interesting man may be responsible for the formation of some of the present laws and the public's attitude regarding addiction to alcohol and other drugs and the social disruption that has been the result of government attempts to control deviant behavior by legislative fiat."

If the content and stress of his message were wrong, he did not err in stating the horrid consequences of drug use.

15

HOBSON'S BATTLES, CONTINUED

After his four terms on Capitol Hill, Richmond Pearson Hobson launched crusades against alcohol and narcotics. But his battles and pronouncements did not begin and end with those causes. He continued to have much to say about military preparedness, economic recovery, social welfare and FDR's actions, to name just a few of his areas of involvement.

From 1919 to 1929, Hobson was a transplanted Southerner and Easterner living on the West Coast, but he still had an impact. In one Los Angeles newspaper poll he was named as one of the twelve "most outstanding and useful citizens in the United States." In July 1926, he received two telegrams from local political leaders asking him to run for the Democratic nomination for California's U.S. Senator. One telegram said, "Fight probably wet and dry. Your record on this issue and long Congressional experience will make you very strong." Hobson begged off: "While head of the narcotic organizations which I have founded I can take no part in the wet and dry fight or in any political struggles whatsoever ... . The narcotic menace has become a problem of utmost importance and urgency ... . My organizations are now at a critical stage in their development when financial support must be made regular and permanent."

Japan was also a menace that was never off Hobson's mind. The Alabaman was derided in 1907 when he prophesied war with Japan. In a 1921 interview, he again predicted war. The circumstances concerned the Pacific island of Yap, which was administered by Japan under a League of Nations mandate.

Hobson predicted that Japan would seize Hawaii, the Philippines, and Guam, blow up the Panama Canal and declare war against America "either before the Atlantic fleet rejoins the Pacific fleet, or in five or six years." Once the Philippines gained independence, Hobson forecast aggressive Japanese moves.

"We must have permanent and immediate control of the sea in the Pacific," he said. "We should have a Navy larger than the combination of navies that Japanese diplomacy can assemble ... . Japan's treatment of Korea and the helpless inhabitants of Formosa should make us turn with horror from the thought of her controlling the destinies of the Filipinos."

The *New York Times* lost no time in mocking Hobson. In "A War Prophet" editorial, the *Times* noted Hobson's previous prophecy in 1907 that "'this Government will either have to eat humble pie or fight.' Nothing happened." The *Times* reviewed Hobson's other failed warlike predictions. "Perhaps Hobson was being cautious now in predicting five or six years," the sarcastic editorial continued. "What should America do?" the *Times* asked. "It is well for a nation to keep its powder dry," concluded the editorial, "but it should not allow itself to be stampeded by hysterical soothsayers."

Japan did not attack within the five or six years, but this did not deter Hobson from speaking out, and after 1930 he saw the "revival" of the menace.

He was a frequent visitor at and took part in the activities of the New York Military-Naval Club, a social club for retired officers. Never forgetting about Japan, in the mid 1930s he helped create the Public Welfare Association, whose the targets were Fascism and Communism. At the Annual Massing of the Colors, held in New York in 1933 to mark Armistice Day, Hobson urged America to take a stand against the "high tide of autocracy" in Europe.

In 1936 he gave a major address, in Saratoga Springs, New York, at the 37th Annual National Encampment of the United Spanish War Veterans. He warned against Fascism and Communism and warned that America itself could be "headed for dictatorship": "Millions even in America, urged on by a new class hatred, and by want, have well-natured designs to seize the wealth of the country and to dynamite our institutions that stand in their way. These hordes with a 'United Front' are on the march in our land headed for dictatorship ... .

"Whether they converge into the bloody road of Communism, or the way of Fascism, their main objective is the overthrow of our American institutions."

Hobson was alarmed about the studies of the Public Welfare Association which showed that

> Communistic autocracy is waging scientific warfare against America under the direction of a general staff, drawing on the resources of a nation ... . Throughout the land a highly financed skillfully standardized policy of pacifism is being directed against all lines of preparedness. In the bloody Soviet, preparation for armaments are being pushed on a colossal scale, unparalleled in history. But in peaceful America, our hatred of war, our very love of peace, our innate Christian idealism are being capitalized through propaganda of a very subtle nature against any forms of preparedness, and are being cunningly maneuvered towards producing apathy, conscientious objection, sabotage and treason of war.

Ironically, Hobson expected a wave of anti-Japanese and anti-Fascist propaganda that would shove into war on the side of Russia: "With the imminence of a Soviet war with Japan and other countries," feared Hobson, "we may expect a recrudescence of, organized anti-Japanese propaganda of internationalism 'against war and Fascism' directed at having America end by entering the pending World War on the side of Russia and the Red."

Because his organization and his family were victimized by worsening economic conditions, Hobson also concerned himself with ideas for economic improvement. At the encampment of the Spanish War Veterans, recommendations were offered for helping solve unemployment, including deporting ten million aliens. Hobson himself attacked the Government's "policy and philosophy of controlled scarcity. Thoughtful citizens should see in this policy and in the regimentation of agriculture and industry the lacing of a straitjacket upon our people, striking at America's inherent superiority.

"This superiority is the boundless production of wealth, engines, and machines set in motion by freedom of enterprise and initiative, and the security of property honestly acquired."

Hobson also turned to more innovative solutions. Many of these ideas were detailed in a 1932 book by his brother-in-law, George H. Hull, Jr., *Perpetual Prosperity: The Hull Plan.* For example, the liquor industry (Prohibition was repealed in 1933) would be owned by the government, which would channel profits to social welfare programs. Other areas of industry would be organized with profits shared between labor and capital. Hobson was enamored with the "Hull Plan" and attracted businessmen worried about Congressman Hugo Black's 30-hour work week. All came to nought, however, when FDR inaugurated the National Industrial Recovery Act, in June, 1933.

Long a believer in the evolution or improvement of man— never held by Hobson to be identical with Darwinian evolution— Hobson sought to initiate, without success, an Institution of Social Evolution to deal with all man's social problems, including alcohol and narcotics. Also failing to attract supporters, in 1934, was his newly formed Safety League of America, designed to educate the public about industrial safety.

Equally without success, in his lifetime, was the advocacy of a Federal Department of Applied Education to "apply the power of education to the treatment of social ills, to the development of social strength and integrity, and to the promotion of social progress and well-being." The bill would also have provided for bureaus within the department that would have been assigned the problems of alcohol, crime, narcotics, public health, and unemployment.

Hobson had taken on President Theodore Roosevelt on the issue of American Naval supremacy. Twenty-five years later he picked his match with President Franklin Delano Roosevelt, this time the issue being "the integrity of the Constitution of the United States." To ensure the 'constitutionality' of his proposals, FDR envisioned loading up the Supreme Court with those favoring his reforms. Hobson, like many other Americans, was angered at this assault on the integrity of the Constitution. At the veterans' gathering in 1936, Hobson attacked the "enemies" of the Supreme Court. It was important to affirm, said Hobson, that "the integrity of the Constitution of the United States rests on the Supreme Court, and the integrity of both rests upon the confidence of the American people.

"A thoughtful citizen can see throughout the land a standardized, highly financed, insidious sustained propaganda against the Constitution, and the 'nine old men' and can detect a half-concealed plan to undermine the authority of the Court."

In 1935, in customary Hobsonian manner, the Alabaman established a new organization, the Constitutional Democracy Association, with Hobson as president and headquarters at 578 Madison Avenue in Manhattan. This group attracted more money and followers—including high ranking retired officers of the Army and Navy as board members—than past ventures. It published a major paper on *Constitutional Democracy*.

Roosevelt's plan would be a "profound mistake," Hobson told members of Congress, who were planning to hold hearings, and promised to return to take part in the hearings. From his small office and staff, in March 1937, Hobson sent letters to all members of the New York State Legislature to help defeat FDR's proposal. Working together with related groups like the Citizens Committee for Protecting the Supreme Court, Hobson suggested that the last Wednesday of March 1937 be celebrated as "Constitutional Democracy Day" throughout America. Before leaving for the hearing in March 1937, in Washington, he wrote his last letter, to President Roosevelt, telling him, "I am not able to go with you on this Supreme Court Fight." For Hobson, said Grizelda in her *Memoirs*, it was a reaffirmation of her husband's favorite lines, from *Hamlet*, "This above all things, to thine own self be true."

On March 17, 1937, he wrote this letter, slept, breakfasted with his family, and put on his coat, ready to leave for his office. He collapsed and died in full view of the shocked family.

Upholding the integrity of the Constitution in a battle that FDR lost was a fitting way for Hobson's work to end. To ensure that this cause would continue, an announcement was sent out after his death from the headquarters of the Constitutional Democracy Association that the Admirals' scheduled time before the Senate Judiciary Committee would be assigned to another member of the Association.

Surprisingly, in his post-Congress years Hobson was involved in 'battles' that should not have taken place. Perhaps none was in such poor form as the battle fought in 1928 on the pages of *The Independent* in Elizabeth City, North Carolina.

George Viett, a journalist from Norfolk, Virginia, wrote a voluminous article critical of Hobson's political activities. It was titled "Richmond Pearson Hobson: A Prohibition Ballyhooloo and War Hero." Actually, the article had little to do with Hobson's war heroism or his work against drink. The crux of the article attacked Hobson's salvaging operations after the war, accusing him of abandoning a ship in a storm. In short, Viett tried to portray Hobson "as something less noble than the hero he was made out to be."

The editor, in that spirit, ran a war portrait of Hobson with a caption that ended, "Today he is 58 years old and doesn't get kissed so often."

Hobson demanded and won an apology in the paper from Viett, who revealed that it was his first apology in his forty-year journalism career. While he agreed to the apology, since Hobson insists his facts are right, he sheepishly conceded that the article was purely part of the process of political assassination that writers engage in: "My article was purely political and designed to be somewhat historical. Employed in the present campaign on behalf of the Democratic nominees, I had conceived a series directed against the political and official records of the stronger of our antagonists in the effort to lessen their public influence upon audiences and the election. To this alone is due my attack upon Mr. Hobson, the campaign also affording opportunity to comply with the request of my cousin."

Grizelda Hobson related two incidents, more than thirty years after the Spanish-American War, that showed just how little many people knew of him. The first told how, after being introduced to Hobson, an English gentlemen said, "I am most happy to meet you, Admiral, but, I say, that must have been a whale of a battle between the *Merrimac* and the *Monitor*. Tell me about it, please."

The second incident continues this theme: "It is sometimes amazing how magnificent is the flight of time! As for solving mystery, it once happened that the Captain was introduced to an audience like this, 'Ladies and Gentlemen: I have the great honor of introducing to you the man who blew up the *Maine* in the battle of Manila Bay.'"

These incidents aside, many Americans did come to know Richmond Pearson Hobson in the years before he died. Regionally, he received honorary degrees from Bob Jones College, Southern University, and Washington and Jefferson College. However, these academic honors did not give him the acclaim he finally earned through two Congressional acts: the conferral of the Medal of Honor and promotion to Rear Admiral.

Grizelda Hobson was surprised to learn that Captain Hobson had never been awarded the Medal of Honor. All of the other participants in the sinking of the *Merrimac*, the enlisted sailors, had long ago received this honor and were, in fact, specifically cited as having served "under Naval Constructor R. P. Hobson" as well as having "distinguished themselves by extraordinary courage." Mrs. Hobson first learned all this in 1930 as she was assembling her husband's files.

According to Mrs. Hobson, Richmond Pearson never thought much of it, and perhaps even considered the medal in his possession. "It was characteristic of my husband," she wrote, "always busy with important duties, to have entirely overlooked the fact that included in the other medals he had, the Medal of Honor was not to be found. I spoke to him about it several times and he always said, 'I think I must have it.' Perhaps it was with my effects in the fire at the Army and Navy Club.'"

The Department of the Navy confirmed Mrs. Hobson's deductions that the Medal of Honor had never been awarded her husband and informed her that, until a change of law in 1915, naval officers were not eligible for the award. What Hobson did receive in 1898 was the Specially Meritorious Medal.

Grizelda Hobson contacted Hobson's congressional friends to rectify the situation. The measure was introduced by Congressman William Oliver, who was the Representative in Hobson's Sixth District, and was passed by Congress in early 1933. The honoree received telegrams from all over America on this honor. Grizelda was especially pleased and proud, and that made her husband even happier. Writes Mrs. Hobson, "I, myself, felt a very special satisfaction,

President Franklin D. Roosevelt presenting Richmond Pearson
Hobson with his Medal of Honor in 1933 in the presence of
the Secretary of the Navy and other government officials
Courtesy: Houston Stokes.

for now he, with his crew, all had the highest award that our country can bestow for bravery. He was very happy indeed over it, mostly because *I* was."

FDR presented the award on April 29, 1933, nearly thirty-five years after the *Merrimac* heroics. Grizelda could not attend because she and her mother could not get back from Florida, where they were visiting relatives. Richmond, Jr., the Captain's son and his brother-in-law, George Hull, were at the ceremonies.

When the honoree was introduced to FDR, the Captain said, "I've heard a great deal about you, Sir," to which the President responded with broad smile, "I've heard a great deal about you."

After a brief introduction, FDR read the citation honoring the former Naval constructor for "distinguishing himself conspicuously by extraordinary courage and intrepidity at the risk of his life and beyond the call of duty on 2 June 1898, by entering the fortified harbor of Santiago, Cuba, and sinking the partially dismantled collier *Merrimac* in the channel under persistent fire from the enemy fleet and fortifications on shore."

More important to Captain Hobson himself and his family, perhaps, was the 1934 Congressional act promoting him to Rear Admiral, placing him on the retired list, and granting him a full pension. According to Gloria Cole, it was Hobson'a sister, Margaret, who was the driving force behind that campaign. The higher title itself was a charming prospect, but more importantly, the family was running short of funds and needed the pension.

The story of Hobson's resignation thirty years before due to health problems incurred in service has already been discussed, and the Navy had a rigid rule against reinstatement after resignation. Nevertheless, in January 1933, a week after the Senate Naval Committee reported favorably on the Medal of Honor, Nevada Senator Tasker Oddie introduced a bill to rank Hobson as Rear Admiral, with thirty years' service, and retirement pay of that grade. As reported by the Associated Press, Tasker wanted to give proper recognition to "an epic deed almost forgotten by modern-day folks."

For Oddie and other supporters, it was "a simple act of justice," but for Hobson it involved many hours, days, and weeks, spent in Washington testifying and making data available concerning his Naval record, especially the circumstances that led to his deteriorating physical condition. "It was all a wearisome task," said Grizelda Hobson.

Hobson was accompanied in Washington by his brother-in-law, George Hull. As reported by Mrs. Hobson in her *Memoirs*, Captain Hobson asked his brother-in-law, "'I wonder if it is worth all this time?'"

Mr. Hull responded, "'Richmond, you owe it to Grizelda and the children to go through with it."

The Captain agreed. "'Yes. That is true. It will make them all so happy.'"

One of Hobson's biggest boosters was former Navy Secretary Charles Francis Adams, who told the hearing that the rank of Admiral "was the one he undoubtedly would have reached if his devotion to the Naval service had not resulted in physical disqualification." But his biggest supporter in the House, in an irony of ironies, was Speaker William Bankhead whose father, John Bankhead, was the driving force in ensuring that Hobson's retirement bill was defeated during 1902-03. William Bankhead had himself defeated Hobson in his last political race in 1916.

The Bill, H.R. 9221, was introduced in the House by Georgia Congressman Carl Vinson, and in the Senate, S. 3380 was introduced by Florida's Park Trammell, chairman of the Committee on Naval Affairs. It passed the Senate on May 28, 1934. As Hobson wrote to Grizelda: "I wish you could have been with me in the Senate gallery as they went down the calendar and bill after bill was 'passed over.' There must have been 90 Senators, more than I have ever seen. At times I was anxious—then I would check up our friends. They were all there, it seemed—and Bennett Clark was in the Chair, and we had practically all the leaders. The Chamber was breathless when the Clerk read my bill and paused—Not a sound! The clerk announced it passed!

"... I hope to have a telegram reach you for dinner. How would you like to be in the Navy? It is *your* doing, I love you, darling."

The bill would have passed the House the next day, but partisan attacks on Roosevelt precluded action. Memorial Day followed, and the historic vote was set for June 2, the 36th anniversary of the sinking of the *Merrimac*.

The Hobson family was surprisingly absent. "It was bitter for us both," Grizelda wrote unhappily in her *Memoirs*, "that I could not have been there to see this event at the end. But even the expense of going to Washington was prohibitive at the moment! The children and I were joyous; even though not there, we could see it all in our minds."

Every House member seemed to be present for the vote, and the galleries were filled. Hobson was literally carried by his former colleagues from the cloak room, where he had been quietly awaiting the vote, to the House floor. The entire House rose and applauded the Admiral's entrance.

The excitement of the moment was captured in a letter from the Admiral to Grizelda and is recorded in the *Memoirs*: "'My precious Little Sweetheart! How I wished for you to be in the Gallery. I retired to the Speaker's Lobby. Every few minutes, a member would come out aglow with pleasure to report speeches. It seems a dozen or more were made. Finally, two came to say it has passed and insisted that I step inside, near the Speaker's desk—and *all arose and applauded*. Wasn't that touching? [Congressman Carl] Vinson [Georgia] asked for unanimous consent, but if objection had been made, he would have moved suspension of the rules and passed it by 2/3 majority. Everybody seemed so happy."

Congressman Vinson's remarks paying tribute to Richmond Pearson Hobson were recorded in the June 4 *Congressional Record*:

> The older Members remember how they considered lightly the warning that Captain Hobson sounded year after year of the approach of the World War as he pleaded for building up the Navy so that America could be the great neutral, able to exert powerful influence to prevent the World War, and if it came, to inspire respect for our rights as a neutral by both sides and thus to safeguard the rights of all neutrals and of civilization. This policy of a peace-loving nation, far from the hatred and strife of other lands, but holding power adequate for our own home defense and the defense of our commerce and vital interests everywhere, is as sound for America now as it was then. The older Members recall the persistency with which Captain Hobson pointed

out the rising importance to America's peace of the control of the sea in the Pacific, and the positive danger of letting that control pass to foreign hands. It was Captain Hobson who secured the authorization of the naval base at Pearl Harbor and raised his voice for the strong fortification of the Panama Canal, and urged year in and year out the assembling of the Navy into one great fleet with its home in the Pacific Ocean.

The older Members recall the incident when the Democratic floor leader, John Sharp Williams, shortly after the first feeble flight of the Wright brothers, taunted his young kinsman, Captain Hobson, with being such a Navy jingo that he would put a fleet in the air as well as on the sea. Captain Hobson's answer was: 'I expect to see the day when great fleets will carry on in the air, and my hope shall be that America in that day will be in aviation the biggest and the best.'

It would not be amiss in these days for Congress to give consideration to Captain Hobson's up-to-date formula for our safety—America as a minimum to maintain power on the sea second to none, and simultaneously power in the air adequate to control the air out to midocean on both oceans at the same time.

The bill was signed by FDR on June 4. Hobson was greeted that day by the Secretary and Assistant Secretary of the Navy in the former's office: "Glad to have you back in the Navy." Secretary of the Navy Claude Swanson told Hobson. "I am going to recommend the President to sign the bill." Commenting on the demonstration for Hobson in the Congress, Swanson observed, "It seems there has been nothing like this in the memory of man!"

Some two years after his Naval reinstatement and promotion, the Admiral—who had not lived in the South for decades—was given a regional honor. He was named Honorary Admiral of the Confederate Navy. The commission was signed by General Harry Renee Lee, commander-in-chief of the United Confederate Veterans.

The honors continued to accumulate after Hobson's sudden death. Tributes were paid by members of the Army and Navy alike. "He was a splendid American citizen," said General John J. Byrne, president of the National Defense League, and Lieutenant George Charette, U.S.N. (retired), one of the Admiral's shipmates on the *Merrimac,* said "[Hobson's] name will live forever in the annals of American naval heroism."

Admiral Richmond Pearson Hobson was buried with full Naval honors at the Arlington National Cemetery. Honorary pall-bearers were: Rear Admiral S.E.W. Kitelle, retired; Rear Admiral Emory S. Land; Rear Admiral William G. DeBose; Rear Admiral Horatio C. Gilmor, retired; Captain C. W. Fisher; and J. W. Powell, a friend from New York. Admiral W. S. Pye, assistant chief of Naval operations, was the Navy's official representative. The full seaman guard of the Washington Navy Yard, and a Navy Band acted as escort to the funeral.

Hobson's body was accompanied from New York by Grizelda Hobson and their three children, Richmond P., Jr., Lucia, and George Hull Hobson. Among those at the service were Ambassador Pedro Martinez Fraga of Cuba, House Speaker Bankhead, and other Alabaman members of Congress.

Margaret Hobson, the Admiral's sister, recorded the service in an unpublished tribute, "The Passing of a Great Man":

> The passing was instantaneous, as though the great clock of Parliament suddenly stopped ticking, and time went on in its eternity. He was as big among men as was Big Ben in the realm of finite time. And the horologe of infinity will carry on the great work to which his heart and mind were dedicated.
>
> The ceremony in Washington was like some triumphal procession in another world. All seemed to feel it ... .
>
> In the little Georgian Chapel at Arlington, the Navy Chaplain read his record as part of the ceremony, while the organ played softly; and Oh, what a record! Rear Admiral William T. Sampson's letter to the Navy Department in 1898 was read in full.

U.S.S. Hobson, DD-464, the destroyer named in his honor
and launched at the Charleston, South Carolina, Navy Yard.
Courtesy: Houston Stokes.

The procession to the grave was headed by a Company of Marines and another of Blue-Jackets. Then came the casket, with flag, epaulets, and sword on top, drawn by six white horses, pall-bearers walking alongside.

At each winding cross-road en route a soldier stood with hand raised in salute. At intervals the boom of a gun firing a salute rang out on the still air. Last at the head of the grave, the bugler standing like a statue, broke the silence with the clear call of the Last Post. When the sound died away, the grim snap of the bugler's hand in salute, before he stepped down the earth from that high place, seemed to say, 'Carry on!'

Then the order was given to the Company of Blue-jackets—'Be prepared to fire three volleys.' With their rifles pointed obliquely to the sky, each volley was fired as the order rang out—'ready, take aim, fire!'

It seemed as though fifty tongues of flame from those rifles in perfect alignment, leaped out to follow the departed one to some place, where someday we will all go.

How glorious the life and how beautiful the tribute to the going of this one!

Charleston, South Carolina . . . 1941

More tributes followed in later years. In September 1941, at the Charleston, South Carolina, Navy Yard, a $5 million destroyer was launched and named *U.S.S. Richmond Pearson Hobson*. The ship was christened by Mrs. Hobson in the presence of other family members. Admiral Allen of the Charleston Yard presided at the ceremonies. The address was given by J. W. Powell, lifelong friend of the Admiral and Special Assistant to the Secretary of the Navy.

On June 2, 1898, Powell had been a cadet commanding a steam launch that had been detailed to follow the *Merrimac* to the harbor entrance and then to rendezvous with Hobson's pulling boat, in which he had hoped to escape with the crew of his doomed vessel. Recalling his friend's exploit, Powell praised the action as "the bravest deed it has been my privilege to witness in a long life, and none can testify more wholeheartedly than when I say, from the bottom of

Hobson, Washington County, Alabama.
Courtesy: Theodore Pearson.

my heart, that we are honoring a great man and a great officer in naming of the destroyer *Hobson*."

The destroyer was converted to a minesweeper and, unfortunately, sank during the Korean War. On April 26, 1952, the *Hobson* was participating in sea maneuvers with the carrier *U.S.S. Wasp*. The *Hobson* mistakenly turned in front of the *Wasp* and was sliced in two. The ship sank in less than 90 seconds and 176 of the 203 crewmen were lost.

Alabama . . . 1942-1990

On May 28, 1942, at the state capital, in the Alabama War Memorial Building in Montgomery, bronze busts were unveiled of two state heroes: General Joseph A. Wheeler and Admiral Richmond Pearson Hobson. The ceremony was conducted under the auspices of the United Spanish War Veterans. Margaret Hobson unveiled her brother's bust.

On May 2, 1943, Magnolia Grove was dedicated as a shrine to the hero of the *Merrimac*. Some 300 friends and relatives visited the 112-year-old antebellum home and saw the wooden nameplate from the *Merrimac*. The dedication fulfilled a legislative mandate passed in 1943: The House and Senate voted to appropriate $7,500 for restoration of the Hobson family home and its 14 acres of magnolia and oak trees, and $1,500 for maintenance.

Two cities in Alabama were named for the legendary hero— Hobson City in Calhoun County and Hobson in Washington County—and in 1990 a monument to the *U.S.S. Richmond Pearson Hobson*, said to be the first monument on record to a combat unit in the Korean War, was dedicated at Waterfront Park in Mobile.

16

AN APPRECIATION OF
RICHMOND PEARSON HOBSON, THE MAN

At Home with the Hobsons—Looking Back . . . 1905-1937

Beyond being a visionary crusader for Prohibition and narcotics control, a Progressive, and a champion of other causes, Richmond Pearson Hobson won the admiration of many as a devoted family member and friend.

His never-wavering love for his wife, Grizelda, has been illustrated numerous times on these pages. Several years after her husband's death, Grizelda commented about her youthful appearance: "People always say to me, 'Mrs. Hobson, how young you look! How is it?' After some years deprived of [my husband's] companionship, I am confident that my 32 years with him are the reason for my 'looking young' and feeling young as well.

"The vibrations of his glorious spirit still encompass me, and I still live with the positive assurance that if we but try to do our part, we are protected by powers beyond our feeble finite understanding."

Typical of Hobson's sentiments, as maudlin as they might seem to readers, was a letter he sent to Grizelda from Washington, as he awaited news of his Admiralty and pension: "It is 29 years now that your little hand has been resting in mine. Of course, we have had some trials, but they have been wonderful years all the same, and I think each year is happier than the preceding, and the happiest are still in store. I love you, my adorable little wife."

Despite a very filled schedule during the Congressional years and after, the Admiral was always close to his children. In 1941,

Lucia Hobson Stokes recalled some of her childhood experiences which are presented in her mother's *Memoirs*: "I remember so well a trip to Bear Mountain [in upstate New York] when we were very small. Daddy produced a pocketful of strong rubberbands, cut forks from low-branched trees, and showed us how to make sturdy sling shots. Our ammunition was plentiful—the large acorns we found strewn on the ground. We spent many hours making the shooting sling shots.

"Later we progressed to hickory bows and feather-tipped arrows. We tracked Indians in forests. We made green cloth scabbards which we carried across our shoulders and filled with hand-made arrows. How much more joy we had ... . Making our own toys [was] much more meaningful than those of the modern child with his myriad of bought playthings."

The Hobson children got their greatest "thrills" from the out-of-door exhibitions that Dad organized. "Dad always fascinated and thrilled all the children of the neighborhood," writes Lucia, "and our house was generally headquarters for every Tom, Dick, and Harry for miles around."

Dad Hobson was a wonderful teacher, raved Lucia. For example, he was a champion fencer at Annapolis, and Lucia was anxious to learn. "Every morning before breakfast and the dash to school," related Lucia, "he and I could be seen advancing and retreating with much flashing of steel blades up and down the driveway to the garage. "

From fencing they went on to shooting. "We all admired good marksmanship," continued Lucia, "and were allowed to rig up a target and practice with a .22 in the garden."

Along with sharpening skills, Hobson sought to instill the proper values. While shooting was fine, remembered Lucia, "It was considered, however, cruel and not really sporting to shoot anything that was not needed for food, as for example, on real camping trips, or to catch fish that were not eaten."

Consideration for others, whether animals or humans, were prime lessons for the Hobson children. We learned at a very early age," said Lucia, "to care for our pets without the usual unintentional mauling and harm that children perpetrate on animals. It was a matter of great pride with us to excel in the care of our pets and to make life as pleasant for them as we knew how—this [we learned] at six or eight years of age."

The first lesson in generosity, Lucia remembered, occurred during Christmas in Washington, when she was three or four. Lucia and her brothers all pleaded to own the decorated Santa at the top of the tree. The boys were invited upstairs for a conference with Dad. When they emerged, together they presented the Santa to Sister.

"[Dad was] ready for a tumble and a rough time with my brothers [as they got older]," narrated Lucia, "and their feeling of real comradeship with him did not in any way lessen his stature in our eyes as a great man and 'the greatest sport of all,' for whom we all had the most profound respect, and in whom we had the greatest confidence, always sure of real understanding.

"The boys always called him 'The Old Sport,' which was the greatest compliment they could pay him. The two boys and their Dad always started the day together with setting-up exercises, heavy dumb bell lifting, boxing bouts and cold showers. Wrestling was popular too and Daddy was ready for them all. It was hard on the furniture but great fun for the boys."

As they grew older, and the family was in Los Angeles, the boys went with their Dad on camping trips into the High Sierras.

The three children, said Grizelda, "were in the most interesting stages of development." Despite the extensive lecture tours and regular trips to New York with his narcotic control organizations, there was a daily exchange of letters between father and children and from each child to him.

"When the day of his homecoming was at hand, there was great excitement and joy in the household. Each child had been waiting his coming to consult him as to some personal project. Lucia's plans were always how she could circumvent the fact of having too slender a bank account to meet the necessary expenditures for Mother's birthday, or an Easter egg party or Christmas. She always consulted Dad as to these details, and he, in turn, would dig down into his pockets for the 'coin of the realm.'

"One can well understand the real companionship that existed between such a father and his children and their admiration and love for him."

George Hobson, the only surviving child, now in his 80s, lives in Falls Church, Virginia. He still has a vivid recall of an incident that happened when he had turned on a street fire alarm and several fire engines answered. Sheepishly, George had gone home and informed his father of every detail.

Father and son conferred solemnly, George recalled. Dad accompanied son to the City Fire Chief and to the City Police Chief. George did all the talking and apologizing. "When the Police Chief meted out my punishment as suggested by Dad, I had to pay a court martial fine of $5 to Dad to be worked off at 15 cents an hour or 33 1/2 hours. But parole was possible after 11 hours!"

George was also taught the value of responsibility through a series of contracts drawn up between his father and him. George was raising animals in the backyard and, in order to increase their stock, he signed a number of contracts with his dad, one of which is reproduced in the *Memoirs*. In consideration of $15, Dad promised to deliver to George 17 pullets and one rooster, white leghorns. George agreed "at his own expense diligently to operate this bunch of birds for profit" in which Dad and son shared.

Much of the responsibility was left with George, who, according to the contract, "shall decide on the methods and details of operations whether to have the fowls lay, set, or be marketed ... and report to Dad weekly upon his operations and to keep a careful record of all proceeds from the sales, eggs, chicks, broilers, or grown birds."

The contracts were signed by both parties and witnessed by Mother Hobson. Contracts were often changed, in which case they were designated "revoked" or "superseded."

George also reminisced about a very anxiety-ridden contract concerning the purchase of a motorcycle. The agreement was designated as a "Solemn Contract," and Mother Hobson recorded the wording in the *Memoirs*: "Dad agrees to finance a used motorcycle, hereby designated as 'Cleveland,' for George, under conditions to be mutually agreed upon, and George agrees to abstain entirely from tobacco in any form, from alcoholic drinks of all kinds, from dope and from gambling as long as he lives."

Although times were more difficult after the Stock Market crash of 1929, when the Hobsons moved from Los Angeles, but their close family life did not suffer. "After doing his full part," said a grateful Grizelda Hobson, "he never let the barrier down to *fear*— thus it always turned out that he attracted whatever he wished. It was unfailing. And, too, those hours, which to come, might have been very dark ones, to him, and to us who trusted and loved him, they were stepping stones along the way to further development.

"Those evenings, all together around the fire, we lived rarely happy hours, never to be forgotten."

Helping Friends and Comrades—Looking Back . . . 1898-1937

Before, during, and after his terms in Congress, Hobson remained faithful to his friends and former comrades. In particular, Hobson maintained a strong friendship with Sumner Kitelle, his one faithful ally who never deserted him during his difficult days at Annapolis.

The war hero also kept in close contact with his seven "*Merrimac* men" and their families. Although they advanced in life, with Naval promotions and honors, they still carried emotional scars following the long hours in the water before their surrender and subsequent imprisonment. The gracious treatment Hobson received from the Spaniards was not accorded to the seven other captives.

No one fared as badly as Francis Kelly. Luckless Kelly, as he became known, had been shell-shocked when he emerged from the coal bunker of the old collier. Evidently, the effects were long-lasting, Years passed without news of Kelly. One day Hobson learned that Kelly was in the middle of the ocean, headed for Europe on a merchant vessel. "Realizing in a dazed sort of phasia that he would be carried as a 'deserter' on the records of the Navy," Grizelda Hobson recorded in her *Memoirs*, "[Kelly] felt so mortified that he wandered all over the earth, for twenty years. Finally, Richmond found his whereabouts, long after the World War, in which he had served, and promptly undertook to have a bill introduced and passed to clear Kelly's name."

Hobson helped change Kelly's luck, with an honorable discharge and reenlistment in the Navy as a machinist's mate, with retirement pay of that rating. While in despair, Kelly had lost his Medal of Honor. A new one was given him, "and his name went down in honor, as it should," wrote Grizelda Hobson.

Daniel Montague, the *Merrimac*'s chief boatswain, did not endure the continued misfortune of Kelly, but he developed a pernicious anemia and by 1909 he lay dying in a Baltimore Naval hospital. Then Congressman, Hobson, arranged for blood transfusions and for all arrangements so his former mate could cling to life as long as possible. As Montague was succumbing to the disease, he asked to see his former commander, and Hobson rushed to Baltimore from Capitol Hill. Montague rallied for a few days and told his wife how kind Richmond and Grizelda had been to him. He and Hobson had a final talk as his life ebbed away. After the boatswain died, Hobson arranged for Mrs. Montague to be granted a pension.

Hobson came to the aid of Kelly and Montague, as well as other friends, colleagues and constituents who needed services and favors. In 1910 Hobson received a letter from Naval officer G.P. Colvocaresses, then living in Litchfield, Connecticut. The Admiral had been Hobson's teacher at the Naval Academy.

Because of bureaucracy, Colvocaresses had been denied his commission as Rear Admiral on the retired list. Hobson saw to it that the enabling legislation was passed. In a letter of June 1911, the Admiral thanked Hobson for his "zeal and perseverance" on this matter: "You have that intimate knowledge of naval conditions and the delicate appreciation of esprit de corps that led you to sympathize with a feeling which perhaps is chiefly sentimental, but, nevertheless, is very dear to us who are no longer in active service."

EPILOGUE

As the public life of Hobson so often showed, the Alabaman had many detractors who loved nothing better than to attack him. And while Hobson did counterattack his enemies, it was always on a political, and not personal, level.

As Grizelda Hobson praises her husband, "Perhaps one of his most uplifting attributes was Richmond's habitual and never-varying good word for whomever was brought under discussion. Sometimes I would say, 'Richmond, won't you offer any criticism about him?' he would smile and reply gently, 'Give him time.'

"This trait became so fixed with him that I am confident now in looking back on it that it generated all about him a feeling of harmony and happiness, and that if it could be isolated and examined, this attitude would even go far as to cause the blood to stir more vigorously, to make everyone around him more peaceful, more content."

As a Progressive Congressman, Hobson was an oft time controversial reformer and visionary legislator on such issues as the direct election of Senators, women's suffrage, the involvement of the Federal Government in education and social welfare, and racial relations.

When he articulated his international concerns, he was labeled a fanatic or lunatic. In truth, he was simply way ahead of his time. In 1895, three years before the *Merrimac* episode, he had written, "Not even the walls of China will be a serious obstacle in the way of Russia's march toward the circumference of three continents." Before the twentieth century ever opened, he had warned Americans of a war that "bids fair to involve all the great nations of Europe ... on a scale incomparably greater than any in the world's history."

As Arthur Postles wrote in "American Nostradamus," Hobson had persistently warned America about the Japanese threat, but even though his concerns came to realization at Pearl Harbor in much the way Hobson had predicted, the press continually lambasted him as "jingo," "enemy of mankind," and "war bird."

But it wasn't all negative. While he lived, Hobson was long idolized by a loyal army of Americans who revered him, not only for the causes that he advocated, but for the genuine spirit behind these causes.

Hobson always thought of himself as a fighter, a warrior engaged in Christian battle. Certainly, his battles for Prohibition and narcotics control, women's suffrage, and racial relations would fall under that banner. A letter Hobson's sister, Margaret, received from a writer named "Miss Nancie" four days after her brother died, spoke of his Christian focus as she recalled Hobson's early life. "It is as a Christian that I love best to think of your brother," she wrote, "for that he was a humble follower of our Saviour is known to all. When he was a lad, barely fourteen years of age, he went with Mr. Nelson and me one night to church in Newborn. He sat in the back seat and, I noticed, was very quiet.

"The next afternoon in conversation with your Aunt Sallie, he revealed that he had made the all-important decision and would be confirmed at his first opportunity. And as he was true to his Church and his Saviour [he did]."

In his crusade for Prohibition, Hobson announced, "I only ask God's Divine favor in proportion as my motives are pure, and my cause is right." But if his causes and crusades were as right as they seemed to be, why has America, for the most part, ignored their hero, Richmond Pearson Hobson?

Hobson's downfall came because he was a political maverick who refused to play 'the game'. He publicly challenged the integrity of the President of the United States and 'violated' loyalty to party and region. It is understandable why he never progressed beyond Congressman. Still, the relative obscurity of Richmond Pearson Hobson is difficult to explain.

While preparing this book, the author called the office of Alabama Governor Fob James in 1997, and no staffer, not even a close aide who was a history minor at the University of Alabama, had even heard of Hobson. What was even more shocking to the author was the lateness of his election to Alabama's Hall of Fame, which didn't take place until the 1990s, more than fifty years after his death and nearly one hundred years after his heroism at Santiago de Cuba.

In a recent issue of *The Alabama Review*, the lack of a comprehensive biography on the life of Hobson was lamented by Theodore Pearson, a retired teacher, superintendent of education, and past president of the Alabama Historical Association. Pearson observed that while the deserving biography has not [yet] been written, "contemporary historians have not [totally] overlooked this fascinating figure in Alabama history ... but they do not satisfy the need for a definitive biography of the Hero of Santiago."

Many Alabama publishers and educators do not seem to agree with Pearson. The University of Alabama Press turned down proposals for this biography of their native son, as submitted by the author and by the current curator of Magnolia Grove. And when the author contacted the former administrator of one of Alabama's colleges—who was being asked to write a foreword to this book in his current prestigious position at another Southern institute of higher education—the former administrator begged off after reading the book because Hobson had clashed with a major benefactor of the college he was previously associated with.

To accentuate Hobson's fleeting fame, Elting Morrison, in his "Dictionary of American Biography," linked the naval hero to others who had earned fame from a single heroic feat: "[Hobson] joined an excellent company of men like Steve Brodie and Charles A. Lindbergh, Jr., who likewise found themselves, by a single exploit, catapulted into prominence in a society that has never been able to define or assimilate the role very well."

Linkage with the Spirit of St. Louis is somewhat understandable, but who, the author of this book wondered, is this Steven Brodie author Morrison mentions? After looking him up, it was found that the "fame" of this man who Hobson was being compared to preceded the heroics of both the naval constructor and aviator Lindbergh. In 1896, Brodie earned celebrity status when—by his own account—he became the first to jump from the Brooklyn Bridge and live. On top of the fact that Brodie's supposed "feat" is in no way comparable to the national heroics of the

Merrimac, the *New York Times,* in Brodie's obituary of 1901, denied the feat ever happened and related how Brodie capitalized on the strength of this imaginary feat as a saloon owner in New York's Bowery and, later, as actor.

In short, Alabamans, other Americans, and time appear to have been quite unfair to Richmond Pearson Hobson. In 1943, Gerald White Johnson wrote, in *American Heroes and Hero Worship,* "Heroes are created by popular demand." America needed a hero during the Spanish-American War, and the dashing Alabaman was right there, at the right time and the right place. When the glow of adulation wore off and the decades passed, America no longer remembered his heroism, nor his service to the country. And because he was more interested in focusing on issues rather than playing 'the game,' his country forgot, too, his exceptional dedication and lifetime commitment to so many controversial issues that would in later years prove vital.

AFTERWORD

This latest contribution to historical literature by Dr. Harvey Rosenfeld is a continuation of this talented author's theme of focusing on impressive people whose fortunes run dry. History, we are always reminded, is written by the winners; Rosenfeld habitually breaks the mold by focusing on unfortunate characters who might be consigned to historical obscurity but who deserve to be remembered. As the founding and current editor of the renowned Holocaust remembrance newspaper, *Martyrdom and Resistance*, Rosenfeld has kept alive the memory—and the dignity and, in countless cases, heroics—of the millions of victims of Nazi genocide.

Another example is Rosenfeld's acclaimed biography, *Raoul Wallenberg: Angel of Rescue*. Wallenberg, the offspring of a celebrated Swedish aristocratic family, took it upon himself to travel to Nazi-era Hungary and, with diplomatic status, took 100,000 imperiled Jews into his protective custody and saved them from the relentless Nazi death machine. Wallenberg's unfortunate fate was to disappear as the Hitler regime collapsed, probably—and ironically—by attracting the suspicion of the invading Soviet authorities.

Indeed, the parallels between the Wallenberg story and the story contained in the preceding pages are remarkable. Both Wallenberg and Richmond Pearson Hobson, by any reasonable contemporary expectation, had the world on a string. Born into prominent families and favored with handsome appearance and gifted intelligence, both were essentially assured of affluence and influence. Hobson's naval adventures in the Spanish-American War gave him the kind of celebrity status that is normally reserved for the most popular movie stars, rock stars, and professional athletes. On the other hand, neither Wallenberg nor Hobson seemed to be particularly attracted to—and certainly were not satiated by—affluence, influence, and comfort. Instead, both were obsessed by their respective visions of the way the world ought to be, and they pledged, in Thomas Jefferson's immortal words, their lives, their fortunes, and their sacred honor in the service of those visions. In so doing, both gave up the opportunity to determine who would write history and how it would be written.

But for a handful of inquisitive historians like Rosenfeld, these two heroes might, in fact, be forgotten by an ungrateful posterity. Fortunately, Rosenfeld has produced another compelling account of "a good decent man, who saw wrong and tried to right it, saw suffering and tried to heal it, saw war and tried to stop it."[1] This is a political system where government officials used (and, increasingly, use) cautious "incremental" methods to develop public policy, and where elected officer-holders elevated (and, increasingly, elevate) their own reelection fortunes over the public interest: But Hobson sought instant, comprehensive, and beneficial change and repeatedly invested all of his political capital to achieve it. He committed himself to social causes and to the achievement of results that were so far beyhond the capacity of any one man that Don Quixote himself might have blushed upon observing Hobson's quests. Reversing the usual protocol of the power-hungry and the social climber, Congressman Hobson would show deferential civility to the most obscure and despised among his constituents, while he would display contempt toward the highest ranking government officials—up to and including the occupant of the White House himself. Having antagonized so many with his boldness, Hobson— the daring and all-but-suicidal perpetrator of the plan to block the Santiago harbor during the Spanish-American War and the two-term U.S. Representative from Alabama's Sixth District—was all but forgotten, even by the substantial majority of contemporary Alabamans. While this is not surprising, it is a most unfair outcome but one which, fortunately, Rosenfeld mends somewhat with this exceptional biography.

In the absence of tributes to those who have selected personal sacrifice in preference to self-aggrandizing acts, there will be less

---

[1] The reader will likely recognize this passage as an excerpt from U.S. Senator Edward M. Kennedy's moving eulogy at the 1968 funeral of his brother Robert.

sacrifice and more self-aggrandizement. Memorials like this book may send a wholesome signal that there is nobility in selfless acts, and that a record of acts of sacrificial heroism will be preserved as a model and ideal for future generations. This account of the life and times of the valiant Rear Admiral Richmond Pearson Hobson is at least as inspiring as it is astonishing. If it inspires people in all walks of life to imitate Hobson's altruism, Rosenfeld's efforts will be more than justified.

Barry D. Friedman, Ph.D.
Professor of Political Science
North Georgia College & State University
The Senior Military College of Georgia/Dahlonega

APPENDIX I:

A CHRONOLOGY OF THE LIFE OF RICHMOND PEARSON HOBSON

1870	Born at Greensboro, Alabama, to Probate Judge James Hobson and Sally Pearson Hobson
1877-82	Private education with Miss Kate Boardman
1882	Enrolled at South University in Greensboro
1885	Entered the U. S. Naval Academy at Annapolis
1889	Graduated from Annapolis, at age 18, with highest honors
1889	As Midshipman, assigned to a two-year of duty as Assistant Navigator aboard the flagship *U.S.S. Chicago*
1890-93	Studied at l'Ecole National Suprieure des Mines and l'Ecole d'Application du Genie Maritime in Paris
1893	Appointed Assistant Naval Constructor at U. S. Navy Department's Bureau of Construction and Repair
1895	Counsel at New York Navy Yard in Brooklyn
1896	Assigned as Officer in Charge of Construction at the New port News Navy Yard
1897	Organized and conducted postgraduate course at U. S. Naval Academy for officers in Construction Corps
1898	Reassigned to the *U.S.S. New York*, the flagship of the North Atlantic Squadron in February
1898	Planned and executed the sinking of the *U.S.S. Merrimac* on June 3, while attached to *U.S.S. New York*; taken prisoner by Spanish Admiral Cervera
1898	Exchanged for Spanish prisoners on July 5
1898	Met his future wife, Grizelda Hull, after momentous presentation at Metropolitan Opera House in New York on August 4
1898	Kissing craze begins in Long Beach, New York on August 5
1898	Promoted to Naval Constructor with rank of Captain on June 23; designated in charge of salvage operations of Spanish vessles wrecked or sunk during the battle of July 3, 1898
1899	Assigned to duty in Far East, directing reconstruction of three Spanish guboats damaged at Manila Bay

1900	Assigned to Cavite, Phillipine Islands, in charge of the Construction Department at Naval Station; developed eye problems, so assigned to Kure, Japan
1900	Returned to U. S.; near death bout with typhoid fever
1901	Assigned to Bureau of Construction and Repair, U. S. Navy Department, in Washington, D. C.
1902	Appointed Superintending Constructor at Crescent Shipyard, Elizabeth, NJ
1903	Resigned from Naval service in January
1905	Married Grizelda Houston Hull, May 25
1907-15	Served four terms as Congressman from Alabama's Sixth District
1914-21	On the lecture circuit campaigning for Prohibition
1921	Organized and served as General Secretary of the American Alcohol Education Association
1926-27	Organized the World Conference on Narcotic Associaton and the World Narcotic Defense Association
1933	Awarded Medal of Honor, belatedly, on April 29
1934	Reinstated into the Navy and promoted by Congress to Rear Admiral on June 4
1937	Died in New York City on May 17 and buried at Arlington National cemetery
1941	*U.S.S. Hobson* launched at the Navy Yard in Charleston, South Carolina
1943	Magnolia Grove dedicated as a State Shrine in Alabama in memory of Richmond Pearson Hobson on May 2

APPENDIX II:

THE HERITAGE OF MAGNOLIA GROVE

James Marcellus Hobson (April 29, 1840-January 31, 1905)
— married Sarah Pearson (February 24, 1843-January 17, 1904) on July 24, 1867
— purchased Magnolia Grove in 1879 for $3,000

Children of James Marcellus and Sarah Pearson Hobson:
Samuel Augustus Hobson, August 3, 1868–September 14, 1962
Richmond Pearson Hobson, August 17, 1870–March 17, 1937
— married Gizelda Hull of Tuxedo Park, NY,
Joseph Morehead Hobson, November 25, 1872–May 6, 1972 1874
Sarah Ann Pearson, July 10, 1874–October 21, 1953
James Marcellus Hobson, Jr., December 17, 1876–December 6, 1940
Florence Pearson Hobson Morrison, October 27, 1878–November 29, 1972
— married James Morrison of Hammond, LA
Margaret Williams Hobson, February 7, 1884–December 21, 1979.

APPENDIX III:
SPEECHES

Women's Right to Vote
U.S. House of Representatves
January 13, 1915

If on any reasonable qualification requirement the vote were denied women simply as it is denied, men would have nothing to say. What are the legitimate qualifications for the exercise of this, the inherent right of free men? It is not might and brute force; it is not physical strength. Some have said, because women do not carry arms they should not be allowed to vote. I answer, neither do men bear children; why should they be allowed to vote? Is the carrying of arms more vital than the bearing of children?

Show me any function that man renders to society and to the State that is more fundamental than women's function of bearing and rearing children and creating and maintaining the home. In the last analysis, the true line of demarcation for determining the qualifications for the franchise is the character. If any gentlemen will demonstrate to me scientifically that women has on the average a lower standard of character than man, I will not advocate the submission of this amendment. But there is no gentleman on this floor, however materialistic is his philosphy of life , who would dare to make such an assertion. On the contrary, it is known of all men, it is the uniform experience of criminal jurisprudence. It is on the records of the courts everywhere that woman on the whole and on the average has a very much higher standard of character than men.

Therefore, if either sex should be disqualified from the exercise of the franchise on the account of sex, it should be the male sex, and not the female. To discriminate against this citizen who has the highest qualifications is indefensible; it is fundamentally wrong.

Next after character comes the qualification of intelligence—educated intelligence. Proofs are overwhelming in the records of our schools— of the graduates from our high schools, of the teachers—showing that women are better educated than men. Women do not get their mental food daily from the headlines of of newspapers on crowded cars ... ; but those who sell standard books and edit standard magazines testify that woman is the reading sex of the race instead of man.

In the test of both intelligence—educated intelligence—and of character woman stands with higher qualifications than man. To deny her the right through the ballot to protect herself and her home and all that she holds dear because of her sex is absolutely indefensible. I understand why this has been so in the past. Governments have grown out of the military institutions of the past when making war was the chief function of the state. Naturally physical strength to bear arms—brute force—was the determining factor in government, as in war. It is natural, when the institution of suffrage was evolved, that it should have been confined to men. But when justification can be shown for continuing this relic of barbarism into the present and future ages where the destroying principle of war is giving way to the conserving, building principle of peace, where the test for fitness to survive in men and in nations is the capacity and willingness to cooperate and to serve; when the greatest is to be the servant of all?

If we fail to vote for this resolution, we not only violate the inherent rights of the sisterhood of States, but we violate the inherent rights of man, dedicated by the principle of immaculate justice. . . .

I wish to lay down a fundamental proposition from which there is no escape. The permanent success of free institutions rests, and can rest, on no other foundation than the average standard of character behind the vote. When the average gets low in the multiplication of degenerate votes, the use of money—the danger of corruption—becomes increasingly menacing. By the use of money and corruption with degenerate votes, tyrants have overthrown the liberties of Rome and Greece, and unscrupulous monopolies are now menacing the liberties of Amerca in cities, in States, and in this Nation. They help create the growing degenerate vote and then supply the corruption money with which to buy these votes and deliver them to politicians and political parties that will do their bidding and leave the people helpless in their hands. If we should give the vote to women, we would of necessity raise the average standard of character and intelligence behind the vote and put this Nation and its institutions upon a sureer and more solid foundation. I do not overdraw this fundamental proposition when I say that in large measure the very perpetuity of our free institutions depends upon our taking some such measure as this to raise the average standard of character behind the vote.

Mr. Speaker, several times today I have been ashamed of my sex. Can anyone conceive of women saying such things as have been said here to-day apparently with gust and self-congratulations, things that show an utter materialistic view of life, where the relation of the sexes was regarded as one of lust, not of the spiritual relationship, of true inspiring love. For myself and the majority of my colleagues, I wish to repudiate this attitude. Man has an immortal soul. It is this spiritual part of man that gives dignity to human life above the life of the brute. In the differentiation of occupation, the woman in the homes, in the schools, in the churches, in the charities, in the tender ministries of hospitals and philanthropy, the women of the race have conserved and developed the spiritual nature of man. The great weakness of politics and government today is that they reflect largely, if not exclusively, the motive and activities of men who are engaged chiefly in business. I do not undervalue the importance of business and industry when I say this influence of government should be less exclusive. The great need of our day is to project woman's sphere, woman's activities, and woman's influence into government, so that questions affecting the home, the protection of the children, and the good morals of society would share with business the attention of public servants, the efforts and aims of public policy.

The only real effective way to accomplish this result is to give the ballot to woman. The effect on public servants is magical. Not two years ago, before equal suffrage was established in Illinois, members of the Illinois delegation in the House were not inclined to give any consideration even for the elemental rights of women, their right to police protection when peaceably parading the streets of Washinton being questioned on the floor of this House. The Illinois delegation is so docile it eats out of woman's hand.

Mr. Speaker, all government exists to promote the evolution and uplift of the Nation and the race. If women had the ballot, it would broaden her views and activities and make her better equipped in heredity to be the mother of man. At the same time it would project women's life more and more into the life of her husband, and not only make a better foundation for a true home but develop more the spiritual side of her husband. Our institutions need woman suffrage. The home needs woman suffrage. Woman needs woman suffrage. Man needs woman suffrage. Woman suffrage is now a crying need for the evolution of the race.... .

Racial Relations
House of Representatives
February 27, 1909

When these crimes were committed at Brownsville, the President of the United States could have ordered all officers and men to remain within barracks and could have avoided a Court of Inquiry, followed by a court martial, which, held on the spot without delay, would no doubt have established the guilt or innocence of all the men, and would have given a regular legal opportunity to every innocent man to establish the fact of his innocence. If, under duly administered oath, any man had refused to tell the whole truth or had been found to have concealed or abetted the guilty, he could have been punished accordingly. By such a regular and legal procedure, the guilty, all of them or part of them, at least, could have been brought to full punishment at the scene of their hideous crime, fulfilling the ends of justice. But the President did not proceed in this regular, legal way. He scattered the men, guilty and innocent alike, to the four winds and thus prevented the innocent from establishing their innocence. These men never had a chance to appear before a Court of Inquiry; never before a court martial; have never been under oath. This bill provides the least that can now be done for the cause of justice.

Mr. Speaker, I saw black men carrying our flag on San Juan Hill; I have seen them before Manila. A black man took my father, wounded, from the field of Chancellorsville. Black men remained on my grandfather's plantation after the proclamation of emancipation and took care of my mother and grandmother. The white man is supreme in this country; he will remain supreme. That makes it only the more sacred that he should give absolute justice to the black man who is in our midst. I submit it to the conscience of my colleagues. This ought not to be made a party measure. We are standing here on the field of eternal justice, where all men are the same. It is justice that links man to the Divine. Whether the heavens fall or the earth melt away, while we live let us be just.

Naval Supremacy
"An Adequate Navy and the Open-Door Policy"
January 29, 1915

The Rights of Peace Versus the Rights of War .... A very illuminating example is now seen of the encroachments of war upon the rights of nations at peace simply and solely because of their preponderance of power over the latter. America's woeful lack of preparation is the fundamental reason for the reversal of the ordinary progress of humanity, the contraction of the rights of peace before the encroachment of the so-called rights of war, based solely upon the preponderance of brute force. It is no exaggeration to say that the condition of preparation for national defense in America is now and will remain the largest determining factor in the preservation of our own peace and the establishment and extension of peace throughout the world.

America's War Policies: A nation's position among the nations of the world and its own world policies are the foundation considerations for working out a policy of national defense.

Danger of Attack in the Atlantic: We have 5,300 miles of Atlantic coast line, and bays and harbors and navigable rivers leading up to the same, upon which are located, within 15 miles of water, the homes of 15,000,000 American citizens and over seventeen billions of American property. On the Gulf coast, we have the homes of nearly 2,000,000 citizens and over eight hundred millions of property; on the Great Lakes, the homes of about 8,000,000 citizens, with about seven and a half billions of property; in the great Mississippi Valley, 11,500,000 citizens and nearly nine billions of property. In addition to our mainland exposure, we must protect Cuba, Puerto Rico, and the Panama Canal.

Danger of Attack in the Pacific: In the Pacific Coast States, the homes of nearly 2,000,000 citizens are exposed, with nearly three billions of property. In addition to the mainland, we have the great treasure house of Alaska, the great interior and islands of Hawaii, together with the Philippine Islands, and also the Panama Canal.

Must Always Protect the Filipinos: Whatever may be our political relations with the Philippine Islands, America will also protect the Filipinos, as she protects the Cubans, against military aggression.

Inadequacy and Impossibility of Defense by Land Forces: As compared with the great nations, our regular standing Army may be considered a negligible quantity. Likewise our militia and reserve. The same may be said of coast fortifications, which are open to capture from the rear because of the lack of a mobile army for their defense. Therefore an enemy in control of the sea could occupy Cuba, Puerto Rico, and Panama, in the Atlantic; Alaska, Hawaii, Guam, and the Philippine Islands in the Pacific, all with little predictable resistance in case of attack in force. In addition to definite occupation of this outlying terriotory, an enemy could raid our mainland caosts in force, occupy and levy upon our great cities without any chance whatever of the effective resistance until long after they could retire with their booty, after destroying our navy yards, shipbuilding yards, arsenals, shipping, and public works. It is vain to imagine that our cities would be spared after the experience of cities abroad. It is likewise vain to imagine that the meager land forces available could make any serious resistance.

America Must Control the Sea: In order to realize the first policy, namely that of security of our vital interests against violence in accord with the dictates of self-preservation, there is no other recourse. America must control the sea in the Atlantic, and thereby keep the European armies in Europe, and must control the sea in the Pacific, to keep the Asiatic armies in Asia; and since these oceans are so far apart and since nations that are liable to attack us in Europe and Asia are liable to establish and have already established alliances, offensive and defensive, we must control the sea in both oceans at the same time.

Protection of Our Commerce and Foreign Markets: America is rapidly becoming a great industrial nation, competing for the markets of the word. The jealousy of industrial nations in this competition is illustrated by the attitude of Great Britain toward Germany before the war. America need not hope to have a fair chancce to gain supremacy in world commerce any more than Germany if she has no more formidable naval strength than Germany had. The alacrity with which our rights as a neutral are invaded and the quickness with which every means in sought to hamper the growth of our merchant marine at the present time clearly show that neither when Europe is at war or at peace will our commercial and industrial expansion over seas be permitted normal and legitimate course unless we have control of the sea. Thus control of the sea must be on the foundation for the security of our property rights on land and on sea.

Menace to Our Institutions: Our Government was established and will have to be maintained in the face of antagonistic institutions of the Old World. Believing as we do in the principle of the rights of self-government and of equality of opportunity, no European and Asiatic monarchy has yet acknowledged the right of sovereign local self-government as vested in our industrial States. There have been 13 cases in our country's history where the subjects of foreign powers have been maltreated in individual States; in 11 cases these foreign subjects suffered violence. The foreign Governments promptly made demands upon our central Government to interfere, and our central Government informed them with regret that it could not interfere. In most cases an indemnity was afterwards made as a matter of humanity but not as a matter of law. In one recent case a foreign Government questioned the right of a State to regulate its own school system, and in another case now pending it challenges the right of a State to determine the question of tenure of lands and property rights. It is not necessary to cite the dangers involved in this case on account of the race question. This, for the security of our institutions as for the security of our homes, our property rights on land and on sea demand that America should control the sea.

The Cause of Justice and Right: In world relations under the dictates of self-preservation the game should be played according to the rules of justice and of right, not the rules of brute force and might. The ascendancy of right is in line with the law of evolution. The progressive development of the higher and nobler faculties of men and of nations. Indeed, cooperation and service should supplant the destroying principle in the relationship of nations as in men. America has already historically become the champion of the right of the weak against encroachments of the might of the strong.

The Monroe Doctrine: Though the Monroe Doctrine may have been conceived with the idea of self-protection for the United States, and though from time to time its justification is based upon considerations of vital interest, nevertheless the spirit of the Monroe Doctrine is our championship of the rights of the weak against the oppressions of the strong and our championship of the principle that among all strong and weak alike there shall be equality of opportunity, fair chance, and no favor. This doctrine cuts off the Western Hemsiphere from the extension of colonial policies of Europe and Asia. It is natural and inevitable that the security of this policy rests, and can permanently rest alone upon the control of the sea ... .

Germany and Venezuela: Germany hoisted her flag over the courthouses of Venezuela against the expressed wishes of America, President Roosevelt assembled our whole fleet at Guantanamo, then requested Germany to haul down her flag. The request was complied with.

Mexico After the European War: When Europe is relieved of the absorbing activities of the great war, what will likely be the attitude of the victorious nation toward Mexico, especially in the event that the allies are victorious and British financial interests are greatly disturbed and injured by Mexican disorder? No one can tell when or in what way the issue may arise, but certain it is that America will be called on to surrender the Monroe Doctrine unless she is able to defend it, and since the countries involved, Mexico and Central and South America, are over the seas this defense will hinge absolutely upon our Navy, whether it is powerful enough to control the sea.

Canada and the Monroe Doctrine: A new complication of the Monroe Doctrine has arisen in the participation of Canada in the European war. If Germany were victorious and gained control of the sea, she would probably send an expeditionary force against the British colonies. In the event of such a force conquering Canada, question would arise whether Germany following her natural inclination to remain should be allowed by the United States to establish a Germany colony on our borders. In case German and American policies should conflict, the question of peace and war—the question of the integrity of the Monroe Doctrine—would hang upon the strength of our Navy. If we want peace with the Monroe Doctrine, we must control the sea.

The Open-Door Policy in China: Amerca has been the champion of the open-door policy in China, beneath which lies essentially the same principle underlying the Monroe Doctrine, namely justice to the weak and equal opportunity to all; respect for the integrity of China and equal opportunity for all nations in their competition for the trade of China.

Russian encroachments through Manchuria continued until Port Arthur was occupied. America promptly protested and practically called on Russia to retire. We had no strong fleet and no military strength behind the fleet we had. Russia ignored our demand and remained and from her remaining came the war between Russia and Japan. Great Britain has shown scarcely more consideration for the integrity of China than Russia. She seized Hongkong after imposing her opium from India upon the unwilling Chinese by war. She has since extended the territory first seized in the mainland in the Kaloon extension. She made a second war on China to further impose opium upon her people, and later seized Wei-hai-wei, though it appears that since the Japanese alliance she has dismantled this station. Germany has shown a similar attitude toward China, especially when she seized Kiaochow and fortified the harbor of Tsing Tau.

Japan and the Open-Door Policy: Japan has shown less regard than all the other nations for the integrity of China. She has annexed Korea, part of the Liao Tung Peninsula with Port Arthur; she has practically annexed southern Manchuria, and now has seized Kiaochow. She went to war against Russia, ostensibly to get Russia out of Port Arthur and out of Chinese territory, but when Russia withdrew Japan remained and never made any pretense of returning the Chinese territory to China. The probabilities amount to almost a certainty that having gone to war with Germany ostensibly to remove Germany from its encroachment upon China, Japan now in Germany's place will never dream of retiring herself.

Japan's Menace to China: Count Okuma, prime minister of Japan, in an article in the *Shin Nippon*, used these words referring to the struggle for existence: "We must be careful to keep this point in mind and prepare ourselves with power to meet the struggle for existence. The people who can not meet the struggle will be crushed ... .

"Thus, those who are superior will govern those who are inferior. I believe within two or three centuries the world will have a few great governing countries and others will be governed by them—will pay homage to the mighty. . . .

"Woe to the nations which are governed. We should now on prepare ourselves to become a governing nation."

These statements are significant in light of the recent dispatches from Japan stating in effect that Japan had practically sent an ultimatum to China because China had naturally ordered the discontinuation of the war zone around Kiao Chao, since war there had ceased, and a later dispatch stating that Japan had taken up negotiations with Peking for the purpose of "determining the development policies of China."

<u>Japan and America</u>: In the same article referred to above, Count Okuma stated: "Although we hold Germany as our enemy, yet we do not forget the part played by Germany ... . In future as in the past we will continue to pay our respect to German knowledge and scientific genius, but we must at all costs fight against the Kaiser's spirit of conquest until we shall have crushed it ... . Our attitude toward the American people will be the same; we shall attack any mistaken ideas or policies without mercy. We do not, of course, hate the individuals. The time has now come when humanity should awaken. The present war has brought about the opportunity. We should free ourselves from the mistaken racial competition arising from prejudice."

<u>Anti-American Propaganda in Japan</u>: The cosmopolitan press and the dispatches to the foreign press from Japan continue more or less the same kind of smooth generalities regarding the Japanese and American relations, but in the vernacular press all kinds of disquieting and misleading rumors are energetically circulated, all tending to arouse enmity and hatred among the Japanese populace, ending in the conviction that war with the United States is inevitable. A similar propaganda against Russia preceded the Russo-Japanese War. Among the rumors and misrepresentations may be mentioned the following: that the United States had territorial ambitions in the Far East and proposed to seize a naval station on the continent of Asia; that the United States is seeking to undermine Japanese commerce and the like. It is authentically reported that when the Japanese troops were mobilized for the expedition against Kiao Chao the soldiers for a long time thought they were starting for war against America.

<u>Another Warning</u>: My warnings to my countrymen as to the dangers in the Pacific Ocean arising from our lack of defensive preparations have been little heeded, and in some quarters have even been ridiculed.

Officers high in the councils of our Government have joined in the scoffing when they themselves knew that code messages had been sent to commandants of our navy yards to be prepared to put their stations on a war basis upon short notice and that our troops in the Philippines protecting the harbor of Manila had slept at thier guns for weeks with the harbor mined hourly expecting an attack by the Japanese fleet. I renew my warning. The only security for permanent peace in the Pacific Ocean is our unquestioned control of the sea in that ocean.

The Pacific Ocean Cleared of American Battleships: When one battleship fleet started around the world I endeavored to have it stopped and remain in the Pacific Ocean. The impression I received led to the firm conviction which I have not since changed, that our fleet was allowed to go to the Pacific Ocean. The impression I received led me to the firm conviction which I have not since changed, that our fleet was allowed to go to the Pacific Ocean by Japan only upon our assurance that it would be out of that ocean by a fixed date. I have felt for some time that our battleship fleet will never go to the Pacific Ocean by Japan only upon our assurance that America would speedily retire from the Philippine Islands. I am further convinced that our first inquiry as to the intentions of Japan in seizing Kiao Chao and the islands in the Pacific Ocean will not be followed up, at least by this administration, and that Japan, as a price of peace, will be given a free hand in China with the prospect of the complete overthrow of the open-door policy, leaving China to its fate to become "governed" nation, while the commerce of America, which in cotton goods fell off over twenty millions in Manchuria after Japanese occupation, will be at the mercy of a competitor, while the complete overthrow of the balance of power in the Pacific Ocean would lead to the inevitable result, war.

The Gravity of the Anglo-Japance Alliance: In determining the movements of our battleship fleet we can not escape leaving one ocean undefeated. We may rest assured that in our negotiations with England that country has in mind both the Japanese Navy and the Japanese Army would be available for cooperation should war result, while in our negotiations with Japan that country will bear in mind that the British fleet or part of it, and possibly the forces of other allies will be available in the Atlantic to prevent our battle fleet from going to the Pacific, insuring Japanese control of the sea and the availability of her overpowering army already on a war footing.

The brief scan of America's policies, the Monroe Doctrine and the open-door policy, based upon the principle of right and justice like America's policies upon the necessity of self-preservation , both meet in the same inevitable conclusion. We must control the sea in the Atlantic and in the Pacific, both at the same time.

Cooperation and Service: In the relations of nations to each other as in the relations of individuals with each other there should not only be justice and right but also cooperation and service, generosity, mercy, charity, good will, brotherhood.

Militarism Versus Industrialism: Two forms of civilization are passing through a test of survival—militarism, with its concurrent institutions, based on monarchy, and a privileged hierarchy of royalty and nobility and bureaucracy, and the system of industrialism, based upon productiveness with institutions free from privilege. America is the Nation that embodies industrialism; Japan and Asia and the great military nations in Europe embody the system of militarism. In a fair competition in times of peace militarism must go down, but industrialism unprepared would as inevitably fall in war. In the interest of humanity, that lies upon the survival of industrialism, America with her vast resources make adequate preparations, taking care always to safeguard her own people against the spirit of militarism.

America the Merciful and the Generous: When Great Britain, France, the Netherlands, and the United States jointly bombarded Shiminosiki and exacted $3,000,000 indemnity from the Japanese Goverment for having closed the straits at that point, the other nations took their equal shares and expended them. America's share was duly received but ere long by a unanimous vote of the American Congress, every dollar was returned to the Japanese Government.

In the Boxer disturbances, the allied nations invading China levied huge indemnities against America's pleading and allotted America $12,000, by a unanimous vote of the American Congress, we returned the last dollar to the Chinese Government.

When our blood and treasure had been freely poured out in Cuba and the world expected us to remain and hold Cuba as a fruit of conquest and a source of revenue, America astonished the whole world by voluntarily giving Cuba her independence. What nation on earth would have been so patient, so long suffering in Mexico as have been the American people?

America the Peacemaker: America is the one great Nation that covets no territory of any other nation. America is the one great Nation that has no enemies. America is the one great Nation that would recoil at the very thought of becoming a "governing" nation. In America, Jews and Gentiles have become reconciled, Protestants and Catholics. America is a blood kinsman of the Anglo-Saxons, of the Germans, of the Frenchmen, of the Austro-Hungarian, of the Italian, of the Russian, the common friend of Celt, Slav, Tenton, Latin. America opened up Japan with the blessing of an elder brother. Shall this great nation of destiny be impotent when it raises its voice for the establishment of such policies as the Monroe Doctrine, the open-door policy, such principles as justice and equal opportunity and rights of the weak? Shall America be impotent when she seeks to restrain the cruel march of war and permit the operation of great organic forces of commerce and industry, of education, the moral and religious forces of the world, to work out the overthrow of war and the ultimate establishment of the era of peace on earth, good will to men?

The Rights of Neutrals Versus the Rights of Belligerents: The swift events are daily bringing into contrast the so-called rights of belligerents and their restraint upon the inherent rights of neutrals. America is the only great nation in the world logically constituted the champion of the latter. The so-called rights of belligerents are founded solely upon might. For instance, Great Britain maintains that she has the right to negotiate unlimited credits and purchase unlimited amounts of war material in America and denies the right of Germany to sell ships to America from which a credit might be derived that, when derived, could not be used to supply war materials. Our Secretary of State takes the position that we ought to be parties to the proposition of giving great military aid to Great Britain and her allies and withholding even commercial aid to Germany, because the British and allied fleets are stronger in might than the Germans and have control of the sea.

A statement was made some time back emanating from the White House, that our Government in bona fide transactions and our citzens in similar transactions could purchase vessels where they pleased, but now we hear no murmur of protest when Great Britain informs us that a ship purchased in good faith from Germany by an American citizen will not be allowed to carry on peaceful commerce over the high seas. Every arbitrary action of the British government in extending the list of contraband and the exercise of search and seizure represents an encroachment for all future time, at least as far as precedents go upon the sphere of neutral rights, simply because the combination of the allies represnts so much power upon the high seas, the limited progress already made in the rights of peace must be turned back. America must fold her hands while her own opportunities for commercial expansion are limited and the evolution of the rights of neutrals, the rights of peace, is set back.

No Chronic Belligerent Should Henceforth Be Allowed Control of the Sea: Great Britain has undertaken for a long time to maintain power upon the sea greater than that of any two nations—in fact, more than double that of any other nation—so that the high seas are practically under the control of a partisan. In the interest of humanity at large and the orderly evolution of peace and right, and especially the development of the rights of neutrals, mimimizing and localizing disruption of war demand that the scepter of the seas shall pass from the hands of Great Britain and hereafter rest in the hands of the great peaceful kinsman of all nations, the United States.

America's Defense Policies: Having reviewed American war policies, we can now proceed to establish our defense policies.

The elements of national defense may be divided into two classes— national resources and national preparations.

The trend of the times is to increase the already preponderant advantages of preparations as compared to potential resources. When Prussia struck Austria in 1866, the war was over in a few months. When Germany struck France in 1870, the same result followed. When Japan struck Russia, the same. In the great world war now raging both factors may be brought into the field, because both sides had ample preparations to insure having a time element sufficient to develop and bring to bear their resources. America's preparations are so utterly inadequate that the prospects are that the blow struck would seriously endanger our chances of being able to bring our resources to bear at all. It is estimated that at least three years would be necessary to create a model army in America, prepared to cope with modern armies abroad, which are kept ready to move on a moment's notice, with transportation facilities sufficient to cross the ocean in a few weeks. Our mobile army being so small and so widely scattered and our militia in the same condition, with the complete absence of any reserve, America must rely on her naval force to insure the time element in which to bring to bear our great resourcs. Fortunately, from our geographical position over seas from the great military nations, naval forces sufficiently powerful can insure us a security greater even than England has enjoyed for hundreds of years, enabling her to escape the necessity of conscription and permitting her to evolve liberal institutions.

Naval Power Versus Military Power: Military power involves large numbers of men organized into armies; naval power consists chiefly in property made up of ships. A dreadnaught today, with its crew of 1,000 men, is ordinarily estimated to be more than equivalent in power to an army corps of more than 40,000 men. Take Germany's case today. Twenty additional dreadnaughts would give her control of the seas and at least cut off the 2,000,000 men England is preparing to place on the Continent drawn from the British Isles and the colonies of the British Empire.

Germany would have access to the resources of the whole world, while England could be starved into submission in a few months. The additional 20 dreadnaughts would be worth to Germany more than a billion of dollars, more than millons of men. It would mean sure victory; in fact, it would have prevented the participation of Great Britain in the war. It would have determined the course of history. A few more battleships in our Navy before the war with Spain would have insured control of the sea without the necessity of the test of war, and would have saved the cost of hundreds upon hundreds of millions of dollars entailed by the war itself. Defense by naval power, therefore, does not involve miliary activities of the people and what few people there are involved are far away from the mass of the people themselves. Thus, there is no tendency to militarism. On the contrary when people can secure their defense by naval power, then industrial activities are uppermost, and their civilization follows the kines of industrialism instead of militarism. It is this great fact in history that has caused all the Republics of the world to be built on naval power. This will account for the fact that it is such countries where defense comes through naval power that free institutions have developed most, as in the case of England. The evolution of the world has been away from militarism and toward an industrial civilization, so the history of the world has persistently hung upon the course of sea power, and the great crises, the great decisive battles, have really been naval and not military.

... The English civilization of Elizabeth overcame the Spanish civilization of Philip II because of the destruction of the Spanish Armada. England came through the Napoleonic wars supreme as against Napoleon because Napoleon could not cross the English Channel. England at Waterloo fought for victory; England at Trafalgar for existence. Anglo-Saxons are associated with the most advanced civilizations in the world, with the most advanced institution of human liberty, because the Anglo-Saxon has held naval supremacy for a thousand years and has not been subjected to military conscription. The future of the world, like the past, is going to be determined by the control of the sea. Industrial nations sufficiently farsighted to make naval preparations to insure their bringing to bear their great resources are the ones that are going to survive as against the nations that continually maintain great armies.

Our Policy for Land Forces: The fact that defense through naval forces where available is more advantageous than defense through land forces does not nullify the importance of the latter nor the necessity of clearly establishing a policy for land forces.

America a Nonmilitary Country: We are a nonmilitary country, and our very civilization demands for its perpetuation that we remain a nonmilitary country. Therefore we can not have and should not have large standing armies, maintained under conscription like the military nations of the world. Our relatively small standing army therefore must be maintained in the highest state of efficiency, and must be kept at such station as to permit of rapid concentration at our vital points of exposure.

Present Policy Wasteful and Inefficient: The policy of maintaining small detachments in scores of points widely scattered is absolutely contrary to such a policy, since it prevents practice in large units and prevents efficiency, and makes rapid concentration an impossibility, while the cost per soldier is increased beyond reasonable limits. There should be two main points on the Atlantic, one on the Gulf, two on the Pacific. Most of the others should be abandoned.

Having such a small standing army increases the importance of maintaining a comparatively large militia and military reserve force.

Military Pay Bill a Necessity: Congress should speedily take measures to encourage the States and the citizenship to develop in numbers and efficiency the National Guard. This, of course, can not be done without the Federal Government's sharing a reasonable amount of the expense necessary. A comprehensive militia pay bill insuring not only expansion but increased regulation and efficiency of the militia is a military necessity.

A Great Citizenry Reserve Force Must Be Developed: We should adopt national policies to encourage the average citizen to secure that minimum amount of military training necessary for a speedy development of the citizen into a good soldier after war comes. This will involve the Federal Government's cooperation in the educational policies of the Nation, and a comprehensive plan for financial aid should be established to apply to all high schools and colleges and even to the seventh and eighth grades in the graded schools. The cost in equipment would, of course, be large, since the Federal Government, in all probability will find it necessary to provide the essentials, but the success of the Boy Scout movement shows that cooperation on the part of the people and the boys would greatly reduce the total cost from what would naturally be the estimate.

Ex-Soldiers and Officers: A definite military reserve should be maintained in such a way as to keep together the bulk of discharged soldiers and collegss, high schools together with the militia and reserve, should be conducted with a special view to preparing a large contingent of officers ready for taking charge of the great volunteer armies in time of war.

Coordination: Our land forces and our policies controlling same should be determined in coordination with our naval forces and the policies controlling the same. The two are essentially supplemental, in proportion as the land forces are weak so the naval forces must be strong ... . It is clear, however, that before any real permanent efficiency and economy can be realized in our natonal defense, we must create an agency competent to investigate the whole question of national defense, whose duty it would be to work out and recommend to the Government a comprehensive policy.

The Council of National Defense Bill: For six years such a measure has been before Congress in the form of a bill to establish a council of national defense. This bill has been twice favorably reported by the Naval Committee of the House. It has been incorporated in the Democratic platform of Baltimore. In the hearings before the Naval Committee Gen. Wotherspoon, president of the Army War College, made the significant statement that under the operation of such a council the efficiency of the Army could be trebled while the expense could be cut in half. Similar testimony was given by other officers in the Army and Navy, and favorable action has been urged by the late President of the United States and by the last four Secretaries of War and by the late Secretary of the Navy. Such a council would only have advisory power, and could not possibly interfere with the jurisdiction of the legilsative or executive branches or with their independent operation. Upon the council would be found with the President the Secretary of State, the highest authority on our world policies; the Secretary of War and the Secretary of the Navy, with their highest technical experts and advisers; along with the chairmen of the committees of the Senate and the House having cognizance of naval and military affairs, foreign relations, and the purse strings.

The President and Secretary of State the Greatest Obstacle of National Defense: The fact that the council of national defense is a plank in the Democratic platform seems to have no influence with the administration. This bill would long since have been a law but for the opposition of the President and the Secretary of State. This opposition to the most vital and fundamental measure; similar to measures that have been taken by all the other nations of the world, opposition that keeps America from making a start, constitutes the President and the Secretary of State the greatest obstacle of their country's defense.

It seems a singular irony that the movement for national prohibition likewise has found greatest opposition from the present administration, To thoughtful men these two questions are the most vital and the most fundamental before the Nation, one affecting the integrity of the Nation within and the other the security of the Nation without. It seems passing strange that measured by these two great causes, we find the highest official of the Nation is the greatest obstacle to progress.

The Country's Greatest Liability: It is far from me to question the patriotism and conscientious devotion of this eminent citizen. This only deepens the tragedy of the situation and the threatening effect of his influence in these two fields of public endeavor. I do not disparage the usefulness of his services in other lines and the beneficient educational influence his life had upon his country. These, again, only deepen the tragedy

Every citizen is entitled to his own appraisal of the relative importance of public questions. To me, however, the first question in importance before this Nation or any other nation is to make and keep the nation sober. The question of next importance before our Nation is to provide an adequate defense, so that as a people we may live in peace and security and work out our institutions at home without molestation and with the minimum disturbance when war exists in other lands, and so that we may without fear be to effectively champion the cause of the weak and the principles of right and justice in the Western Hemisphere, and even ultimately in the Eastern Hemisphere, thus insuring the survival of industrialism, bringing about the passing of militarism, causing war to steadily recede, so that at last peace can reign throughout the earth, free institutions can be developed in all lands, leading toward the ultimate goal of the brotherhood of man under the fatherhood of God.

Nothing is so much needed in this country as for the public to be appraised of the truth that really bears upon great public questions. If there were any chance of my being mistaken about the obstacles in the path of these two great lines of national progress, I would not raise my voice; but being in the heart of the public movements in both lines, I have felt only too heavily the power of the obstacles represented by the President. My conception of duty as a public official is to do the duty, whatever it may be, without flinching, though it be a "to his own hurt." It is only when the truth is fully known to our people that the real obstacles in the path of progress can be appreciated, and a beginning made toward ultimate realization of a great objective. If national prohibition and national defense are the greatest questions in America, as I believe them to be, then the President of the United States instead of being our greatest asset is our country's greatest liability.

I am fully aware, Mr. Chairman, what these words of mine mean, and the effect they will have in the minds of millions of partisans, particularly those who exalt party because party constitutes for them the ladder to climb the offices of preferment and eminence. There are some who place self above party and party above country, even without being conscious of their own subconscious classification. I look upon all parties as human agencies organized fundamentally to promote the public welfare. If our country were at war in the presence of a deadly foe, whether within or without, the patriotic citizen would subordinate self, and if necessary subordinate party. Others may differ with me, but I do not believe that in our country's whole history, whether in peace or in war, we have ever been confronted with a more critical situation.

Our Naval Policy: ... My previous investigations led to the final conclusion that America should always maintain in the Atlantic Ocean a fleet equal of the fleet of any military nation of Europe possessing a big standing army, and that we should maintain permanently in the Pacific a fleet as large as the fleet of any military nation of Asia possessing a large standing army. Formerly, this standard demanded that our Navy in the Atlantic should be equal to the navy of Germany, and that our Navy in the Atlantic should be equal to the navy of Japan. The war in Europe, as previously pointed out, has shown that Great Britain is not a nation whose relation with other nations permits her to be safely trusted to dominate the waters of the world. In the interests of our own peaceful commerce when warlike nations are at war, in the interest of the rights of peace for all nations as against the usurped rights of belligerents based on might, the interests of neutrals, the interests of peace throughout the world now demand that our two fleets in the Atlantic and Pacific should always at least equal the Brtish Navy and during the continuation of the Anglo-Japanese alliance they should be together equal to the navy of Great Britain and the navy of Japan combined. This should be the foundation upon which to determine our naval program.

Our Naval Program: The true naval program for our country at this juncture should be to speedily take measures to render the Navy that we have efficient and to adequately increase its strength. The great lacking of the Navy as a whole today is that naval administration in our country has been developed almost wholly in times of peace. Not since we have had a Navy Department beyond an embryo stage has our country ever engaged a powerful naval foe. It is not surprising therefore that the organization of the Navy Department, based upon seven bureaus, has not included an agency for coordinating all the elements of the Navy and for preparing plans and directing their execution in time of war in order to insure naval victory. Every navy department and every military department of every other nation of the world has such an agency; ours alone is lacking.

Chief of Naval Operations: In my judgment, the most important part of the present bill is the paragraph establishing a chief of naval operations, with15 assistants. The enactment of this legislation would represent the real beginning of ultimate efficiency for the Navy we have, whatever its size. It is needless to remark that the efficient navy is beyond all comparison to the economical navy. Whatever the size of an organization, nothing is so wasteful in its operation as inefficiency. . . .

Our Fleet is Blind: Although the field of operations of our fleet must cover inevitably not a narrow channel nor a comparatively small sea, but the great extent of an ocean, nevertheless today we have no scouting ship, either weak or strong, and consequently our fleet is blind. All other navies have eyes in the form of not only scout ships properly adequate to the task of scouting on the high seas, but great battle cruisers that can make swift "reconnaisance in force" over long distances. Irrespective of the qualities to be developed on the part of fighting ships, the imperative need of the fleet we have today is two great battle cruisers of about 40,000 tons displacement making more than 30 knots, carrying the heaviest guns afloat, and sufficient armor to keep out armor-piercing projectiles at usual battle ranges, with a radius of larger than that of any vessel afloat. In addition to these we should provide at least four scout ships proper, three for the Atlantic and one for the Pacific.

Increase in Enlisted Men: To make our Navy efficient for the vessels that we now have and would expect to commission instantly on the outbreak of war would require at least 20,000 additional enlisted men. The report from the commander in chief of the battleship fleet, on the findings of various boards, shows an "alarming" shortage of enlisted men. The admiral [Rear Admiral Austin M. Knight] refers to the findings [in a speech before the Efficiency Club of New York City] as follows: "These boards have now completed their work and the result has developed an alarming shortage of officers and men that are required to efficiently man our ships for battle. The reports of all these boards were made independently and are singularly unanimous in their conclusions, presenting a more serious shortage than could have been anticipated by either the Navy Department or the fleet until brought to light by this searching investigation.

"The reports of these boards show that in 21 battleships in commission and now composing the Atlantic Fleet there is a shortage of 5,219 men and 339 officers required to fill all stations necessary to efficiently fight the ships in battle."

The least we can do at this session of Congress is to provide for additional men to make up this deficiency on the battleships alone now in commission. Taking into account the fact that we have a comparatively small ocean-going merchant marine, a small Naval Militia, and as yet no naval reserve at all, we should endeavor to have our complements on our ships in commission relatively larger than on the ships of other nations. I shall offer an amendment at the proper place to begin by the authorization of an increase of 5,000 men in the enlisted force of the Navy. This would entail an additional provision of a little over two millions of dollars and would ultimately require about three millions a year.

The Building Program: In order to approximate a Navy equal to the Japanese Navy and the German Navy combined, and equal to and ultimately superior to the British Navy, we should adopt a consistent program of six capital ships per year, and I trust that sooner or later we may reach this basis. Knowing, however, that this Congress will not provide such a program, at the proper time I shall move to increase the number of battleships from two to four, in addition to offering an amendment of a new paragraph to provide for two battle cruisers. I will not discuss at length the characteristics of these capital ships, but the experiences in the present war confirm the contention I have consistently made for many years before the Naval Committee and before this house that our capital ships should have superior speed along with the most powerfulguns.

Auxiliaries: It is a corollary or an axiom that with the capital ships we must provide auxiliaries in sufficient numbers to make the capital ships most effective and balance the fleet.

The Question of Submarines: The submarine has rapidly demonstrated its power in the course of operations in Europe, a demonstration that shows that the defense from torpedo attacks heretofore provided is not adequate. As yet the use of destroyers and picket boats seems to have been the only available defense. There are indications, however, that other means of defense may be developed. Nevertheless, the great usefulness of the submarine is fully demonstrated, and its numbers should be rapidy increased.

Capital Ships Determine the Control of the Sea: It should be borne in mind that however useful auxiliaries may be, it is the preponderance of captal ships of the latest type that gives a nation control of the sea—the all-determining factor in the course of the world. No matter how many submarines Germany possessed, no matter how many auxiliaries of other types she possessed, the heavy preponderance of the allies' capital ships insures them the control of the high seas and recourse to the resources of the world.

Experimentation: The question of types of ships and of the qualities of each type involves evolution and change, particularly during and immediately following war. Orderly and useful developments of complicated implements of war entails laborious, patient experimentation. The organization of the Navy Department contains no agency to conduct such experimentations, and only at intervals does a bureau appoint a board for such special purposes. The Committee on Naval Affairs of the House has had a subcommittee on ordnance experiments cooperating with the Navy Department for several years in the development of ordnance materials. The results of the investigations are naturally of a confidential nature, but their importance can be overestimated. In the conduct of these investigations a member of the Senate Committee on Naval Affairs has been frequently present. I trust that this special subcommittee work may be continued after my leaving Congress and may become a joint subcommittee of the two naval committees, and may have cooperating with it a corresponding board of the Navy Department, which could be provided by slight extension of the present board appointed to conduct experimentation on torpedo shells. . . .

Air Craft: I can not close, Mr. Chairman, without urging—what I have urged for a number of years—the systematic development of experimentation and building of air craft of all types. The utter decadence of aviation in our Army and Navy is due to lack of sympathetic legislation of Congress. I remember with painful vividness the defeat several years ago of a measure brought to the floor of the House from the naval committee to simply cooperate with private individuals to establish in Washington a laboratory and plant for experimentation in aeronautics. I hope the day will come some day when America—the great peacemaker, the great Nation championing the cause of free institutions and of humanity, championing the cause of the weak; our great peace Nation of America—will not only be mistress of the seas but mistress of the air.

"An Adequate Navy and the Open-Door Policy," continued
February 5, 1915

...Our fleet today is without eyes. It can not see a hundred miles. It ought to see across the Atlantic Ocean and as far from the Pacific Coast to the Hawaiian Islands and from there to Asia. It is the only Navy in the world whose fleet has no scouting vessel, and has no vessel that can be used for an ocean scout. The great battle cruisers and special scout crusers are the eyes of the fleets of Europe. The former can make reconnaissance in force. That is, they can fight while they scout.

The only scout vessels we have are the antiquated type of the *Birmingham* class, that can not keep the seas—little, small cruisers that ought to be used as gunboats or put into the discard. So today our fleet, which lacks aeroplanes with which to scout, and lacks Zeppelins, with which to scout, and which lacks enough torpedo-boat destroyers to care for the defense of the fleet, has neither battle cruisers to scout with nor any scouts proper. We maintain the 21-battleship fleet in a condition where it simply could not fight on equal terms with a 21—battleship fleet of any other country. Our fleet is in a condition of inferiority that is exceedingly serious. The General Board urged that we provide four scouts in this bill, two for each division of the fleet. Instead of that we not have a single one. I am not going to dwell on it. This is a proposition not to increase Navy. You voted down those propositions. The proposition is whether we are going to make the Navy we now have efficient or not, and on that basis I give the membership a chance to vote.

[The amendment offered by Hobson follows]: "There is herby established a council of national defense consisting of the President of the United States who shall be ex-officio president of the council; the Secretary of State, who shall preside in the absence of the President; the Secretary of War; the Secretary of the Navy; the chairman of the Committee on Appropriations of the Senate; the chairman of the Committee on Foreign Relations of the Senate; the chairman of the Committee on Military Affairs of the Senate; the chairman of the Committee on Naval Affairs of the Senate; the chairman of the Committee on Appropriations of the House of Representatives; the chairman of the Committee on Foreign Affairs of the House of Representatives; the chairman of the Committee on Naval Affairs of the House of Representatives; the chief of General Staff of the Army; by the Secretary of the Navy; the president of the Army War College; and the president of the Navy War College.

"The chairmen of the several committees of the Senate and House of Representatives herein named shall act as members of the council until their successors have been selected.

"Said council shall report to the President, for transmission to Congress a general policy of national defense and such recommendations and measures relating thereto as it shall deem necessary and expedient

"Said council shall meet at least once in each calendar year on such date or dates as it shall fix; PROVIDED, that in time of war said countries shall meet only upon the call of the President of the United States; PROVIDED FURTHER, That special meetings may be called by the president of the council; AND PROVIDED FURTHER, That the council may summon for consultation at any of its meetings any citizen of the United States, and upon request by the council the Secretary of War and the Secretary of War and the Secretary of the Navy shall order any officer of the Army, Navy, or Marine Corps to appear before the council for consultation.

"For carrying out the purposes of this act, there is hereby appropriated out any funds in the Treasury not otherwise appropriated, the sum of $20,000, to be available until expended, and to be expended upon vouchers signed by the president of the council; PROVIDED, That all necessary expenses of the chairman of committees of the Senate and of the House of Representatives, when called to attend meetings of said council when Congress is not in session, and the necessary expenses of all persons summoned shall be paid from this appropriation, upon approval by the president of the council."

APPENDIX IV

WRITINGS

"Information Gathered Abroad by Students" (1893)

"A Study of the Situation and Outlook of Europe" (*Proceedings of the U. S. Naval Institute*, 1894)

The Disappearing Gun Afloat (1895)

"The Yacht *Defender* and the Use of Aluminum in Marine Construction" (1896)

*The Sinking of the **Merrimac*** (1900)

"America Must Be Mistress of the Seas" (1902)

"Why America Should Hold Naval Supremacy" (1903)

"Paramount Importance of Immediate Naval Expansion" (1906)

Buck Jones at Annapolis (1907)

"Arbitration and Armaments" (1908)

"Diplomacy and the Fleet" (1908)

In Line of Duty (1909)

"America's War Policy" (1910)

"Fortification of the Panama Canal" (1911)

The Great Destroyer: Alcohol (1911)

"Our Country's Destiny" (1913)

"America and the World War" (1917)

"The Great Reform" (1918)

"Alcohol and the Human Race" (1919)

The Perils of Narcotics (1925)

"The Yellow Peril" (1927)

BIBLIOGRAPHY

Books

Brown, Charles H. *The Correspondents' War.* New York: Charles Scribner's Sons, 1967.

Brown, William 0. *The Lower South in American History.* New York: B. P, Smith, 1930.

Hagan, Kenneth J., ed. *In Peace and War: Interpretation of American Naval History*, 1775-1978, Greenwood: Wesport, CT., 1984.

Hobson, Richmond Pearson. *Alcohol and the Human Race.* New York: Fleming R. Revell Co., 1919.

_____. *Buck Jones at Annapolis.* New York: Appleton, 1907.

_____. *The Disappearing Gun Afloat.* Annapolis: U.S. Naval Institute, 1895.

_____. *In Line of Duty.* New York: Appleton, 1907.

_____. *The Perils of Narcotics.* Los Angeles: Richmond P. Hobson, 1924.

_____. *The Sinking of the "Merrimac": A Personal Narrative of the Adventure in the Harbor of Santiago de Cuba, June 3, 1898, And of the Subsequent Imprisonment of the Survivors.* New York: Century Co., 1899.

Morrison, Elting E. "Hobson, Richmond Pearson" in the *Dictionary of American Biography.* 1958 ed.

Turk, Richard W. "Introduction," *The Sinking of the "Merrimac"* by Richmond Pearson Hobson. (1899 reprint). Annapolis: Naval Institute Press, 1988.

Tutweiler, Juli S. *Richmond Pearson Hobson: The Preparation for His Life Work.* Livingston, AL: Hobson Campaign Club, 1903.

Newspapers and Periodicals

"The Boyhood of Hobson as Told by his Mother." *The Saturday Evening Post.* 72 (March 11, 1899), 585.

Feare, Varian. "Magnolia Grove Keeps Early Charm." *The Birmingham News-Age Herald.* 27 September 1936, 11.

Hobson, Richmond P. "America Must be Mistress of the Seas." *North American Review.* 177 (October, 1902), 544-557.

_____. "If War Should Come."*Cosmopolitan*, 44 (May, 1908), 584-593; (June, 1908), 38-47; 45 (September, 1908), 383-387.

_____. "A Summary of the Situation and Outlook in Europe: An Introduction to the Study of the Coming Wars." *Proceedings of the United States Naval Institute.* 21, (April, 1895), 349-385.

James Joseph H. "Richmond Pearson Hobson." *Alabama Historical Quarterly.* 5 (Winter, 1943), 447-451.

Johnson, Evans C. "Oscar Underwood and the Hobson Campaign." *Alabama Review*. 16 ((July, 1963), 125-40.

Morton, Louis. "Military and Naval Preparations for the Defense of the Philippines During the War Scare of 1907." *Military Affairs*, 10 (Summer, 1949), 95-104.

Pearson, Theodore B. "Research Needs and Opportunities: Richmond Pearson Hobson—Naval Hero, Reformer, and the Most Kissed Man in America." The *Alabama Review*. 50 (July, 1997), 174-80.

Pittman, Jr., Walter E. "The Noble Crusade: Richmond P. Hobson and the Struggle to Limit the International Narcotics Trade," 1920-1925. *Alabama Historical Quarterly*. 34 (Fall/Winter 1972), 181-193.

Postle, Arthur S., "Hobson: The American Nostradamus," *Louisville Courier Journal*, May 29, 1949, Sect. 3:3.

"R. P. Hobson, Alarmist." *Army and Navy Register*. 44 (December 5,1908), 12.

Scott, Anne P. "A Progressive Wind From the South, 1906-1913," *Journal of Southern History* 29 (February, 1963), 53-70.

Shaw, Barton C. "The Hobson Craze." *Proceedings of the United States Naval Institute* 102 (February, 1976), 54-60.

Sheldon, Richard N. "Richmond Pearson Hobson as a Progressive Reformer." *Alabama Review*. 25 (October, 1972), 243-61.

Snowbarger, Willis E. "Pearl Harbor in Pacific Strategy, 1898-1908," *Historian*. 19 (August, 1957), 361-84.

Turner, Sue F. "Ghosts Held no Fears for Mammy Tappy." *The Montgomery Advertiser*. 19 May 1940, 10.

Speeches

Hobson, Richmond Pearson. "An Adequate Navy," U.S. House of Representatives, January 20, 1915.

_____ . "Open Door Policy," U.S. House of Representatives, February 6, 1915.

Unpublished Manuscripts, Dissertations and Theses

Hobson, Gizelda Hull. *Memoirs*. Unpublished manuscript, 1951

Hutchens, James A. "The Chief Justiceship of Richmond M. Pearson, 1861-1871." Master's thesis. University of North Carolina, 1960.

Pittman, Jr. Walter. "Richmond P. Hobson, Crusader." Ph.D. dissertation. University of Georgia, 1969.

Pittman, Jr., Walter, "Richmond Pearson Hobson and the Fight for a Big Navy." Master's thesis, Mississippi State University, 1961.

Sheldon,, Richard N. "Hobson: the Military Hero as Reformer in the Progressive Era." Ph.D. dissertation, University of Arizona, 1970.

INDEX